No Experience Necessary

for this comprehensive book that leaves nothing to chance. No previous knowledge on the part of the reader is assumed. In plain English you will be told exactly what a pinch is, how to break an egg, what to do when you use too much salt, what brands are best, how to cope with emergencies.

You will be given the essentials for a well-stocked cupboard, you will learn what cut of meat to buy for a certain dish, how to truss a chicken, how to scallop potatoes. And more. Lots more. From roast beef to crabmeat Newburg, here's the story of how to cook succulent food the fast and easy way. You'll even learn how to boil water.

THE I NEVER COOKED BEFORE COOKBOOK

"Simple, clear, reassuring and full of recipes that will make you into an overnight cooking sensation."—GLAMOUR

THE I NEVER COOKED BEFORE COOK BOOK

by *Jo Coudert*

A SIGNET BOOK from
NEW AMERICAN LIBRARY
TIMES MIRROR

For Jane K. Coudert and Marianne K. Herdic
The born cooks in the family

This is an authorized reprint of a hardcover edition published by Stein & Day Publishers.

SIGNET TRADEMARK REG. U.S. PAT. OFF. AND FOREIGN COUNTRIES
REGISTERED TRADEMARK—MARCA REGISTRADA
HECHO EN CHICAGO, U.S.A.

SIGNET, SIGNET CLASSICS, MENTOR, PLUME, MERIDIAN AND NAL BOOKS *are published by The New American Library, Inc., 1633 Broadway, New York, New York 10019*

12 13 14 15 16 17 18 19 20

PRINTED IN THE UNITED STATES OF AMERICA

Contents

Foreword

The telephone rang just as I was sitting down to dinner. Although I have long since persuaded myself that I am not one of Pavlov's dogs to respond to a bell unless it is convenient, it seemed best to answer this time in the event that it was my date of the evening with a change of plans. Instead, it was Rob.

"I've got a ham," he said. "What'll I do?"

He sounded a little panicky. He had lost his wife about a year before, through an act of the courts, and his nine-year-old son came to stay with him each weekend. For quite awhile, the boy was intrigued with the idea of eating three meals a day in restaurants, but eventually it began to pall. Rob, knowing not the first thing about cooking and with a coffeepot his only utensil, took to heating up TV dinners for them at home. His son obviously liked eating in, and Rob himself enjoyed it. But the variety of TV dinners is not endless, and it became apparent that Rob was going to have to venture beyond their safety.

Hence the telephone call.

I knew just how he felt. At the time I was growing up, when I might have absorbed some knowledge of cooking from being around the kitchen and asked to peel carrots or stir something on the stove, my mother and father ran a country club, where we had our meals, and my nearest approach to the kitchen was to read the funnies to the dishwasher during his afternoon break. Accordingly, like Rob, there had also come a time in my life when I was suddenly on my own and had not the slightest idea of how to put a meal together.

Unlike Rob, I could not eat out; two weeks' salary out of every four was going on rent. I ate at home: baked beans, canned hamburgers, canned peas, and hot dogs. This was before the days of frozen foods, and I dared buy only something that had a label on it saying how it should be cooked.

I might have gone on this way indefinitely, barring overt malnutrition, but such a limited diet drives one to accept any and all dinner invitations, and dinner invitations sooner or later must be reciprocated. Since guests cannot be served canned hamburgers and baked beans (although I eventually found a way of doctoring the latter to turn them into an excellent buffet dish), I asked a friend how to broil chicken. The third time it didn't turn out at all badly.

I bought several cookbooks, cut recipes out of newspapers and magazines, and asked anyone who served a dish I liked how it was made. This is not to say, however, that this was the start of my turning into a gourmet cook. It seemed to me then, as it still seems to me now, that the point of cooking, except for people whose profession or hobby it is, is to do it very well but very easily. While it is necessary to eat and therefore it is pleasantest to eat food that looks handsome and tastes good, on the other hand there are things I would far rather do than spend time in a kitchen. And while I think that the most civilized form of entertaining is four well-chosen guests at a well-appointed table, neither do I want to do this if it involves a day of preparations or possible disaster if the cocktails stretch beyond the time planned for.

But cookbooks, I found, are intended for people with time to cook—and, surprisingly often, for people who already know how to cook. They tell you only the several right ways of making things, not the easy way and not the infallible way, the two things I was really interested in knowing. One day, for instance, I followed a recipe for Beef Stroganoff, and after painstakingly adding one ingredient after another and stirring constantly over a low flame, I suddenly said to myself, "Oh, my goodness, it's beef gravy. Why didn't they say so in the first place?" Now I buy a can of beef gravy and make Stroganoff that is unfailingly delicious in something less than one-quarter of the time.

Thus, gradually, I learned the short cuts, and in the process I also became quite a good cook, for the short cuts reduced the uncertainty quotient; my cream sauce may lump but Campbell's soup never does. Over the years, I have substituted, invented, experimented, and learned, plagiarizing from friends and professionals alike, and finally arriving, after a winnowing process, at the repertoire of recipes in this book.

It occurred to me to set them down after I had told Rob that, no, the ham didn't need parboiling first; yes, a 350 degree oven was right; and, no, it didn't have to cook for longer than an hour. I returned to my dinner, ate three bites, and got up to answer the telephone again; he had forgotten to ask how to do the sweet potatoes and the peas. By the time we had covered this, my lamb chop was sadly cold, and the cat, who is well-behaved but passionately fond of asparagus, had grown tired of waiting for his share of the stalks and had eaten them and the tips as well. I settled down to the salad and began to wonder what cookbook I could buy Rob that would answer his needs.

Here was a man with no interest in cooking beyond necessity, with no knowledge of what equipment to buy to launch himself, with no awareness of the prepared foods available that could save him time and trouble, no way of knowing which brand was superior to another, no basic sense of food preparation, no ability, in short, to buy a bag of groceries, choose a recipe, follow it, and be assured that a reasonably successful meal would arrive at the table. He needed a cookbook that would tell him all this.

I could not think of one.

In such a moment is yet another cookbook born. The justification for this one is the possibility that there are many Robs in this world who would like to do their cooking painlessly and with the full advantage of someone else having made the mistakes and picked up the oddments of information that can be so helpful, who would like clear directions on how to cook the basic foods, who are well aware that foods can be braised, flambéed, and souffléed but who are really only interested, at this stage of their lives, in getting a decent, well-cooked meal on the table with the least amount of trauma.

A friend of mine tells a story of her first attempt to roast a turkey. The cookbook she consulted gave the instruction: "Baste every half hour." This she conscientiously did—removing the stitches that held the skin in place over the stuffing and putting new ones in. Another friend describes her bafflement and the pictures conjured up when she first tried to follow a recipe that started with the instruction: "Dredge a chicken." And yet another friend, when I told him of the plan for this cookbook, countered with a favorite family story of his sister leaving on her wedding trip and suddenly leaning out of the car window to call in anguished tones, "Ma, how do you cook?"

The intention of this cookbook is to answer the question of how to cook without the use of any unfamiliar terms and in complete specifics. What is taken for granted in other cookbooks is spelled out here; no previous knowledge on the part of the reader is assumed. The recipes are basic, simple, and, barring unforeseen mishaps which can happen to the best of cooks failure-proof. There are numbered steps to follow. Cooking times for both the main dish and accompanying vegetables are given, so that the greatest fear of the novice, that of not being able to get everything done at the same time, is answered. In order to be able to ignore the problem of timing altogether when there are guests, a chapter on casseroles for company is included. The use of leftovers is coped with wherever relevant. There are, of course, seventeen ways of cooking almost anything, but for the most part sixteen of the seventeen have been ignored in favor of the one uncomplicated way, alternative recipes being given only when these are equally good, equally straightforward, and can add an interesting variety to the menu.

The book makes no claims to being exhaustive. There are foods not mentioned at all, either because I have not found a way to prepare them with certain success or because they strike me as being more trouble than they are worth. Too, if a food available commercially is comparable to what can be made at home, I have said this and omitted the recipe. I have even, at the risk of stepping on some very large toes, named the particular brand names that I find best. The choice is prejudiced, of course; I have only my own taste to go by; but my most frequent complaint on reading a cookbook is that it is not explicit enough and I have at least tried to avoid that sin.

There is a story of a youngster being asked her opinion of a book on rhinoceroses. "It is good," she said, "but it tells me more about rhinoceroses than I care to know." So, I have tried, too, to avoid that pitfall and have included in this book only what Rob needs and cares to know about cooking. If I have succeeded, he will cook not only adequately but well from here on in, perhaps even coming to take a fair amount of pleasure in it as he finds it is neither a formidable nor a tiresome task. And so, I hope, will everyone else who has never cooked before.

CHAPTER 1 HOW TO . . .

HOW TO READ THIS COOKBOOK

Ingredients: Each recipe is prefaced by a list of ingredients so that you can tell at a glance what you need to have on hand before you start, and in what amount, and the amounts are repeated again in the numbered steps to be followed in the actual cooking so that your eye need not bounce back and forth between the list and the directions, a maneuver I find exasperating when trying to follow a recipe. Not every ingredient used in the recipe is mentioned in the list of ingredients, however; this, for two reasons. There is nothing so off-putting as a long list of item after item; it makes the recipe seem hopelessly complicated whether it actually is or not. And it seems reasonable to assume that certain things, such as salt and butter and flour, are always on hand even in the most sparsely outfitted kitchen. Also not listed is the pinch of this or that herb called for in so many recipes. Herbs are very inexpensive and a small box lasts for a long time; thus, it is suggested that the basic ones listed on page 18 be purchased so they are always available when needed.

A neighbor asked why she heard the typewriter morning and night, and when I told her that I was writing a cookbook, she said, "Oh, I do hope it isn't one of those ones with herbs and wine." Feeling somewhat defensive, I admitted that both were mentioned frequently. "Oh, dear," she sighed, "I don't know how to use them and it makes everything so complicated." The answer is, of course, that you don't have to know how to use them; you just follow the recipe. They are simply flavoring agents, like salt or Worcestershire sauce, which both add a touch of their own and bring out the flavors of the other ingredients. Because they are flavoring agents, not essential ingredients, another answer is that they can be omitted, but it then follows necessarily that the dish will be flatter, not as interesting and not as professional. I hope, then, that the user of this cookbook will at least give them a try, putting aside any notion that it is complicated or effete to cook with herbs and wine until the results have been sampled in a few dishes. The other side of the coin is that they must not be allowed to dominate any dish; if you are aware of their presence, there is too much in. Like a good make-up job, they should enhance, not cover up. The postscript to the small story of my neighbor is that she then asked if I wanted her most successful recipe, which proved to be shrimp in garlic sauce, so apparently she was not quite as helpless with herbs as she imagined.

Seasonings: A pinch of herb, a dash of cayenne pepper, salt to taste may sound like vague directions, and indeed they are, but often that is as specific as a recipe can be. The sense of taste varies; likes and dislikes vary. Seasoning is a matter in which the cook's own judgment must be exercised, and, actually, all good cooks taste as they go along. The best advice is to add less than you think will be needed, taste, and keep adding more in small increments until your taste tells you the right point has been reached.

Because you can always add more but cannot subtract ingredients already in, stay on the light side with initial amounts of all flavoring agents. A pinch of herb, for example, is not as much as you can grasp between your thumb and forefinger; it is one layer between the two fingers. When adding herbs, sift them in by rubbing the fingers back and forth; this crushes the herbs slightly to release the flavors. For ingredients like prepared mustard, measure by level spoonfuls. Cayenne pepper and dry mustard are particularly powerful ingredients, so be extra cautious about amounts of these. Some recipes call for a clove of garlic; the garlic bulb is divided into distinct sections and one of these sections is a clove.

Measurements: On the whole, it is wise to be accurate in all measurements. Use a level cup or spoonful unless the recipe specifically says otherwise. As you grow more at home in the kitchen, you will surprisingly quickly develop a sense of what is important and what is not, as well as an instinct about amounts. You will realize, for example, that 2 tablespoons of butter in a white sauce means just that, but 2 tablespoons of butter in which to cook onions means enough butter to keep them from sticking to the pan and burning. A little more or a little less of this or that seldom makes any drastic difference, so be accurate but relaxed.

Most butter (and margarine) is packaged now with measurements on the wrapper, but if you find you need to measure a half cup of butter, the easiest way of going about it is to put a half cup of water in a measuring cup and then add butter until the water reaches the 1 cup mark. In measuring brown sugar, always pack it down firmly. In measuring a cup of flour, rap the bottom of the cup against the table so that the flour packs in closely.

Butter: A great many of the recipes in this book start with the direction: "Melt 2 tablespoons of butter . . ." or include the instruction: "Rub the inside of a casserole with butter. . . ." In almost every instance, "margarine" may be read in place of "butter." Margarine is not as good when served melted and hot with artichokes or lobster, not as good in Hard sauce or Hollandaise sauce, and not quite as good when used in place of a pat of butter on top of a hot vegetable, but it does very well in every other situation.

Sour Cream: When sour cream is called for in a recipe, it is commercial sour cream that is meant, not simply cream that has gone sour. This is probably a superfluous warning, but I remember the time when I did not know the difference and the results were rather disastrous. It is a pity that sour cream did not acquire a more attractive name somewhere along the line, for it is delicious and does marvelous things to many a dish that would otherwise be ordinary. If you are not familiar with it, don't hesitate to try it.

Cans: Many of the recipes call for a can of this or that. In such an instance, do not add the juice in the can unless the recipe specifically directs you to do so. Although all the cookbooks I have ever used give some such direction as, "Add a No. 2 can of . . . ," I have not designated the size of cans in this cookbook, for the very good reason that I don't know a No. 2 can when I see one, and I figure if I have managed to cook for years without this information, it cannot be essential. So far as I am concerned, there are three sizes of cans, small, medium, and large, and that is how they are described here.

Timing: The biggest fear that haunts the inexperienced cook seems to be how to get everything done on time. It is not an ungrounded fear, but neither is it a very large problem. A few months' experience at cooking will end it forever, but in the meantime, for guidance, the cooking times of a suggested menu accompany the recipe for every main dish. A look at these will tell you when each food must be started in order for all to come out even. Again, however, some judgment must be exercised by the cook, for the size of the pan, the height of the flame, and the state of the food (old vegetables take longer than new) can make the cooking time vary. Keep an eye on how things are going, prod with a knife occasionally to check the degree of tenderness, and if one thing or another seems to be getting ahead or falling behind, raise or lower the fire accordingly.

HOW TO READ OTHER COOKBOOKS

Cooking terms, unless they appear in a context in which they will be self-explanatory, have not been used in this book in an effort to make all directions completely intelligible to the non-cook at first reading. But if the non-cook finds that he is turning into a cook and that his interest is piqued by other recipes he comes across, it will be useful to him to know the following definitions.

Bake: This means to cook in an oven above the flame, as does roasting. It is a difference in usage, but not technique, that one bakes a cake but roasts a turkey.

Baste: Basting is to pour a liquid over something that is in the process of cooking in order to keep it from drying out. Either the juice from the food itself that has collected in the bottom of the pan or an extra liquid, such as water or wine, may be indicated.

Brown: In reference to meat or poultry, this means to cook until the outside is a rich brown color. Most often, this is an initial step in the cooking process and is achieved by putting the meat in a little fat in a skillet on top of the stove and cooking on all sides until it is brown. The rest of the cooking, aimed at getting the meat done through, is then proceeded with. Browning has two purposes: it makes things look more appetizing and it seals in the juices. In relation to casseroles, on the other hand, browning means to cook in the oven, either over or under the flame as directed, until the top is a golden tan color. Whether browning is the first or last step in the cooking process (the recipe will indicate which) it simply refers to the color of the food.

Broil: This is cooking in the oven under the flame.

Chop: To chop is to cut into pieces. The size of the pieces is usually indicated by "finely chopped" or "coarsely chopped."

Cube: To cube is to cut into small pieces the shape of a cube.

Dice: This is the same as to cube except that it indicates the pieces should be even smaller.

Dredge: To dredge is to coat with flour. If the direction is to dredge in seasoned flour, this means flour to which salt and pepper have been added. Crumbs, such as bread crumbs or cracker crumbs, may be indicated in place of the flour.

Dust: This is to coat very lightly with flour or sugar or a similar substance.

Fold: This is used in the sense of folding in an ingredient, i.e., adding it not by stirring but with a few gentle overlapping strokes.

Fry: To cook on top of the stove in a skillet with fat of some kind.

Grate: This involves rubbing the food against a grater so that it is cut into very tiny pieces.

Grill: This is the same as to broil.

Marinate: To marinate a food is to soak it in some liquid, the liquid being referred to as the marinade.

Mince: To chop very fine.

Pan-Broil: To cook in a skillet on top of the stove without fat or with a very minimal amount of fat rubbed on the pan and then discarded.

Parboil: This indicates that the food is to be cooked first in boiling water and then the cooking completed in another form. For instance, roast potatoes are often parboiled first and then put around a roast in the oven to complete their cooking.

Poach: When a food is cooked gently in just enough liquid to cover it, it is referred to as poaching.

Roast: To cook in an oven.

Sauté: To sauté a food is to cook it very gently in a skillet on top of the stove and in a minimal amount of fat.

Sear: This is rapid cooking in a preheated skillet over a high flame and is an initial stage in cooking meat, when indicated, in order to seal in the juices.

Shred: To shred is to cut into narrow strips.

Simmer: This is gentle, slow cooking, with the food itself or the liquid in which it is being cooked not quite bubbling or bubbling only occasionally.

Thicken: To thicken is to add an ingredient to a mixture that will change it from a thin liquid to one of the consistency of soup or gravy. Flour and egg yolks are the most frequently used thickening agents. The direction to cook until thickened means that the thickening agents are already present and the mixture will become less liquid as it is cooked and stirred. Usually the transition is quite abrupt.

Truss: To truss is to tie the legs and wings of a chicken or turkey, or other fowl, close to the body with a piece of string.

HOW TO EQUIP A KITCHEN

UTENSILS I: These are the absolute essentials. If you are not feeling particularly flush, check the ten-cent store first; almost all these things are on sale there.

3 saucepans—small, medium, and large. Or 1 saucepan and 1 double-boiler. It is easier to cook successfully with heavy saucepans than light ones, and well-fitting lids are a necessity. Thus, if your budget can manage it, this is the place not to skimp on quality.

2 skillets—small and large. Skillets are the same as frying pans, and my own preference is for the heavy cast-iron ones.

2 knives—small and large. One of the hoaxes perpetrated on the American public is that stainless steel knives are

good. They are handsome, but they do not hold a cutting edge in anything like the fashion that a carbon-steel knife does.

1 slotted spoon. This is a large spoon with holes in it that is used to remove foods from the liquid they were cooked in.

1 long-handled fork. This is necessary to avoid burns when, for instance, taking a chop out of the broiler.

1 strainer or sieve or colander. These are approximately the same thing.

1 measuring cup. A tin one is more useful than a glass one, for it can also be used to heat small quantities of things, such as butter.

1 parer. There are several types of parers on the market, but the type that pares, cores, and has a melon-baller on the opposite end is the most versatile.

1 casserole. Perhaps the ten-cent store has a good-looking one, but if not, splurge in a department store because so often it will go directly from the oven to the table and it should be handsome to look at. Earthenware ones hold the heat best, but metal ones with baked-on enamel can go over a direct flame on top of the stove with less risk. If you can afford it, buy individual-size casserole dishes, called ramekins, at the same time. They are not essential but are often very convenient.

2 pot holders

3 Pyrex baking dishes—small, medium, and large. These can double as mixing bowls.

Vegetable brush. For scrubbing baked potatoes.

Roasting pan with a rack

Can opener

Pancake turner. Useful for turning over many things in addition to pancakes.

UTENSILS II: These are extremely useful, but not directly essential.

Toaster. See page 192 for how to make toast without a toaster.

Pressure cooker. Life can go on without one of these, but they are so marvelous for vegetables that I recommend at least putting it on your Christmas list if you don't want to make the purchase yourself.

Grater. A four-sided grater with openings of different sizes is inexpensive and handy to have.

Timer. This gadget makes life easier in two ways; you don't have to keep an eye on the clock, and when guests are present, the ring of the bell allows you to get up in the middle of a sentence, not wait, worrying that the rolls may be burning, until there is a pause in the conversation.

Meat grinder. The only advantage in having a meat grinder is in using up leftovers, but that is a very large advantage indeed. The end of a roast can be chopped fine with a knife, but it is a tedious job and the result is not the same as running the meat through a grinder. Plan to buy one at the first opportunity.

Potato masher. This ten-cent store gadget makes the best mashed potatoes, but you won't need it if you use prepared mashed potatoes. Too, a completely effective substitute is pressing the boiled potatoes through a sieve, using the back of a tablespoon.

Garlic press. Useful but not essential because garlic powder can be used, or a fresh garlic glove can be sliced very thin or mashed with a fork to release the flavor.

Meat thermometer. This is a thermometer that is inserted into a roast before it goes into the oven and indicates when the meat is done.

Baster. A syringe with which liquid can be drawn from the bottom of the roasting pan and released over the roast is useful, but a tablespoon can do the same job.

Measuring spoons. Another ten-cent store item which is handy but not indispensable because you can use an ordinary teaspoon, for example, and judge with your eye an eighth of it.

Meat loaf pan. Until you get one of these oblong pans, you can use a baking dish or an iron skillet.

Muffin, cake, and pie tins. The need for these is essential if you plan to make muffins, cakes, or pies, completely nonessential if you don't, although a pie tin is useful for warming rolls and for such things as baked apples.

Top-of-the-stove oven. This, which is, in effect, a flat pan with a very high lid, saves lighting the oven and heating up the kitchen when you want to make baked potatoes or a small baked dish of some kind.

Electric broiler. These come in all sizes and all degrees of elaborateness. Mine, which cost about nine dollars, is in almost constant use for chops, steak, fish, chicken, broiling tomatoes, browning rolls, etc. It is easier to clean and much less fuss than the oven broiler.

UTENSILS III: The following have their advantages but are not in the least necessary.

Electric mixer. The person who makes a great many cakes has the greatest use for this.

Electric blender. This is fun for making both alcoholic and

vegetable cocktails, and is excellent for concocting soups and sauces.

Electric frying pan. My aunt says she couldn't get along without hers, but I don't know why not. Perhaps it is because she is much fonder of fried foods than I am.

Waffle iron. Frozen waffles are not as good as fresh, but they will do in lieu of going out and buying a waffle iron.

Pepper mill. There are those who swear by freshly ground pepper (and coffee), but grinders are niceties, not essentials.

Electric grill. This makes good sandwiches and pancakes, but both can also be made just as well in a skillet.

HOW TO STOCK A CAN CUPBOARD

The following list looks rather formidable in its length, but not everything need be bought at once and items will collect as you decide to try one or another recipe and buy the necessary ingredients. A painless way of stocking the cupboard initially is to buy two cans of each thing instead of only one when you are planning a meal. For instance, if your shopping list includes a can each of mushrooms, tomatoes, and pineapple, buy two and put one away in reserve. Replace the items in the can cupboard as used rather than waiting until there is a specific need for them.

STAPLES

Salt
Pepper
Paprika
Sugar, white and dark brown
Flour
Salad oil (Wesson or Mazola)
Vinegar (Heinz, plain)
Catsup or chili sauce (Del Monte)
Mayonnaise (Hellmann's)
Mustard, dry and prepared (Gulden)
Evaporated milk
Worcestershire sauce
A-1 sauce
Gravy Master or Kitchen Bouquet
Bread crumbs
Dried onion flakes
Bouillon cubes
Grated cheese (Parmesan, American, and Swiss)
Noodles, broad and narrow
Spaghetti
Dry sherry
Dry vermouth
Tomato sauce (Progresso)
Syrup
Rice (Uncle Ben's or Minute)
Jelly
Dehydrated potatoes
French dressing (Hellmann's Old Homestead)
Paper towels
Aluminum foil
Saran wrap
Waxed paper
Plastic bags

HERBS

Oregano
Garlic (fresh and powdered)
Thyme
Bay leaves

SPICES

Curry powder
Nutmeg
Cinnamon

CANNED VEGETABLES

White potatoes
Sweet potatoes
Peas (Le Sueur's)
Tomatoes (Del Monte)
Mushrooms (B in B)
Corn (Le Sueur's shoepeg)
Artichokes (Regina Mia)
Beets
Asparagus tips

CANNED SOUPS (Campbell's, condensed)

Cream of mushroom
Cream of tomato
Consommé

CANNED GRAVIES (Franco-American)

Beef
Chicken

CANNED MEAT AND POULTRY

Frankfurters
Chicken (R & R)
Hash (Broadcast)

CANNED SEAFOOD

Tuna fish
Crabmeat
Shrimp
Lobster
Sardines (Portuguese)
Clams (Doxsee)

CANNED FRUITS

Grapefruit
Mandarin oranges
Black cherries
Pears
Peaches
Pineapple
Applesauce

Note: Put brown sugar in a jar with a tightly fitting lid to keep it from getting hard. Keep flour in the refrigerator to keep it from getting wormy.

HOW TO STOCK A REFRIGERATOR

MAIN COMPARTMENT

Eggs
Milk
Meat (in current use; store excess in freezing compartment)
Bacon (can be kept in freezing compartment if not used frequently)
Parsley (wash it, shake off excess water, and put it in a jar with a lid; it will keep for weeks)
Butter
Olives, pickles, etc.
Grease jar (grease should not go into the plumbing system; it is best disposed of by pouring it into a jar kept for the purpose in the refrigerator, or in a can or waxed carton, which can be thrown away intact when full)

Note: All opened cans, leftovers, etc., should be put in the refrigerator. Cover leftovers so they do not pick up odors. Cans of fish or anything with a strong smell should be covered with aluminum foil. If opened cans are to be stored for more than twenty-four hours, it is safer to transfer their contents to a covered glass or plastic container.

VEGETABLE BIN

Lettuce
Radishes
Carrots
Green pepper
Fruit
Onions and potatoes (if there is room; if not, store in a dark place)

Note: If your refrigerator does not have a vegetable bin, these things can, of course, be stored in the main part of the refrigerator. In either event, they will keep best if put away in plastic bags or wrapped in aluminum foil or Saran wrap. Plastic bags now come in a roll and are endlessly useful for storing things.

FREEZING COMPARTMENT

Meat (if not planned for use within twenty-four hours, store in freezing compartment; wrap in aluminum foil, in individual-size portions if feasible, e.g., chops, ground meat, pieces of chicken, so that only as much as is required for one meal need be thawed at a time)
Frozen Vegetables (particularly if you are cooking for one or two, keep an assortment of different kinds on hand and break off just what you need for one meal; in this way, you can get the necessary variety into your menu)
Frozen Onions (a package of the frozen chopped onions that are now available are extremely convenient to keep on hand)
Ice Cream
Frozen Turnovers (either for yourself or in reserve in the event of unexpected company)
Frozen Soup (frozen shrimp soup is particularly useful to keep on hand as an easy and delicious substitute for cream sauce)
Frozen Fish (trout, scallops, shrimp, crab, for an emergency and to vary your own menu)
Frozen Fruit Juices (after mixing, keep in main compartment of refrigerator; many fruit juices taste better if slightly less water is used than is called for by the directions)
Rolls (if you are not going to use up a whole box of Brown 'n' Serve rolls at one time, they keep well frozen and need not be thawed before browning in the oven)
Bread (if a loaf of bread tends to go stale before you use it up, it can be kept in the freezing compartment and then slices toasted before using)
Leftovers (wrap in plastic bags, aluminum foil, or put in plastic containers; wrap

very tightly to exclude all air; if you are cooking for one or two people, you can halve the work by making a double quantity of a dish and freezing the extra for a second meal at a later date)

Ice Cubes (store in polyethylene bags, for the convenience of being able to reach in and get out just one or two and/or the times you need extras for a party; if the ice cubes are "dry" when put in, they will not stick together)

HOW TO DEFROST THE REFRIGERATOR

Wrap frozen foods in several thicknesses of newspaper, and put a heavy layer of newspaper over the top shelf of the main compartment to catch water dripping from the freezing compartment. Fill the ice trays with hot water and put them in the freezing compartment to hasten thawing of the frost. It is a great temptation to hurry the defrosting process along by knocking off large chunks of frost; this should not be done, but if you cannot resist, do not use a sharp-pointed instrument, such as a knife or ice pick, because of the danger of putting a hole in the cooling coils. When the refrigerator is free of frost, wash it out with baking soda and hot water. A gadget called an Infra-Red Defroster has come on the market which is said to do the defrosting job in minutes.

HOW TO REGULATE AN OVEN

If you do not have an automatic regulator on your oven, an oven thermometer becomes a rather necessary purchase. It does not do the work of a regulator, but it tells the temperature of the oven so that you can make the necessary adjustment in the height of the flame. In general, a flame turned one-quarter of the way up is a slow oven, halfway up is medium, all the way is high. By a slow oven is meant 250° to 300°, medium indicates 350° and high is 400° to 450°.

HOW TO MEASURE

2 tablespoons is 1 ounce
4 tablespoons is ¼ cup
8 tablespoons is ½ cup
16 tablespoons is 1 cup
2 cups is 1 pint

As a rough estimate, 1 cup of (uncooked) rice serves four people, 1 8-ounce package of spaghetti serves four people, 3 cups of (uncooked) noodles serves four people. Figure on ⅓ to ½ pound of meat per person, ¼ to ½ chicken per person, ¼ duck per person. There are approximately 4 servings in a package of frozen vegetables, and 4 servings in a large can of vegetables. A pie should give 6 servings, a cake 8 or more. In a quart of liquor there are 21 drinks, in a fifth 16, using a standard jigger measure of 1½ ounces.

HOW TO SEPARATE AN EGG

Holding the egg over a bowl, crack the shell in the middle. Turn the egg so that the larger end is down and then separate the shell into two halves. Some of the white will overflow into the bowl below, while the yolk will stay in the bottom half of the shell. Pour the yolk carefully into the empty half of the shell, allowing more of the white to drip off. Continue this transfer of the yolk back and forth between the two half shells until all, or most, of the white has dripped into the bowl. A bit of white remaining with the yolk makes no difference, but if any of the yolk gets into the white, the white will not whip. Unused yolks should be covered with cold water and placed in the refrigerator; unused whites should be stored in a covered container in the refrigerator. Both will keep for several days in this fashion. Add the yolks to scrambled eggs, the whites to soufflés.

HOW TO MAKE FOOD LOOK APPETIZING

Paprika and parsley are a cook's best friends. They take only a moment to add, but it would be worth doing even if it were more troublesome, for they are the important finishing touch that makes the food appealing to the eye. The fresh, perky green of parsley sprigs can be used lavishly to surround a roast or a chicken on a platter, or more sparingly as single sprigs on beets or a lamb chop, for example, or the parsley may be chopped and sprinkled over any light-colored food, such as cauliflower. Paprika, too, singly or in combination with parsley, should be used on light-colored food, mashed potatoes and creamed dishes especially. Since neither parsley nor paprika shows up on green vegetables, the final touch for the latter is a pat of butter. Parsley, as mentioned elsewhere, should be washed after purchase, the excess water shaken off, and then stored in a covered jar in the refrigerator, in which fashion it will keep a long time.

Color contrast in the foods themselves is equally important if a meal is to look appetizing, and menus are best planned with this in mind. Red cabbage and red beets are a poor choice for the same meal, for example, as would be peas and spinach or cauliflower and rice, while spinach and noodles, on the other hand, are appealing because of their contrasting colors. The textures of foods should also be taken into account. Two foods that are similar in texture, although of different families, such as lima beans and mashed potatoes, do not go well together.

One last admonition: hot foods should be hot, cold foods cold.

CHAPTER 2 HOW TO COOK MEAT

To the inexperienced cook, meat seems the most formidable part of the menu to prepare well, but this is not really true. A roast, as the recipes in this chapter indicate, is a perfectly simple matter, and steaks and chops are difficult only in that they must be watched so that they do not overcook. Although the novice is apt to postpone attempting a roast until he has gained some confidence in the kitchen, it probably should be the first thing he tries as it stands the best chance of turning out well.

The most crucial factor in having meat be tasty and tender is in the buying of it. Suggestions are given as to what qualities to look for in choosing a piece of meat, but the most certain guarantee of getting a good cut is to make friends with the butcher. He will know far better than your eye can tell you which piece of meat will be excellent and which indifferent. This is particularly true in the case of beef, which is the chanciest meat to buy. Lamb, veal, and pork present less risk, and ham almost none at all.

Included with each recipe for meat in this chapter is a suggestion for vegetables that go well with it and their cooking times so that getting everything done on time need not be a matter of guesswork. Instructions on how to cook the vegetables appear in Chapter 7 and can be located quickly by checking the Index.

A few general tips: to estimate the amount of meat to buy, plan on ⅓ to ½ pound per person; lining the broiler or roasting pan with aluminum foil can save a lot of cleaning up later; do not salt beef before cooking; overcooking or too rapid cooking dries meat out.

BEEF

ROAST BEEF

A roast of beef is just as easy to cook as it is to eat. Choose a three-, five-, or seven-rib roast according to your needs, calculating ⅓ to ½ pound of meat per serving. Look for a piece which has a rich, deep-red color. Dark beef is well-aged and will be tenderer and have more flavor than a piece which is lighter and brighter. The fat on the roast should not be excessive in amount and should be creamy in color, and the meat itself will be best if it has flecks of fat distributed through it.

RECIPE: ROAST BEEF

Timing of menu: Multiply the number of pounds the roast weighs by 20 minutes per pound. Roast potatoes, 50 minutes. Roast carrots, 50 minutes.

1. Turn the oven on at least 10 minutes ahead of time and set it at 325°.

2. Put the roast in a roasting pan with a rack. And that is all, unless you want to add the interesting and, in this instance, subtle flavor of garlic by peeling and cutting in slivers 1 or 2 cloves of garlic and inserting them at intervals in the meat in stab cuts made with the tip of a knife.

3. Roast the meat 20 minutes per pound for rare, 25 minutes per pound for medium, and 30 minutes per pound for well-done. Do not baste, i.e., do not pour any liquid over the meat. Do not season; salt toughens beef.

Roast potatoes and carrots are an excellent and easy accompaniment. Add a teaspoon of salt to a pot of water sufficient to cover the vegetables, and set it on the stove to boil. Peel the potatoes and carrots and cut the potatoes in half. Boil for 20 minutes, take out of the water, and 30 minutes before the roast is due to come out of the oven, place the vegetables around it in the roasting pan.

OR: Add a can of white potatoes and a can of white onions half an hour before the roast is done. (Canned carrots are not very good.)

4. Put the roast on a warmed platter, salt and pepper it, and let it stand for 10 minutes before carving; less juice will run out, and the meat will be firmer, and thus easier to carve, if this is done. Put the vegetables in a covered dish or pot to keep warm.

Gravy

1. Put 1 tablespoon of flour and 6 tablespoons of water

in a jar with a tightly fitting lid, and shake vigorously.

2. Remove the rack from the roasting pan. Pour off all but what looks to your eye to be about 3 tablespoons of fat; the fat will be in a transparent layer on top of the meat drippings and can be poured off by tilting the pan and letting it run slowly from one corner.

3. Put the roasting pan over a medium flame on top of the stove, and stir energetically with a spoon to loosen all the meat drippings from the bottom.

4. Give the flour and water mixture another shake, and, slowly, a little at a time, pour into the pan, stirring constantly. Stop adding it as soon as the gravy is as thick as cream soup.

5. Shake salt and pepper in, while continuing to stir; keep tasting until the amount of salt is right. To get a marvelously dark gravy color, add a capful of gravy coloring (Gravy Master), no more because it will make the gravy sweet.

6. Continue to cook gently, stirring often, for 5 minutes or until ready to serve. If the gravy becomes too thick, add water (or dry white wine); if it is too thin, add more of the flour-water combination.

Leftover Roast Beef

- See the recipes for Beef Stew and Beef Hash. Cooked beef may be used in place of raw in the recipe for Beef Stroganoff.
- Cold sliced roast beef is delicious, as you know. Take it out of the icebox sufficiently ahead of time so that the meat is at room temperature when served; otherwise, some of the flavor will be lost.
- Slices can be wrapped in aluminum foil and stored in the freezing compartment for later use.
- When the roast is down to odds and ends, put these through the meat grinder. If there is a lot, make some into a sandwich spread by mixing with mayonnaise and chopped pickles. With the remainder, make a tasty version of hash. Melt 2 tablespoons of butter in a skillet, lightly cook chopped onion (¼ cup to 1 cup of meat) until it is transparent, add the meat and a tablespoon of A-1 sauce. Stir well and heat through, adding salt to taste.

EYE OF THE ROUND

Eye of the round is a rolled roast of beef, that is, there are no bones and the meat is tied in a circular shape. It is not as tender as a rib roast, but it is nevertheless exceedingly good. Cook it in exactly the same way as the directions given for roast beef. Or, if you have doubts about its tenderness, treat it as a pot roast.

POT ROAST

A pot roast is usually bottom round, occasionally eye of the round, and a cut weighing about 3 pounds is the best buy. Because pot roast must cook for a long time, there is a risk of its drying out; hence the instructions to wrap it in aluminum foil.

Timing of menu: Pot roast, 3 hours. Broad noodles, 12 minutes. Frozen broccoli, 8 minutes.

RECIPE: POT ROAST

3-lb. pot roast	½ cup dry red wine
2 cans sliced mushrooms	1 cup chopped onions

1. Sprinkle the pot roast thoroughly with salt and pepper and garlic powder.
2. Melt 2 tablespoons of butter in a skillet over a high flame. Put the roast in this, and turn it over when it is brown on one side. Turn at intervals until it is brown all over.
3. Take the roast out of the skillet and set it in the center of a large piece of heavy-duty aluminum foil. In the same pan the roast was browned in, gently cook 1 cup of chopped onions and 2 cans of sliced mushrooms until the onions are transparent.
4. Fold the edges of the aluminum foil up around the meat so that it makes a kind of cooking pot. Put the onions, mushrooms, and ½ cup of dry red wine into the foil with the meat. Close the foil over the top of the roast and seal it tightly by folding over all the edges.
5. Bake this package in a 300° oven for 2½ hours.

Gravy

1. Shake together in a jar 1 tablespoon of flour and 6 tablespoons of water.
2. Remove roast from the aluminum foil and put it on a warmed platter. Pour the juices from the foil into a skillet.
3. Turn the fire on under the skillet, and when the juices are bubbling, slowly pour some of the flour-water combination in, stirring constantly so that the gravy does not lump and adding only enough of the flour-water combination to arrive at the consistency of cream soup.
4. Add 1 capful of gravy coloring (Gravy Master). Season to taste with salt and pepper.

Leftover Pot Roast

- See recipes for Beef Stew and Roast Beef Hash.
- Warm up slices in leftover gravy.
- Put the tag end of the meat through the meat grinder, and use to stuff green peppers or tomatoes (see recipes).
- Use slices for either hot or cold sandwiches.

STEAK

To my way of thinking, a Porterhouse or T-bone steak is superior to a Sirloin, for it is apt to be more tender, have a better flavor, and there is less waste. As when buying roast beef, look for a piece with a rich red color, with creamy fat and not too much of it, and with flecks of fat interspersed through the meat itself. Try to get a piece not much under an inch thick; better no steak at all than too thin a one.

Timing of menu: Mashed potatoes, 25 minutes. Steak, 10 minutes. Frozen asparagus spears, 8 minutes.

RECIPE I: BROILED STEAK

1. Turn the broiler on full 10 minutes before the steak is to go in. If you spread a piece of aluminum foil on the broiler, it will be less trouble to clean afterwards.
2. Make a few diagonal cuts in the fat around the steak so that it will not curl up in the cooking. If it sounds good to you, you can spread Gulden's prepared mustard over the steak.
3. Turn the broiler flame down slightly, and insert the steak 3 inches below the flame.
4. Broil 5 minutes on one side; turn and broil 5 minutes on the other. At this point, test for the desired degree of doneness by making an incision near the bone with a sharp knife; if the meat looks too rare, continue the cooking until the color is to your taste.

RECIPE II: PAN-BROILED STEAK

An alternative method of cooking steak, and claimed by some to be the better method, is to pan-broil it in a heavy skillet on top of the stove.

1. Get the skillet very hot and rub it lightly with a small piece of fat cut from the steak; do this by spearing the fat on a fork.
2. Put the steak in, and sear it on one side; if the pan is very hot, it will take only a minute or two until the underside is sealed and brown.
3. Turn the fire down halfway and turn the steak over.

When the second side is a rich brown, turn it over again.

4. Timing the cooking depends completely on how thick the steak is and how rare you like it. After 5 minutes, begin checking on doneness by cutting near the bone and examining the color of the meat.

Gravy

Add to the drippings in the broiler or skillet 2 tablespoons of water, a can of drained sliced mushrooms, and a tablespoon of A-1 sauce or a lesser amount of Worcestershire sauce. Stir and let bubble up briskly. Taste for enough salt. Salt and pepper the steak, and pour the gravy over.

To Carve

In a T-bone steak the bone runs down the middle. The side with the smaller area of meat is the tenderloin. Cut it in strips about 1 inch wide, and do the same thing with the opposite side, serving each person one slice from each side. The tail is usually considerably less tender; so reserve that for seconds.

Leftover Steak

There probably will not be any, which is a good thing because steak is not done a service by being warmed up.

- Slice it thin for a steak sandwich.
- Warm it quickly in a can of (Franco-American) mushroom gravy, arrange the meat on toast, and pour the gravy over.
- If there are just a few pieces left, cube them and add them to a package of frozen Beef Bourguignon, stretching what otherwise is a too skimpy portion for two into ample servings.
- If you estimate that the tail is not needed in the original serving, cut it off before broiling the steak and, for another meal, put it through the meat grinder (or ask the butcher to do this); it makes first-rate hamburger. If it has been cooked, grind it up with some onion, melt 2 tablespoons of butter in a skillet, add the meat and onions, salt and pepper, and a teaspoon of Worcestershire sauce. Cook gently for 5 minutes, stirring occasionally.

MINUTE STEAK

These thin, individual-size steaks should be pan-broiled.

Timing of menu: Hash-brown potatoes (Pillsbury), 25 minutes. Broiled tomatoes, 15 minutes.

RECIPE: MINUTE STEAK

1. Melt 1 tablespoon of butter in a skillet. Let the pan get quite hot and throw in the steaks.
2. Cook 2 minutes on one side, 1 minute on the other.
3. Add salt and pepper, and serve.

FLANK STEAK

This is also called London Broil, and the only trick here involves the carving.

Timing of menu: Steak, 10 minutes. Broiled mushrooms, 10 minutes. French-fried potatoes, 10 minutes. Frozen green beans, 7 minutes.

RECIPE: FLANK STEAK

1. Turn the broiler on full 10 minutes before the steak is to go in.
2. Cut a clove of garlic in half, and rub the cut sides over the meat. Or sprinkle the meat with garlic powder. Brush the meat with salad oil.
3. Cover the broiling pan with aluminum foil, and place the steak 2 inches below the flame.
4. Cook 5 minutes on each side.

To Carve

Salt and pepper the steak, and put a pat of butter on top. Carve by holding the knife at an acute angle to the meat and slicing thinly across the grain. This is important, for if it is cut in any other way, the meat will be tough.

PEPPER STEAK

For pieces of meat labeled Round Steak, Rib Steak, Shoulder Steak, Chicken Steak, etc., you are best off not treating them as steak proper. They are tougher and take a bit more cooking. The following is a tasty way of coping with them.

Timing of menu: Pepper steak, 30 minutes. Rice, 30 minutes. Frozen wax beans, 8 minutes.

RECIPE: PEPPER STEAK

1 pound steak
1 green pepper
1 onion
1 tomato
1 tablespoon soy sauce
1 tablespoon sherry
1 teaspoon cornstarch

1. Peel and dice 1 onion, or use ½ cup of frozen chopped onion. Dice the green pepper.

2. Cut up the meat into 1-inch cubes, discarding any fat or gristle.

3. Heat 2 tablespoons of salad oil in a skillet and brown the meat in it, flipping the pieces over so they get brown on all sides.

4. Add the chopped onion and pepper.

5. Add 1 tablespoon of soy sauce, 1 tablespoon of sherry, and ⅛ teaspoon of garlic powder.

6. Put a lid on, turn the flame down low, and cook for 10 minutes.

7. Mix, in a cup, 1 teaspoon of cornstarch and 2 tablespoons of water, and stir this until smooth. Add to the skillet, stirring constantly, and let the mixture boil (you may have to turn the flame up temporarily to bring it to the boiling point).

8. Cut a fresh tomato into 8 wedge-shaped pieces and add to skillet.

9. Put the cover back on and allow to cook gently for 15 minutes.

10. Serve over rice. This amount is sufficient for four people.

HAMBURGER

There are a variety of ways of cooking hamburger and a variety of ingredients that may be added to it to vary the taste. One thing to remember is to handle the meat as little as possible, that is, when you are shaping the meat into patties, do not press and push and knead; pat them lightly and quickly into shape and then leave them alone. For hamburger that is to be used in any form of hamburger patties, buy top round, preferably ground to your order; if you are adding the hamburger to something else, spaghetti sauce, for instance, you can settle for ground chuck or whatever is being packaged under the name of chopped meat. To store hamburger, make it into individual-size patties, wrap each separately in aluminum foil, and put in the freezing compartment of the refrigerator. Thaw before using (if you forget to do this, see Recipe II).

Timing of menu: Baked potatoes, 1 hour. Broiled tomatoes, 15 minutes. Hamburger, 12 minutes.

RECIPE I: BROILED HAMBURGER

1. Light the broiler and put it on full flame 10 minutes ahead of time.

2. Salt and pepper the chopped meat, and shape into patties about 1 inch thick. Brush patties with melted butter or salad oil.

3. Lower flame halfway, and put the hamburgers 3 inches below the flame.

4. Cook for 6 minutes. Turn and cook for 6 minutes on second side. Check for desired degree of doneness by gently inserting a knife or fork in the center of the patty and parting the meat until you can see whether it is sufficiently cooked in the middle. Let it cook longer if necessary.

RECIPE II: PAN-BROILED HAMBURGER

1. Melt a pat of butter in a skillet. Let pan get quite hot, short of burning the butter. Put the hamburgers in and sear on both sides. When second side is brown and sealed, reduce flame halfway. Allow to cook 5 minutes on each side. Check for doneness.

OR: If, in cooking hamburgers this way, you find that they get too hard a crust, add 4 tablespoons of water to the pan after the patties have been seared on both sides. I have more success in general with this method, particularly if I have forgotten to thaw the patties completely ahead of time. (If the meat is still frozen to any degree, the cooking time must be lengthened. If solidly frozen, put a lid on the pan after searing and cook gently, adding more water if the pan becomes dry.) There is usually juice left in the pan when the meat is cooked in this way, and, with the addition of a bit of chili sauce or dry red wine, salt, and a good stirring while it bubbles up, this makes a tasty gravy to pour over the hamburgers.

RECIPE III: CHEESEBURGER

1. Broil the hamburgers according to Recipe I.

2. When the second side is brown, add a slice of American cheese, and continue to broil until the cheese is melted. A slice of tomato on top of the cheese is also good.

RECIPE IV: MARINATED HAMBURGER

1. Add salt and pepper to the hamburger when you shape it into patties. Put the patties into a bowl, and pour a cup of dry red wine or a cup of (commercial) French dressing (Hellmann's Old Homestead) over them. Cover the bowl, and put it in the refrigerator for no less than 1 hour, preferably several, turning the patties at least once.

2. Melt 2 tablespoons of butter in a skillet and add 2 tablespoons of the wine or French dressing. Pan-broil the ham-

burgers in this, 6 minutes on each side.

3. If there is enough wine or French dressing left in the pan after cooking, pour this over the hamburgers before serving. Otherwise, add more to the pan, cook quickly, stirring until it bubbles up, and then pour over the meat.

RECIPE V: HAMBURGER SMOTHERED IN ONIONS

1. Peel and slice 1 medium-size onion for each serving. Press the center of each slice so that the slice comes apart into individual rings, and put the rings into a large skillet with enough water to cover generously.

2. Add 1 tablespoon of A-1 sauce for each onion.

3. Cook over a high heat. When about one-third of the water has boiled away, it will be time to start the hamburgers, either in the broiler or in a second skillet.

4. The onions are done when the water in the pan has just about cooked away. If the onions get ahead of the hamburgers, add more water to them; if they are behind, turn the flame under them higher so that the water boils away faster.

5. Heap the onions upon the hamburgers. Mashed potatoes complete a delicious triad.

Hamburger with Additions

- When shaping the patties, add crumbled bits of Roquefort cheese.
- Add a teaspoon of dried onion flakes to each patty.
- Mix a pinch of oregano or thyme into each patty.
- Sprinkle patties with garlic salt or garlic powder.
- When shaping patties, add a teaspoon of chili sauce, catsup, or barbecue sauce to each.
- Paint patties with prepared mustard before cooking.
- If pan-broiling, add a can of sliced mushrooms plus a little of the juice the last 5 minutes of the cooking time.

MEAT LOAF

Hamburger, when baked, becomes a meat loaf, with the advantage that ground chuck, which is considerably less expensive than ground round steak, can be used, and, too, the additions necessary in concocting a meat loaf make the meat stretch further. To say nothing of the fact that meat loaf in itself can be very, very good, as witness the following easy recipes. The recipes will serve four people.

Timing of menu: Meat loaf, 1 hour. Baked potatoes, 1 hour. Beets, 30 minutes to 1 hour.

RECIPE I: MEAT LOAF

1½ pounds ground beef
1 cup corn flakes
1 egg
1 can condensed cream of tomato soup
½ cup chopped onions

1. Turn the oven on to 350°.

2. In a large bowl, mix together the meat, 1½ teaspoons of salt, ¼ teaspoon of pepper, 1 cup of corn flakes, 1 egg, ½ cup of chopped onions (use the frozen ones if it is more convenient), and ½ of the can of cream of tomato soup. You will probably need to use your hands to get the ingredients thoroughly mixed.

3. Transfer the mixture to a meat loaf pan (about the shape of a loaf of bread and purchasable in the ten-cent store) or mound it in a heavy iron skillet. Pour the remaining tomato soup over the top. Decorate the top with strips of (raw) bacon if you like.

4. Bake for 1 hour in a 350° oven.

RECIPE II: MEAT LOAF

1½ pounds ground beef
1 cup milk
3 slices bread
1 egg
½ teaspoon prepared mustard
2 tablespoons Worcestershire sauce
¼ cup dried onion flakes

1. Turn the oven on to 350°.

2. Crumble 3 slices of bread and soak them in 1 cup of milk.

3. Mix together, handling as little as possible consonant with getting the ingredients well mixed, the meat, the bread, 1 egg, ½ teaspoon of prepared mustard, 2 tablespoons of Worcestershire sauce, ¼ cup dried onion flakes. Add 1½ teaspoons of salt and a healthy sprinkling each of garlic powder, pepper, and paprika.

4. If you do not have a meat loaf pan, form the mixture into a rounded mound in a heavy iron skillet or any pan that can go in the oven.

5. Bake at 350° for 1 hour.

Leftover Meat Loaf

• Slice and warm up in beef bouillon (canned or made with a bouillon cube) or dry red wine and a little water.

• Break into chunks, and add to canned spaghetti sauce to make a meat sauce for spaghetti.

• Mix chunks into 1 or 2 cans of (Franco-American) macaroni, put into a baking dish, cover the top with sliced tomatoes, sprinkle heavily with grated American cheese, and bake in 350° oven for half an hour.

- Use cold in sandwiches.

BEEF STEW

A delicious beef stew may be made either starting from scratch or with the leftovers from a beef roast. A recipe for each approach is given. If there are odds and ends of leftover vegetables in the refrigerator, such as peas, beans, or corn, toss these in too. The recipes will make four servings.

Timing of menu: Beef stew, approximately 45 minutes for uncooked meat (after meat has been marinated overnight); 20 minutes for cooked. This is a complete meal in itself; just add a green salad, and everything is ready.

RECIPE I: BEEF STEW FROM SCRATCH

1 pound stew meat	2 cans beef gravy
1 cup red wine	1 can white potatoes
1 can small white onions	1 can carrots

1. Trim all the fat and gristle off the meat, and cut the meat into cubes. Put the meat in a bowl, and add 1 cup of dry red wine, 1 bay leaf, and 1 sliced clove of garlic. Cover the bowl and let it stand in the refrigerator overnight. Give it a stir now and again so that all the meat gets soaked.
2. Melt 2 tablespoons of butter in a skillet and cook the meat, turning often, just until it is brown on all sides. Sprinkle salt and pepper over.
3. Add the wine (without the bay leaf and garlic), 2 cans of beef gravy, 1 can of white potatoes, 1 can of small white onions, and 1 can of carrots.
4. Cook gently for 20 minutes. Taste and adjust seasoning.

RECIPE II: BEEF STEW WITH LEFTOVER MEAT

Leftover roast or steak	1 can onions
1 package frozen mixed vegetables	1 can white potatoes
	1 or 2 cans mushroom gravy

1. Cut the meat into cubes, removing all fat. Use a minimum of 2 cups of meat, more if you have it.
2. Put into a large skillet, and sprinkle the meat with salt, pepper, and garlic powder.
3. Add 1 package of frozen mixed vegetables (uncooked), 1 can of white potatoes, 1 can of onions, and 1 or 2 cans of mushroom gravy, depending on how much is needed

to cover everything. Add 2 tablespoons of catsup or chili sauce.

4. Let the stew cook, just bubbling gently, until everything is heated through and the vegetables are tender. Taste for correctness of seasonings.

Leftover Stew

- Just warm it up. It gets better as it goes along.

ROAST BEEF HASH

Both of the following recipes utilize leftover roast beef or pot roast in a dish which seems to be a particular favorite of men, perhaps because it is both tasty and filling.

Timing of menu: Recipe I takes about 30 minutes; Recipe II must cook for 45 minutes. Beets, 45 minutes. This plus a salad will be enough, for potatoes are in the hash.

RECIPE I: ROAST BEEF HASH

3 cups leftover roast
2 cups cooked potatoes (boiled or roasted or canned)
½ cup chopped onions
¼ cup chopped green pepper
1 cup beef gravy
⅓ cup tomato paste

1. Either chop the meat into small pieces, or put it through the meat grinder.
2. Cut the potatoes into small cubes.
3. Add the potatoes, ¼ cup of chopped green pepper, and ½ cup of chopped onion to the meat, and stir in ⅓ cup of tomato paste and 1 cup of beef gravy. Mix well, and add 1 teaspoon of salt and a good sprinkling of pepper.
4. Melt 2 tablespoons of butter in a heavy skillet, and add the hash. Stir occasionally until the hash is heated through.
5. Then let cook undisturbed until there is a nice brown crust on the bottom. Fold the hash in half with a broad knife or a pancake turner and serve.

RECIPE II: ROAST BEEF HASH

leftover cooked beef (or lamb)
1 raw potato for each cup of meat
beef gravy
onion
green pepper

1. Turn the oven on to 350°.
2. Cut all the fat off the meat. Peel the potatoes and onion and cut the green pepper into slices. Decide on the amount of potatoes and onion by figuring on one small to medium-sized potato to a cup of meat, ¼ of an onion to each

potato; do not add more than 1 green pepper and use less if the quantity of meat and potato is small.

3. Put the meat, potatoes, onion, and green pepper through the meat chopper, using the coarsest blade of the grinder so that everything comes out in small chunks, not pulp.

4. Salt and pepper this mixture well, and add 1 teaspoon of catsup and ½ teaspoon of A-1 sauce for every potato used.

5. Stir in canned or leftover beef gravy in an amount just sufficient to moisten the mixture.

6. Rub butter on the bottom and sides of a casserole or a heavy iron skillet, and press the hash in firmly.

7. Bake the hash, covered, in a 350° oven for 30 minutes. Take the lid off, and bake it 15 minutes more.

For recipes for Beef Stroganoff and Beef Bourguignon, see the chapter on Casseroles for Company.

LAMB

ROAST LEG OF LAMB

Like all roasts, a leg of lamb is absolutely simple to cook, and, when young and tender, makes superlative eating. Buy not too large a one, a 3 to 6 pound cut, so that you know it is from a young lamb. Lamb is lighter in color than beef and should have a fresh, firm look to it. Calculate one-half pound of meat per serving.

Timing of menu: Multiply the number of pounds the leg of lamb weighs by 30 minutes per pound; the total is the cooking time needed. New potatoes, 20 minutes. Petit pois (canned peas, Le Sueur), 10 minutes.

RECIPE I: ROAST LEG OF LAMB

1. Turn the oven on to 325° 10 minutes in advance.

2. Wash the roast under running cold water, and dry it off with a paper towel. Sprinkle liberally with salt and pepper. Rub skin with thyme. Or insert slivers of garlic in stab cuts made in the meat with the tip of a knife. Or sprinkle with garlic powder.

3. Roast 30 minutes pei pound in a 325° oven.

RECIPE II: ROAST LEG OF LAMB

This method is my favorite for the roast stays moist and juicy, and wonderful gravy can be made.

1 sliced onion | 1 can stewed tomatoes

1. Preheat oven to 325°.
2. Rub the roast with salt and pepper. Sprinkle a few pinches of garlic powder over, or thyme, or marjoram.
3. Line roasting pan with aluminum foil, set the roast on it, and pour over it a can of stewed tomatoes. If you do not have a can of stewed tomatoes on hand, use a can of tomato juice or V-8 juice. Add 1 sliced onion or 1 cup of frozen chopped onion.
4. Roast 30 minutes per pound in a 325° oven.

Gravy

Whether following Recipe I or II, make gravy in the same way. Remove the leg of lamb from the roasting pan, and put it on a warmed platter. Let it stand for 10 minutes before carving so that the meat becomes firm.

1. Remove the foil and rack from the pan. Pour off the transparent fat by tilting the pan and letting the fat run out of one corner; do this slowly so that the meat juices stay behind. Depending on the leg of lamb, there may not be much fat, and it may not be necessary to do this.
2. Put the roasting pan over a low flame on top of the stove.
3. Shake together 1 tablespoon of flour and 6 tablespoons of water in a jar. Add this in a thin stream to the roasting pan, stirring constantly. Stop adding the flour-water when the gravy reaches the consistency of cream soup.
4. Taste for salt and pepper, and add what is needed. Put in 1 capful of gravy coloring (Gravy Master).
5. After gravy begins to bubble gently, cook for 5 minutes, stirring frequently.

Leftover Leg of Lamb

- Serve cold sliced lamb garnished with parsley. Remove the meat from the refrigerator enough in advance so that it is at room temperature for serving.
- Cut off slices, and freeze them for later use.
- If Recipe II has been used and there is enough gravy left, cube some of the meat, add it to the gravy, warm both thoroughly, and pour over hot buttered noodles.
- If there is a lot of gravy left, cube the meat, mix it with the gravy, add leftover cooked potatoes and vegetables (or canned ones), and you have lamb stew.
- See recipe on page 39 for a different version of Lamb Stew.
- Put chunks of lamb through the meat grinder, along with a quarter of an onion. Melt 2 tablespoons of butter in a

skillet, add the ground lamb and onion, mix in 2 tablespoons of chili sauce, and heat through, stirring now and again.

• Substitute lamb for beef in Recipe II for Roast Beef Hash.

• Add cubed pieces of lamb to 1 can of (Franco-American) macaroni. Mix in well 1 teaspoon of prepared mustard. Sprinkle bread crumbs and grated Parmesan cheese on top. Bake 20 minutes in 350° oven, or until top is nicely browned.

• See recipes for Lamb with Red Wine, Lamb with Currant Jelly, and Lamb Curry.

• Grind up the odds and ends of the roast, and use it to stuff green peppers or tomatoes (see recipes).

• Use sliced lamb in sandwiches, or grind it with a pickle, mix with mayonnaise, and use as a sandwich spread.

LAMB CHOPS

Loin chops are far and away the best kind of lamb chops and, unfortunately, also far and away the most expensive. Rib chops have only a bite or two of meat on them, and shoulder chops are considerably less tender and have a stronger flavor. Since shoulder chops need all the help they can get, try them with Recipe II. Broil loin and rib chops.

Timing of menu: Baked potatoes, 1 hour. Mixed frozen vegetables, 10 minutes. Broiled lamb chops, 10 minutes or less; Recipe II, 45 minutes.

RECIPE I: BROILED LAMB CHOPS

1. Turn the broiler on full 10 minutes in advance.
2. Turn the flame halfway down. Cover the broiling pan with aluminum foil. Place the chops 3 inches from the flame.
3. For 1-inch thick chops, broil 3 minutes on each side for rare, 4 minutes on each side for medium, and 5 minutes on each side for well done. Salt and pepper before serving.

An old cookbook I have says lamb is never served rare. Nonsense! A leg of lamb is best when the meat still has traces of pink in it, and lamb chops are never finer than when their centers are quite, quite rare.

RECIPE II: SHOULDER LAMB CHOPS

4 or 6 lamb chops
2 medium-size tomatoes
2 medium-size onions
1 package dried herb salad dressing mix

1. Melt ½ cup of butter in a skillet.
2. Put in the lamb chops and sprinkle over them 1

package of (Good Seasons) herb salad dressing mix. Cook over a medium flame until the chops are nicely browned on both sides.

3. Peel and slice 2 medium-size onions, or use 1 cup of frozen chopped onions. Add onions to the skillet. Allow to cook for 15 minutes, along with the chops.

4. Cut in quarters 2 medium-size tomatoes, and add these to the pan. Cook 20 minutes longer.

5. Remove the chops to a platter, salt and pepper them, and pour the sauce from the skillet over. Boiled or mashed potatoes go nicely with the sauce.

For a lamb chop casserole made with orange juice, see the chapter on Casseroles for Company.

LAMB STEW

Recipe I is for already cooked lamb, and it is a way of using up a leg of lamb when it gets down too far for slicing. Lamb stew can also be made from uncooked meat, of course, and Recipe II describes the best and least elaborate method I know. Be careful here to remove every possible bit of fat as it can make the stew greasy and give it an unappetizing flavor. Each recipe makes three to four servings.

Timing of menu: Lamb stew, Recipe I, 45 minutes; Recipe II, 1 hour and 15 minutes. Thin noodles, 10 minutes. Fresh asparagus, 10 minutes.

RECIPE I: (COOKED) LAMB STEW

3–4 cups cubed cooked lamb
½ cup chopped onion
⅓ cup dry vermouth
¾ cup sour cream
1 can condensed cream of tomato soup

1. Preheat oven to 350°.

2. Salt and pepper the pieces of lamb, and put them in a casserole. Add ½ cup chopped onion and 1 can of condensed cream of tomato soup to the casserole, and stir them together well.

3. Bake for 30 minutes in a 350° oven.

4. Remove casserole from the oven, and put it over a low flame on the top of the stove. Stir in ⅓ cup of dry vermouth and ¾ cup of sour cream. Heat through, being careful not to let it boil. Taste for seasoning; it may need more salt and pepper.

RECIPE II: (UNCOOKED) LAMB STEW

1 pound boned lamb shoulder meat
1 tomato

1. Trim the fat off 1 pound of boned lamb shoulder meat, and cut the meat into cubes.

2. Spread a piece of waxed paper on a table, and dust it with 2 tablespoons of flour, 1 teaspoon of salt, and ¼ teaspoon of pepper. Roll the cubes of meat in this to coat them.

3. Melt 3 tablespoons of butter in a skillet, and brown the meat, stirring frequently so that all sides of the cubes get brown.

4. Add ½ cup of boiling water to the skillet, 1 fresh tomato cut into small pieces, and ¼ teaspoon of marjoram.

5. Turn the flame low, and cook for 1 hour.

6. If you like, add 2 tablespoons of dry white wine or dry vermouth the last minutes of cooking. Serve the stew on a bed of noodles.

(LEFTOVER) LAMB IN RED WINE

Two more ways of using up the end of a roast lamb, both interesting, are given in this and the following recipes. Pork or veal may also be substituted in these recipes for the lamb. The amounts serve two people.

Timing of menu: Rice, 30 minutes. Lamb dish, 15 minutes. Spinach, 5 minutes.

RECIPE: LAMB IN RED WINE

2 cups leftover lamb (or pork or veal)
1 can beef gravy
2 tablespoons dry red wine
1 can sliced mushrooms
6 black or green olives

1. Dice the meat, removing the fat and gristle as you do so.

2. Put in a pan 1 can of beef gravy, 1 can of sliced mushrooms, and 2 tablespoons of dry red wine.

3. When this combination has heated through, add the diced meat.

4. Slice 6 black or green olives, and sprinkle over the top.

5. Allow to get thoroughly hot, and serve over rice.

(LEFTOVER) LAMB IN CURRANT JELLY

This recipe is equally good with ham, pork, or veal. Follow the same menu as for Lamb in Red Wine.

RECIPE: LAMB IN CURRANT JELLY

2 cups cooked lamb (or ham or pork or veal)
1 can beef gravy
3 tablespoons currant jelly

1. Dice the meat, removing the fat and gristle as you do so.

2. Combine 1 can of beef gravy and 3 tablespoons of currant jelly. Heat, while stirring, until jelly has melted.

3. Add the meat. The dish is done when the meat is hot.

(LEFTOVER) LAMB CURRY

A friend of mine has a wide reputation for lamb curry, and the following is her recipe. It serves four.

Timing of menu: Lamb curry, 1 hour. Rice, 30 minutes.

RECIPE: LAMB CURRY

3 or more cups leftover lamb
2 tablespoons curry powder
½ small onion
2 tablespoons dry sherry
1 large stalk celery
½ cup chopped parsley
1 bay leaf

1. Henriette says she buys a 6 to 7 pound leg of lamb, has 4 people to dinner, and what is left of the leg is what she later uses to make curry for a second dinner for four. So, let us say 3 cups of cooked lamb is minimum but use as much more as you have on hand. Cut the lamb into cubes. Chop ½ of a small onion, or use ¼ cup frozen chopped onion.

2. Melt 3 tablespoons of butter in a skillet, and add to it the meat and onions.

3. Boil 1 cup of water and add to the skillet. Put in 2 tablespoons (Madras) curry powder, ½ cup of chopped parsley, 1 large stalk of celery chopped, 1 bay leaf, and 2 tablespoons of dry sherry.

4. Cover and cook gently, stirring occasionally, until the mixture is almost a paste, which will take at least an hour. If the mixture gets too dry, add more boiling water.

5. The curry is served on rice, and with it Henriette serves side dishes of chutney (available in jars); green pepper and hard-boiled egg chopped together; bananas soaked in Cointreau; grated coconut; chopped peanuts; crumbled cooked bacon; and sliced tomatoes covered with sliced onion rings.

VEAL

Veal is quite similar to lamb and may be cooked in all the ways that lamb can, but because it has a blander flavor than lamb, it also lends itself to some dishes that are special to veal alone. In color, veal is lighter than lamb and darker than pork, which is cream-colored. Choose a piece with a fresh, clear color and with firm, white fat. Estimate one-third to one-half pound of meat per serving.

ROAST VEAL

Timing of menu: Multiply the number of pounds by 25 minutes to estimate the total cooking time. Baked potatoes, 1 hour. Zucchini, 5 minutes.

RECIPE I: ROAST VEAL

1. Preheat oven to 325°.
2. Rinse the meat in running cold water, and dry with a paper towel.
3. Rub the meat all over with salt and pepper and a small amount of thyme or garlic powder.
4. Place on rack in foil-lined roasting pan, and put in oven.
5. After 30 minutes, pour 2 tablespoons of dry vermouth over the meat, and repeat this at 30 minute intervals thereafter.
6. Roast for 25 minutes per pound in a 325° oven.
7. When the roast is done, transfer it to a warmed platter, and surround it with parsley and baked potatoes. Pour off the fat in the roasting pan by tilting the pan and letting it run slowly off one corner. Use the wine remaining as a sauce for the meat.

RECIPE II: ROAST VEAL

Follow steps 1 through 4 above, but pour a can of stewed tomatoes and 3 tablespoons of dry vermouth over the meat before it goes in the oven. Occasionally, while the meat is cooking, spoon some of the liquid in the bottom of the pan up and over the meat.

Gravy

Follow the directions for Roast Leg of Lamb Gravy, page 37.

Leftover Roast Veal

- See recipe for Veal Stew.
- Substitute veal for lamb in recipes for Lamb in Red Wine and Lamb in Currant Jelly.
- Gently and quickly warm slices in leftover gravy. Add ⅓ cup of sour cream to the gravy at the last minute.

• Mix cubed meat in a casserole with cooked noodles and 1 can of stewed tomatoes. Add 1 teaspoon of salt and ½ teaspoon of sugar. Sprinkle bread crumbs and grated Parmesan cheese over the top and bake in a 350° oven for 20 minutes.

• Store extra slices in the freezer.

• Use cold in sandwiches. For hot sandwiches, spread slices on toast, and pour over hot leftover gravy or canned beef gravy.

VEAL CHOPS

Veal chops, not considered very interesting in themselves, are usually cooked in combination with other things, as witness Recipe III. A nice loin chop, however, may be broiled in the same fashion as a lamb chop and will be quite good. Rib chops are considerably smaller than loin, and you had best count on two of these per person.

Timing of menu: Broiled veal chops, 25 minutes (Recipe II, 30 minutes; Recipe III, 40 minutes). Frozen lima beans, 10 minutes. Artichokes and tomatoes, 10 minutes.

RECIPE I: BROILED VEAL CHOPS

1. Light broiler 10 minutes ahead of time.
2. Place chops on aluminum foil 3 inches from a medium flame.
3. Broil about 12 minutes on each side. But keep watch that they do not get overdone and dried out; they may take a shorter time. If the surface of the chop begins to lose its moist, juicy look, make a cut near the bone; meat that is white, not pink, indicates that the chop has cooked enough.
4. Salt and pepper the chops before serving.

RECIPE II: PAN-FRIED VEAL CHOPS

1. Put a tablespoon of flour on a piece of waxed paper, and sprinkle it well with salt and pepper. Pat the chops in this until they are lightly coated.
2. Melt 2 tablespoons of butter in a skillet, and when it is hot, add the chops. Permit the chops to become brown on both sides.
3. Lower the flame, put a cover on the skillet, and cook gently for 20 minutes. Test for doneness by making a small cut near the bone and examining the color of the meat; it should be white, not tinged with pink.

4. Remove the chops from the pan. Add 3 tablespoons of dry vermouth to the pan, stir briskly, scraping up any bits of meat clinging to the bottom of the pan, and let sauce boil up. Pour this sauce over the chops.

RECIPE III: VEAL CHOPS WITH WINE AND MUSHROOMS

4 veal chops
1 can sliced mushrooms
½ cup chopped onions
½ cup dry vermouth
1 cup consommé
1 cup sour cream
1 tablespoon tomato paste

1. Salt and pepper the chops, and lightly coat them with flour. Melt 3 tablespoons of butter in a heavy skillet, and cook the chops in this until they are nicely browned on both sides.

2. Take the chops out of the skillet, and put them aside for the time being. Add ½ cup of chopped onions (fresh or frozen) to the butter left in the skillet (add more if necessary), and cook the onions until they are transparent. If you wish to use fresh mushrooms in place of the canned, sauté these along with the onions.

3. Sprinkle in 1 tablespoon of flour, and stir until it is smooth. Cook over a very low flame for 5 minutes.

4. Pour in one cup of consommé (canned). Add 1 cup of sour cream, 1 drained can of sliced mushrooms, 1 tablespoon of tomato paste (canned), ½ teaspoon of salt, and a sprinkle of cayenne pepper. Stir well. When hot, add ½ cup of dry vermouth. Stir again. Taste and add more salt if necessary.

5. Put the veal chops in the sauce. Have the flame very low, cover the skillet, and cook for 30 minutes. Do not try to hurry this dish; too much heat is a disaster for it. Substitute noodles for the lima beans in the menu so that you have something with which to sop up the interesting gravy.

VEAL STEW

As in the instance of beef and lamb stew, veal stew may be made from either uncooked or leftover cooked veal. A very special type of veal stew is to be found in the chapter on Casseroles for Company. The recipes given here make three to four servings.

Timing of menu: Veal stew, Recipe I, 20 minutes; Recipe II, 30 minutes. Noodles, 10 minutes (veal and noodles seem to have a special affinity, and both of these stews are delicious over a bed of either wide or narrow noodles). A green salad is enough to complete the meal.

RECIPE I: (LEFTOVER) VEAL STEW

2 or 3 cups cooked veal
1 cup chopped onions
2 tomatoes
1 can mushrooms
¼ cup dry sherry
¾ cup sour cream

1. Remove any gristle from the veal, and cut the meat into cubes.
2. Melt 2 tablespoons of butter in a skillet. Cook 1 cup (or 1 medium-size) chopped onion until transparent. Remove from pan with a slotted spoon so as to leave the butter behind.
3. Cut up into small chunks 2 fresh tomatoes, and gently cook them in the butter for 5 minutes.
4. Put the onions back in, add 1 can of mushrooms, and the meat. Salt and pepper all.
5. Add ¼ cup of dry sherry (use dry vermouth or any dry white wine if sherry is not at hand). Stir everything together.
6. Let this simmer for a few minutes until it is nice and hot. Then add ¾ cup of sour cream. Stir and let cook a minute or two longer, but do not permit to bubble. Taste for sufficient seasonings.

RECIPE II: (UNCOOKED) VEAL STEW

1 pound veal
1 can condensed cream of mushroom soup
½ cup heavy cream
½ cup dry vermouth
1 can white onions

1. Trim the piece of veal of any fat or gristle, and cut the meat into cubes the size of dice.
2. Melt 2 tablespoons of butter in a skillet, and cook the meat in this, stirring occasionally, until the meat is brown on all sides.
3. Salt and pepper the meat, and sprinkle a pinch of thyme over it.
4. Add 1 can of condensed cream of mushroom soup, ½ cup of heavy cream, ½ cup of dry vermouth, and 1 drained can of white onions.
5. Cook this very gently until hot. Do not let it bubble.
6. Taste for seasonings, and pour over cooked noodles.

VEAL SCALLOPINI

Very thin slices of veal are used in veal scallopini, and they should be pounded to flatten them still further. If the butcher has not done this, cover the head of a hammer with a piece of cloth, and do the pounding yourself.

Timing of menu: Veal, Recipe I, 15 minutes; Recipe II, 45 minutes. Potato balls, 15 minutes. Frozen peas, 5 minutes.

RECIPE I: SAUTÉED VEAL SCALLOPINI

1. Melt 2 tablespoons of butter in a skillet.
2. Add veal slices; lightly squeeze lemon juice on each.
3. Simmer for 7 or 8 minutes on each side over a low flame, or until veal is tender.

RECIPE II: BAKED VEAL SCALLOPINI

1 pound thinly sliced veal
2 fresh tomatoes
1 can sliced mushrooms
½ cup Chablis or sauterne
½ cup grated Parmesan cheese

1. Preheat the oven to 400°.
2. Heat 3 tablespoons of olive or salad oil in a skillet, add a peeled clove of garlic, and put in the veal cut into 1 inch wide strips. Cook it gently until it is delicately browned.
3. Cut 2 tomatoes into thick slices and add these.
4. Put in the can of mushrooms, ½ cup of sauterne or Chablis, and ½ cup of grated Parmesan cheese. Stir.
5. Transfer all of this to a casserole and bake in a 400° oven for 30 minutes. This amount serves four people.

A SAUCE FOR VEAL

For Veal Scallopini and Veal Chops, the following is an absolutely delicious sauce. The friend who wrote out her recipe at my request appended a note, much underlined, that only *fresh mushrooms* and *real butter* would do.

RECIPE: ONION AND MUSHROOM SAUCE FOR VEAL

¼ pound mushrooms
2 tablespoons chopped onion
4 tablespoons sour cream

1. Melt 2 tablespoons of butter in a skillet, and gently cook 2 tablespoons of chopped onion in this until transparent.
2. Peel ¼ pound of mushrooms, slice them, and add to the skillet, cooking over a medium flame for 10 minutes.
3. Add 4 tablespoons of sour cream, lower the flame under the skillet, stir occasionally, and cook only until the cream is hot.

HAM

Baked ham is an easy matter these days, for the hams sold now are precooked and need only be put in the oven. Half a ham, which is usually sufficient even for a party, comes as either a butt end or shank end. The shank end has considerably more bone in it, and thus the butt end is the better buy, although more expensive per pound. If you want a smaller quantity of ham, rolled roasts are available under the names of smoked shoulder, smoked butt, and smoked tenderloin. These small hams may be cooked in exactly the same way as baked ham. Look for meat with a fresh pink color; avoid any with tannish colored areas in the meat.

BAKED HAM

There will be a brown skin on the ham, and you may cut it off before or after cooking or not at all; I usually leave it on unless it looks too tough and leathery. With the small rolled roasts, cook as is. Canned ham is also baked according to the following directions. It is expensive to buy but has no waste because the bone has been removed.

Timing of menu: Multiply weight of the ham by 20 minutes per pound. Acorn squash, 1 hour. Fresh asparagus, 10 minutes.

RECIPE: BAKED HAM

1. Turn the oven on to 300°.
2. Line roasting pan with aluminum foil and place ham in it with the fattier side up.
3. Sprinkle the ham with ground cloves.
4. Mix together into a thick paste brown sugar and fruit juice (orange, pineapple, tangerine, pear, or peach). Paint the ham with this paste.

   OR: Just put the ham in the oven as is, and when it is done, take it out, cut off the outside skin, stud the ham with whole cloves, and then paint with the sugar-fruit juice mixture. Return the ham to the oven until the outside is glazed a deep brown.
5. Bake the ham in a 300° oven for 20 minutes per pound.
6. If you like, add slices of pineapple or halved peaches or pears to the roasting pan for the last half hour of cooking, and then arrange them around the ham on serving platter.

Leftover Ham

• Use cold and sliced for further meals and for sandwiches.

• See recipes for Ham Custard, Ham and Asparagus Casserole, Tomatoes Stuffed with Ham and Mashed Potatoes, and Poached Eggs and Asparagus.

• Fry slices of ham in butter just long enough to heat them through.

• Make ham pancakes by following the directions for batter on a package of pancake mix. Dip thin slices of ham into the batter, and cook on a greased griddle or in a skillet.

• An interesting baked potato and ham dish may be made by scooping out baked potatoes from their skins, mashing the potatoes with butter, milk, and salt and pepper, adding chopped ham to the potatoes, and then mounding the potatoes back in the skins. Sprinkle grated cheese over, and heat in the oven or under the broiler until the cheese is melted and beginning to brown.

• Ham chopped fine may be added to baked corn custard.

• Substitute ham for lamb in recipe for Lamb with Currant Jelly.

• Warm slices of ham in 1 can of condensed cream of mushroom soup and 2 tablespoons of sherry. Serve on toast.

• Cube 2 cups of ham, and put in a casserole with 1 can of condensed cream of mushroom soup, 3 hard-boiled eggs cut in quarters, and 3 tablespoons of sherry. Cover the top with bread crumbs and grated cheese, and bake in a 350° oven for 20 minutes.

• Dice ham, and mix with 1 or 2 cans of (Franco-American) macaroni, cover the top with slices of American cheese and sliced tomatoes, and bake in a 350° oven for 30 minutes.

• Put odds and ends of ham through the meat chopper with a few pickles. Mix with mayonnaise and use as a spread for sandwiches or canapés.

• Cut ham into very small pieces, and add to scrambled eggs or to an omelet.

HAM STEAK

A slice of ham, about ¾ of an inch thick and preferably labeled center-cut, makes a completely easy and delicious dinner, and yet every time I serve it, one or another guest exclaims he has never had it before, so apparently ham steak is not too well known. The usual size of ham steak serves three to four people; if you are cooking for one or two, prepare only the amount needed, as it is not good warmed over.

Timing of menu: Mashed potatoes, 20 minutes. Ham steak, 15 minutes. Frozen broccoli, 8 minutes. The flavor of mashed potatoes goes particularly well with the sauce on the meat.

RECIPE: HAM STEAK

1. Pour into a skillet about ½ inch of fruit juice: orange or tangerine or pineapple. Add 2 tablespoons of brown sugar. The juice of canned pineapple or peaches may also be used and peach halves or pineapple slices cooked along with the ham.

2. Make a few slashes in the fat around the steak to keep it from curling. Put the ham steak in, and cook over a medium flame, turning once or twice, until the sauce has cooked down to a thick syrup.

3. Serve, pouring the sauce over the ham.

HAM CUSTARD

Ham Custard and Ham and Asparagus Casserole are two solutions to the problem of using up a baked ham, which can be quite a problem as there is a lot of meat on a ham.

Timing of menu: Ham Custard, about 35 minutes. White onions, 20 minutes. Frozen peas, 5 minutes.

RECIPE: HAM CUSTARD

2 cups cooked ham, ground fine
1 small can corn Niblets
1 cup heavy cream
2 eggs
2 tablespoons dry sherry

1. Turn the oven on to 325°.

2. Separate the yolks from the whites of 2 eggs (see page 22). Beat the yolks well with a fork.

3. Put the ham and egg yolks in a bowl, and add 1 small can of corn Niblets, 1 cup of heavy cream, 2 tablespoons of dry sherry, and a pinch each of marjoram and thyme.

4. With an egg beater and in a separate bowl, beat the egg whites until they are stiff. Fold these into the mixture, that is, slide them in gently, and, using a fork, fold over the mixture several times until the egg whites are mixed in.

5. Butter a baking dish, place the mixture in this, and bake in a 325° oven for 35 minutes, or until firm.

HAM AND ASPARAGUS CASSEROLE

Another use for leftover ham, and a simple and tasty one. The recipe serves three.

Timing of menu: Ham casserole, 30 minutes. This, plus a salad and French bread, makes a meal.

RECIPE: HAM AND ASPARAGUS CASSEROLE

2 cups diced ham	4 hard-boiled eggs
1 package frozen asparagus	1 can chicken gravy

1. Put 4 eggs in a saucepan with water to cover. Cook the eggs for 5 minutes after the water begins to boil. Run them under cold water, peel, and slice them.
2. Cook 1 package of frozen asparagus in boiling water for 4 minutes.
3. Butter the inside of a casserole or baking dish. Put a layer of asparagus on the bottom, next a layer of sliced hard-boiled eggs, next a layer of ham cut in small pieces. Repeat these layers until all the ingredients are used up.
4. Pour 1 can of chicken gravy over the casserole.
5. Bake in a 350° oven until the casserole is bubbling, about 20 minutes.

BAKED FRESH HAM

This is actually uncured ham, that is, pork, and it makes a fine roast. Leave the skin on, and when carving, slice the meat thin.

Timing of menu: Multiply the number of pounds the roast weighs by 40 minutes per pound. Roast potatoes (boil in salted water for 20 minutes, then add to the roasting pan 30 minutes before the roast is due to be done). Chopped carrots, 20 minutes. Applesauce.

RECIPE: BAKED FRESH HAM

1. Turn the oven on to 325°.
2. Rub the roast with salt and pepper and either oregano or thyme.
3. Place it in a roasting pan lined with aluminum foil.
4. Cook it 40 minutes per pound. Do not baste.

Gravy

1. Pour off most of the fat in the roasting pan.

2. Mix 1 tablespoon of flour and 6 tablespoons of water in a jar, and shake well.

3. With the roasting pan over a low fire on top of the stove and while stirring, slowly pour in the flour-water mixture. Stop adding it when the gravy is as thick as cream soup.

4. Add salt and pepper and 1 capful of gravy coloring (Gravy Master).

5. Continue to stir, and allow to cook at least 5 minutes. Double check on the seasonings: the gravy must have enough salt and pepper in it to taste really good.

Leftover Fresh Ham

• This makes truly fine sandwiches, either hot or cold. For a hot sandwich, warm slices of the meat briefly in the leftover gravy, arrange them on unbuttered bread or toast, and pour the gravy over.

• Add canned potatoes, white onions, carrots and peas to the leftover gravy and 3 cups of meat cut in bite-size pieces to make a stew. The addition of 1 tablespoon of grape or currant jelly does rather interesting things. If you run out of gravy before you run out of meat, a can of beef gravy will substitute well.

• Arrange slices of the meat on halves of toasted English muffins, put 1 slice of tomato on each, and top with a slice of Cheddar cheese. Put under the broiler until the cheese is melted.

• Cube the meat and add it to a casserole of hot buttered noodles. Mix together 1 can of chicken gravy and 3 tablespoons of sherry and pour over. Top with bread crumbs and bake in a 350° oven until bubbly, about 20 minutes.

• Add cubed meat to an undiluted can of (Campbell's) frozen shrimp soup. Mix in 2 tablespoons of dry vermouth. Heat, and pour over a bed of rice.

• Arrange slices on toast. Put a poached egg on top of the meat on each piece of toast and pour hot tomato sauce or undiluted cream of tomato soup over. Serve with grated Parmesan or Swiss cheese to sprinkle on top.

PORK

When buying pork, look for meat that is creamy-colored and for fat that is white. A loin of pork roast is often less expensive than other roasts and equally good. There is probably no need to repeat the well-known warning that pork should always be thoroughly cooked; no traces of pink should remain in the meat.

ROAST LOIN OF PORK

This roast looks like a series of uncut pork chops, and you can estimate the size you need by figuring on two chops per serving.

Timing of menu: Multiply the number of pounds in the roast by 40 minutes per pound. Roast potatoes (boil the peeled potatoes for 20 minutes in salted water and add them to the roast 30 minutes before the meat is due to come out of the oven). Stewed tomatoes, 10 minutes. Applesauce.

RECIPE: ROAST LOIN OF PORK

1. Light the oven and set it at 325°.
2. Sprinkle the fat side of the roast heavily with salt and pepper. If you wish, rub in thyme, marjoram, or oregano.
3. Place the roast on rack in a foil-lined roasting pan, and cook for 40 minutes per pound.

Gravy

Follow the directions given for Baked Fresh Ham Gravy, being sure to pour off most of the fat, of which there will be a great deal.

To Carve

Cut down between the bones to make thick slices the size of pork chops.

Leftover Roast Loin of Pork

Divide the remaining roast into chops, and warm in leftover gravy. Serve with mashed potatoes.

PORK CHOPS

Pork chops cooked in the following way are superior to broiled or fried pork chops because, despite the length of time needed to insure that the pork is completely done, the chops do not dry out in the cooking. The number of chops that can be cooked at the same time in this way is limited by the number that will fit into the skillet, usually no more than three. Thus, if you have more than this number of people to feed, you should follow the recipe for Pork Chop Casserole that is given in the chapter on Casseroles for Company.

Timing of menu: Pork chops, about 30 minutes. Mashed potatoes, 25 minutes. Frozen string beans, 7 minutes.

RECIPE: PORK CHOPS

1. Turn the fire on under a skillet. Cut 1 or 2 pieces of fat from a chop, and rub them, speared on a fork, over the bottom of the pan.

2. Put in the chops, and leave them alone until they are nicely browned on the underside. Turn them over, and brown the second sides.

3. Sprinkle salt, pepper, and ¼ teaspoon of sugar on each chop. Turn them over, and let the sugar brown; this takes about 1 minute. Sprinkle the other side similarly, and turn over to brown. Sugar burns readily, so keep an eye on them; you want a rich brown color, not black.

4. Add water to the pan, a sufficient amount to come level with the top of the chops. Cook over a flame high enough to keep the water bubbling briskly. Turn the chops once in the course of cooking.

5. The chops are done when the water has cooked away to a dark brown gravy in the bottom of the pan. This gravy is excellent over mashed potatoes or just a plain piece of bread. If it happens that your attention has been elsewhere and you remember the chops only when you hear a sizzling sound, remove the chops immediately and add about a quarter of a cup of water to the pan, stir well, and cook over a high flame until you arrive back at the gravy a second time.

OR: This gravy is fine as is, but if you want to dress it up still further, add 3 tablespoons of Madeira wine and ⅓ cup of sour cream to it. Let this gravy stay on the fire until it is hot, but do not permit it to boil.

LIVER

If liver is not a favorite dish of yours, try it this way, and see if you don't find it surprisingly good. Calf's liver is, of course, the best. A package of frozen liver is convenient to keep on hand for those times when you can't think of what to have for dinner.

CALF'S LIVER

Timing of menu: Baked potatoes, 1 hour. Onions (not a strict necessity but smothered in onions is the best way to eat liver in my opinion), 20 minutes. Frozen mixed vegetables, 10 minutes. Liver, 10 minutes.

RECIPE: LIVER AND ONIONS

1. Slice 1 small to medium-sized onion for each serving

of liver. Cover generously with water, and add ½ to 1 teaspoon of salt and 1 tablespoon of A-1 sauce. Let the water boil briskly, and cook the onions until the water has almost boiled away, about 20 minutes.

2. Ten minutes before the onions are due to be done, cover the bottom of a heavy skillet with a layer of salt, and put over a rather high flame.

3. When the salt is just beginning to brown, throw in the slices of liver. As soon as they are brown on the underside, turn them over, and reduce the flame.

4. Cook about 4 more minutes on each side. If, like me, you do not like bloody liver, puncture the pieces lightly with a fork from time to time so that the blood runs out.

5. The salt usually does not adhere to the liver. If any has, scrape it off with a knife before serving. Mound the onions over the liver.

CHICKEN LIVERS

Save the livers from chicken, freeze them, and when you have enough for a meal, cook them in the following way. Or use (Swanson) frozen chicken livers. Or buy fresh livers from your butcher. For Chicken Livers in Cream, see page 111.

Timing of menu: Chopped carrots, 20 minutes. Frozen lima beans, 10 minutes. Chicken livers, 8 minutes.

RECIPE: SAUTÉED CHICKEN LIVERS

1. Melt 2 tablespoons of butter in a frying pan.

2. When it is hot, add the chicken livers and a generous dash of A-1 or Worcestershire sauce.

3. Sauté the livers until they are cooked through (cut one open to check on the timing; they are done when they are a light tan color all the way through).

CHAPTER 3 HOW TO COOK POULTRY

CHICKEN

Chicken is the cook's best friend. It can be cooked in a quite amazing number of ways, combines well with almost anything, and responds to as little or as much trouble as you want to take with it. It is possible to ruin a chicken in the cooking of it, but not easily. Short of burning it or letting it get dried out, you can hardly go wrong. And it is a safe dish to serve company. I have never had a guest whose diet, no matter how circumscribed, did not permit chicken.

For all practical purposes, "broilers" and "fryers" are the same thing; you can broil a fryer or fry a broiler. They are young chickens weighing from 1⅓ to 3 pounds. Roasting chickens are larger, weighing between 3 and 5 pounds. Stewing chickens may weigh from 3 to 8 pounds and are old birds that take a lot of cooking. You can buy a cleaned chicken whole, halved, quartered, or in parts, just the breasts or just the legs, for example. In whatever form it is, buy it on the basis of a firm, meaty look and the presence of some fat. Avoid any with old, yellow, tired-looking skin.

When you get the chicken home, take out the package of "innards." Save the liver, and feed the rest to the cat; there are things that can be done with the heart and neck and gizzard, but they are not really worth the trouble unless you are an experienced cook. Hold the chicken under cold running water, and with the back of your thumbnail or the back of a spoon, ream out any traces of organs clinging to the meat, for these give a bitter taste to the chicken. Usually the lungs are still in place; so check particularly along the backbone for dark red areas and wash them away completely.

The basic ways of cooking chicken are given in this chapter, along with suggestions for using leftovers. But because of the many ways chicken can be used in splendid casserole dishes, be sure also to check the chapter on Casseroles for Company.

FRIED CHICKEN

There are two ways of frying chicken, one just plain, the other with a light coating of flour. The flour makes a bit more of a crust on the chicken, but otherwise there is little difference. Use a chicken cut in quarters or chicken in parts.

Timing of menu: Fried chicken, 40 minutes. Mashed potatoes, 20 minutes. Petit Pois (peas) (canned, Le Sueur's), 5 minutes.

RECIPE: FRIED CHICKEN

1. Melt 2 tablespoons of butter and 2 tablespoons of salad oil in a heavy skillet or casserole over a medium-high flame.

2. Salt and pepper the chicken all over. Or put 2 table-

spoons of flour, 1 teaspoon of salt, and ⅛ teaspoon of pepper in a paper bag. Shake the pieces of chicken, one at a time, in the bag.

3. Place the chicken pieces in the hot fat, and allow all pieces to brown on all sides. I find that letting them go to a rich brown color, rather than stopping at a golden tan, does more to seal in the juices and insures the chicken being tender.

4. When the chicken is well browned, turn the fire down quite low and cover the pan.

5. Allow to cook about 20 minutes, or until the chicken is tender. Test for doneness by inserting a knife into the thickest part of a leg. If the meat still feels springy and resistant, it is not done.

OR: Brown the chicken on top of the stove as directed, and then put it in a casserole with 3 tablespoons of water or 3 tablespoons of white wine or dry vermouth, cover the casserole, and bake in a 400° oven for 30 minutes.

BROILED CHICKEN

Broiling chicken requires even less attention than frying it, since all you do is put it under the broiler and turn it once in the course of cooking. For a generous serving, buy broilers split in half, and count on a half for each person.

Timing of menu: Broiled chicken, 30 minutes. Mashed potatoes, 25 minutes. Artichokes and tomatoes, 10 minutes.

RECIPE: BROILED CHICKEN

1. Turn on the broiler.

2. Rinse the chicken halves under cold running water, dry them thoroughly with paper towels, and rub them with butter. Salt and pepper them well.

3. Line the broiling pan with aluminum foil, and place the pieces of chicken on it skin side down. Broil the chicken 3 inches below a medium flame.

4. After 15 minutes, turn the pieces over, and broil on the second side for an additional 15 minutes.

5. After 30 minutes total cooking time, test for doneness by inserting a sharp knife in the thickest part of the leg. If the juice that runs out is clear, the chicken is done; if it is pink-tinged, cook it longer. If the chicken begins to look dry at any time during the cooking, brush it with melted butter.

ROAST CHICKEN

Again, an extremely simple way of cooking chicken. Squab may also be cooked this way, but the temperature of the oven should be higher, 450°, and the cooking time shorter, 45 minutes. For roasting, the chicken must be whole.

Timing of menu: Roast chicken, multiply the weight of the chicken by 20 minutes per pound. Baked potatoes, 1 hour. Fresh spinach, 5 minutes.

RECIPE: ROAST CHICKEN

1. Preheat the oven to 350°.
2. Rinse the chicken inside and out under cold running water, and dry it well. Peel an onion and place it, whole, inside the chicken. Tie the legs of the chicken together with a piece of string.
3. Rub the outside of the chicken with butter and sprinkle it well with salt and pepper.
4. Put the chicken in a roasting pan lined with aluminum foil, and roast it 20 minutes per pound. Occasionally pour a little melted butter or white wine over it so that it will not dry out in the cooking. Cooking is complete when you prick the leg with a knife and the juice runs clear.

STEWED CHICKEN

If the chicken is an old bird, it had best be stewed. (Or if you wish to have cooked chicken as a start on any one of a number of dishes.) A pressure cooker does very nicely by a stewed chicken, but if you do not have one, follow the directions here.

Timing of menu: Stewed chicken, about 25 minutes per pound (the age of the chicken makes a difference in the cooking time; test with a fork for tenderness to determine when done). Boiled potatoes, 30 minutes. Frozen string beans, 7 minutes.

RECIPE: STEWED CHICKEN

1 stewing chicken	1 carrot
1 onion	1 stalk celery

1. Rinse the pieces of chicken under cold running water.
2. Put in a pot with 1 peeled onion, quartered, 1 peeled carrot, and a stalk of celery. Add a bay leaf and 2 teaspoons

of salt. Cover the chicken with water.

3. Bring water to a boil, turn the fire down, and simmer the chicken until tender.

Gravy

Good chicken gravy is rather difficult to achieve, so you may wish to settle for warming until piping hot a can of (Franco-American) chicken gravy. Or you can try the following method:

1. Remove the pieces of chicken and vegetables from the pot, and skim off the fat that is on top of the water. Turn up the fire to full flame so the water in the pot boils rapidly.

2. In a separate pan, melt 3 tablespoons of butter.

3. Add to the butter, stirring constantly, 2 tablespoons of flour.

4. When the butter and flour are well mixed in a paste, slowly pour in 1 cup of the chicken broth, still stirring all the time.

5. Taste and adjust seasoning. Permit to cook at least 5 minutes, stirring often so that the gravy does not lump.

Leftover Chicken

With leftover fried, broiled, roasted, or stewed chicken, slice what you can, and then remove the rest of the meat from the bones, discarding the skin.

• See recipes for Chicken Stew, Chicken in Shrimp Sauce, Chicken Tetrazzini, and Chicken and Asparagus Casserole.

• Use for Chicken a la King (see recipe). Or warm a package of frozen Chicken a la King, and add 1 tablespoon of dry sherry and bits of leftover chicken to it.

• Arrange slices of chicken on toast, baking powder biscuits, corn muffins, or on a bed of rice. Add 1 tablespoon of dry vermouth and 1 bay leaf to a can of chicken gravy, heat, remove the bay leaf, and pour the gravy over the chicken.

• Use cold in chicken salad (see recipes).

• Alternate layers of canned macaroni in cream sauce with layers of chicken and layers of cooked asparagus in a buttered baking dish, ending with a layer of macaroni. Sprinkle the top with bread crumbs and grated cheese, and bake in a 375° oven for 20 minutes.

• Cook frozen broccoli or artichoke hearts 2 minutes less than the directions on the package call for. Arrange in a buttered baking dish, and lay the chicken over it. Spoon enough (Kraft's) Cheez-Whiz over all to cover thickly.

Sprinkle with bread crumbs and paprika, and bake in a 400° oven for 15 minutes.

VARIATIONS ON (UNCOOKED) CHICKEN

Each one of these recipes is more delicious than the next, which means that each is impressively good. Try them all, and settle on the ones that most please you as special dishes to keep in mind when you are having guests for dinner. None of them will suffer from being partially cooked, turned off, and then put back on the fire again for last-minute completion. Use broilers or fryers cut in pieces for these recipes unless otherwise designated. One quartered chicken serves four people, barring a guest with a very large appetite. In the latter event, you may wish to add two extra chicken breasts or legs to the recipes; the recipes need not be changed otherwise. More recipes for chicken are to be found in the chapter on Casseroles for Company.

CHICKEN IN CREAM AND MADEIRA

Timing of menu: Chicken, 45 minutes. Rice, 30 minutes. Tossed salad.

RECIPE: CHICKEN IN CREAM AND MADEIRA

1 quartered chicken
1 cup heavy cream
1 can sliced or whole mushrooms
¼ cup Madeira
¼ cup brandy

1. In a casserole or heavy skillet with a lid, melt 2 tablespoons of butter and 2 tablespoons of salad oil.
2. Salt and pepper the chicken pieces, and put them in the hot oil. Brown each piece well on both sides.
3. When all of the chicken is brown, cover and cook over a low flame until tender when tested with a knife; this should take about 20 minutes. If the cooking is to be completed later, stop at this point.
4. Warm ¼ cup of brandy in a separate pan, pour over the chicken, strike a match to ignite the brandy.
5. When the flame of the brandy has died out, add ¼ cup of Madeira wine, 1 cup of heavy cream, and 1 drained can of sliced or whole mushrooms.
6. Make sure that everything is well mixed together. Let it cook over a low flame until it is thoroughly hot, but be very careful not to let the sauce boil.
7. Serve the pieces of chicken, and pour the sauce over.

BAKED CHICKEN IN SOUR CREAM

Timing of menu: Chicken, 1 hour and 15 minutes. Broiled tomatoes, 15 minutes. Frozen peas, 5 minutes.

RECIPE: BAKED CHICKEN

1 quartered chicken
1 onion
1 cup sour cream

1. Preheat oven to 325°.
2. Put 2 tablespoons of butter and 2 of salad oil in a skillet over a medium flame.
3. Put 2 tablespoons of flour, 1 teaspoon of salt, and ⅛ teaspoon of pepper in a paper bag. Shake each piece of chicken in the bag individually.
4. Add the chicken to the skillet, and brown it on all sides.
5. Transfer the chicken to a casserole. Hold cooking up at this point if you wish.
6. Grate one onion and add it to the chicken. If you do not have a grater, chop the onion as fine as possible.
7. Put in 1 cup of sour cream.
8. Cover the casserole with a tightly fitting lid, and bake the chicken in a 325° oven for 1 hour, turning the pieces of chicken over once in the course of cooking.

CHICKEN BREASTS WITH WHITE GRAPES

Timing of menu: Chicken, 45 minutes. Rice, 30 minutes. Chopped carrots, 20 minutes.

RECIPE: CHICKEN BREASTS WITH WHITE GRAPES

4 chicken breasts
1 bunch seedless white grapes
1½ cups dry vermouth

1. Turn on the oven to 400°.
2. Melt 4 tablespoons of butter in a casserole on top of the stove, and cook the chicken, well sprinkled with salt and pepper, in the butter until the pieces have browned on all sides.
3. Pour 1½ cups of dry vermouth over the chicken.
4. Put a lid on the casserole, and transfer it to the oven. Let it bake for 10 minutes.
5. Add 1 bunch of seedless white grapes, and continue the cooking until the chicken is tender, which should take about 15 minutes more.

CHICKEN IN RED WINE

Timing of menu: Chicken, 45 minutes. Rice, 30 minutes. Green beans in sour cream, 20 minutes.

RECIPE: CHICKEN IN RED WINE

1 quartered chicken	1 clove garlic
1 dozen green olives	¼ cup chopped onions
½ cup red wine	¼ pound fresh mushrooms

1. Salt and pepper the chicken well, and brown the pieces in 4 tablespoons of butter.
2. Remove the chicken from the skillet. Put in ¼ cup of chopped onions and 1 clove of garlic cut in half.
3. When the onions are transparent, remove the garlic and sprinkle in 2 tablespoons of flour, stirring briskly so that it does not lump.
4. Still stirring add ½ cup of dry red wine. When this is well blended, put in ¼ pound of fresh mushrooms and 1 dozen green olives cut in half.
5. Replace the chicken, cover the pan, and cook over a gentle heat for 20 minutes, or until the chicken is tender.

CHICKEN AND ONIONS

Timing of menu: Chicken, 1 hour. Potato balls, 15 minutes. Frozen mixed vegetables, 10 minutes.

RECIPE: CHICKEN AND ONIONS

1 quartered chicken	¼ cup dry vermouth
2 Bermuda onions	poultry seasoning

1. Preheat the oven to 400°.
2. Peel and slice 2 Bermuda onions, and spread them over the bottom of a casserole.
3. Lay the pieces of chicken over the onions, and sprinkle the chicken with plenty of salt and pepper and paprika, plus 3 pinches of poultry seasoning (this you will find on the herb shelf at the grocery store and it is called simply "Poultry Seasoning").
4. Add ¼ cup of dry vermouth to the casserole, cover, and bake at 400° for 45 minutes.
5. Remove the lid from the casserole, and bake an additional 15 minutes, or until tender.

CHICKEN IN SHERRY

Timing of menu: Chicken, 40 minutes. Thin noodles, 10 minutes. Broiled tomatoes, 15 minutes.

RECIPE: CHICKEN IN SHERRY

1 quartered chicken
1 cup dry sherry

1. Heat 2 tablespoons of butter and 2 tablespoons of salad oil in a casserole on top of the stove.
2. Salt and pepper the pieces of chicken, and cook them in the butter and oil until they are nicely browned on all sides.
3. Add 1 cup of dry sherry, lower the flame, put a lid on the casserole, and cook gently until the chicken is tender, which should take about 20 minutes.
4. If you like, you can add a can of sliced mushrooms or some sliced green olives in the last moments of cooking.

GARLIC CHICKEN

Timing of menu: Chicken, 40 minutes (but chicken must marinate overnight in the refrigerator). Rice, 30 minutes. Frozen succotash, 10 minutes.

RECIPE: GARLIC CHICKEN

1 quartered chicken
1 cup sour cream
1 teaspoon Worcestershire sauce
2 cloves garlic

1. In a bowl big enough to hold all the pieces of chicken, put 1 cup of sour cream, 1 teaspoon of Worcestershire sauce, and 2 sliced cloves of garlic. Add 1 tablespoon of lemon juice, ½ teaspoon each of salt, pepper, and paprika, and, if you have it on hand, ¾ teaspoon of celery salt.
2. Put the pieces of chicken in the bowl, and turn them several times until they are well saturated with the sauce. Cover the bowl, and let stand in the refrigerator overnight, turning the chicken at least once more.
3. When ready to cook the chicken, discard the marinade. Melt 2 tablespoons of butter and 2 of salad oil in a skillet, and brown the chicken on all sides. When the pieces are brown, put a lid on, and cook until the chicken is tender, about 20 minutes.

CHICKEN WITH PARMESAN CHEESE

Timing of menu: Chicken, 1½ hours. Buttered spaghetti, 12 minutes. Fresh spinach, 5 minutes.

RECIPE: CHICKEN WITH PARMESAN CHEESE

1 quartered chicken
1 cup dry white wine
1 cup grated Parmesan cheese
1 tablespoon prepared mustard
1 cup heavy cream
½ cup bread crumbs

1. Melt 4 tablespoons of butter in a casserole on top of the stove. Add the pieces of chicken, first sprinkling them well with salt, pepper, and paprika.

2. Put a lid on the casserole, and cook the chicken gently over a low flame until it is browned and tender, 45 minutes to an hour.

3. When the chicken is done, take it out of the casserole. Line the broiling pan (remove the rack) with aluminum foil, and arrange the pieces of chicken on this. Light the broiler but do not put the chicken in yet.

4. Add to the casserole 1 cup of grated Parmesan cheese, and let this melt over a low fire, stirring to mix it with the juice left in the casserole from the chicken.

5. When the cheese has melted, add 1 cup of dry white wine, 1 level tablespoon of (Gulden's) prepared mustard, and 1 cup of heavy cream. Stir constantly until the mixture is just about to boil. Taste to see if it needs salt.

6. Pour this sauce over the pieces of chicken, and sprinkle bread crumbs over. Put the chicken under the broiler just long enough for the bread crumbs to become a golden brown.

BROILED CHICKEN WITH MOZZARELLA CHEESE

Timing of menu: Chicken, 45 minutes. Baked corn custard, 30 minutes. Frozen string beans, 7 minutes.

RECIPE: CHICKEN WITH MOZZARELLA CHEESE

chicken breasts
sliced mozzarella cheese
1 can sliced mushrooms

1. Paint the chicken breasts with salad oil, and salt and pepper them. Put them under the broiler, and cook for 15 minutes on each side.

2. Remove the skin (it will pull off easily), cover the meaty side of the chicken with sliced canned mushrooms,

and lay a slice of mozzarella cheese on each breast.

3. Return to the broiler for just long enough to melt the cheese. Before serving, decorate with paprika and parsley.

BARBECUED CHICKEN

To barbecue a chicken, paint it with (Crosse and Blackwell's Smoky) barbecue sauce and broil (page 56) or roast (page 57) it, applying more sauce several times in the course of cooking.

VARIATIONS ON (COOKED) CHICKEN

The following recipes are some of the things that can be done with cooked chicken. Leftover turkey can equally well be substituted in any of these dishes. If you want to make any of these recipes but have no leftover chicken or turkey on hand, cook the chicken first according to the recipe for Stewed Chicken on page 57, but reduce the cooking time quite considerably if you are using a young chicken rather than one for fricasseeing.

CHICKEN STEW

Timing of menu: Chicken stew, 15 minutes. Baking powder biscuits (frozen), 10 minutes. Green salad.

RECIPE: CHICKEN STEW

chunks of cooked chicken	1 can carrots
1 can white potatoes	1 tablespoon dry vermouth
1 can white onions	1 or 2 cans chicken gravy

1. Put everything together in a pot, using either 1 or 2 cans of chicken gravy as needed. Add a bay leaf and cook gently until piping hot. If you have any leftover vegetables on hand, such as peas or lima beans or corn, add these too. Or add sliced mushrooms or sliced olives or (precooked) artichoke hearts.

2. Brown frozen baking powder biscuits in the oven according to the directions on the package. Break them in half, and either put them, split side down, on top of the casserole in which you serve the stew or pour the stew over them.

CHICKEN A LA KING

Timing of menu: Acorn squash, 1 hour. Chicken, 20 minutes. Frozen broccoli, 8 minutes.

RECIPE: CHICKEN A LA KING

1 cup cooked chicken
1 tablespoon sherry
1 egg yolk
1 can mushrooms
1 cup milk
3 tablespoons cream
1 teaspoon lemon juice

1. Make a white sauce by melting 1 tablespoon of butter and sprinkling in 1 tablespoon of flour. Do this over a very low flame, and stir constantly until the butter and flour are blended in a smooth paste. Then add 1 cup of milk, a little bit at a time, always stirring. As the sauce begins to bubble, it will thicken, so do not worry if it starts looking very thin. Allow to cook for 5 minutes, stirring very often.

2. Add ¾ teaspoon of salt and a dash of paprika, and put in the chicken (at least 1 cup; more if you have it), 1 drained can of mushrooms, and 1 tablespoon of dry sherry. Taste to check that there is enough seasoning. Let this mixture cook gently until thoroughly hot.

3. This next step must be done just before the meal is ready to serve. Take the yolk of 1 egg (see page 22 for how to separate an egg) and 3 tablespoons of cream and beat them together with a fork. Stir into the chicken mixture, add 1 teaspoon of lemon juice, and cook only enough longer for everything to be hot; do not let the mixture boil.

4. Serve over toast, biscuits, or waffles, or in pastry shells (available frozen or in bakeries).

CHICKEN TETRAZZINI

Timing of menu: Chicken, 45 minutes. Stewed tomatoes, 10 minutes. Green salad.

RECIPE: CHICKEN TETRAZZINI

2 cups cooked chicken
8 ounces thin spaghetti
1 can mushrooms
1 cup cream
⅓ cup grated Parmesan cheese
1 cup chicken bouillon

1. Cook thin spaghetti according to the directions on the package. Drain it, and put it in a buttered baking dish.

2. While the spaghetti is cooking, turn the oven on to 375°.

3. Melt 2 tablespoons of butter in a saucepan and sprinkle in 2 tablespoons of flour. Do this over a very low heat, and stir constantly to blend the two together without any lumps.

4. Gradually pour in 1 cup of chicken bouillon (canned or add a cup of hot water to a chicken bouillon cube). Cook

gently, stirring, until this sauce is thick and smooth.

5. Add 2 cups of diced chicken, 1 can of mushrooms (including the juice in the can), and 1 cup of cream. Stir and allow to heat through, but do not let boil. Add ½ teaspoon of salt, and taste to see if more is needed.

6. Add this mixture to the spaghetti in the baking dish, sprinkle the top heavily with grated Parmesan cheese, and bake in a 375° oven for 25 minutes, or until top is nicely browned.

CHICKEN AND ASPARAGUS CASSEROLE

Timing of menu: Chicken and asparagus, 25 minutes. Broiled eggplant, 7 minutes. Grape and melon ball salad.

RECIPE: CHICKEN AND ASPARAGUS CASSEROLE

sliced cooked chicken
1 package frozen asparagus spears
1 can condensed cream of chicken soup
1 tablespoon dry sherry
½ teaspoon Worcestershire sauce
½ cup grated Parmesan cheese

1. Turn on the oven to 425°.
2. Cook a package of frozen asparagus spears according to the package directions.
3. While the asparagus is cooking, in another saucepan put 1 can of condensed cream of chicken soup, ¼ cup of grated Parmesan cheese, 1 tablespoon of dry sherry, and ½ teaspoon of Worcestershire sauce. Stir this together and heat.
4. Arrange the asparagus spears on the bottom of a baking dish, casserole, or individual casserole dishes. Lay the slices of chicken over the asparagus. Pour the sauce over all, and top with ¼ cup of grated Parmesan cheese.
5. Bake in a 425° oven for 15 minutes, or until the top is lightly browned.

CHICKEN IN SHRIMP SAUCE

The amount of noodles to be used in this recipe depends on the amount of chicken. For each serving of chicken, use a full handful of noodles.

Timing of menu: Chicken, 25 minutes. Serve with French bread and a tossed salad.

RECIPE: CHICKEN IN SHRIMP SAUCE

pieces of cooked chicken
1 can petit pois

1 can frozen shrimp soup
thin noodles

2 tablespoons dry vermouth or sherry

1. Turn on the oven to 350°.

2. Cook the noodles according to the package directions, and while they are cooking, warm 1 can of (Campbell's) frozen shrimp soup. When the soup is hot, add 2 tablespoons of dry vermouth or dry sherry to it and sprinkle in ⅛ teaspoon of garlic powder.

3. Put the noodles into a casserole. For the next layer, add 1 can (large or small, depending on the quantity of chicken and noodles) of (Le Sueur's) peas, and, if you have it on hand, 1 can of drained sliced mushrooms. The next layer is the chicken. Pour the shrimp sauce over.

4. Bake for 15 minutes in a 350° oven.

TURKEY

Turkeys come in small sizes now, so there is no need to wait for a holiday and many guests at the table to enjoy them. A small turkey makes an excellent alternative to the Sunday dinner roast, it is fine for company, and looks handsome in the center of a buffet table. Best of all, a turkey is perfectly simple to roast. In buying a turkey look for a rounded, plump one with fresh, clear skin. Buy a 6-pound turkey for four to six people.

ROAST TURKEY

Timing of menu: Multiply the weight of the turkey by 25 minutes per pound to arrive at total cooking time. Mashed potatoes, 25 minutes. Tiny white onions, 20 minutes. Frozen peas, 5 minutes. Cranberry sauce.

RECIPE: ROAST TURKEY

1. Turn the oven on to 350°.

2. Wash the turkey under cold running water inside and out, and check to make sure you have removed the package of liver, etc.; sometimes this is tucked under the skin at the neck and is not readily visible. Dry the turkey with paper towels.

3. The turkey may be cooked either stuffed or unstuffed. If unstuffed, rub the inside cavity with salt, and put a whole peeled onion in it. Tie the legs of the turkey together with a piece of string. If you wish to stuff the turkey, buy 2 packages of (Pepperidge Farm) stuffing. Follow the directions on the package, but add to the stuffing 1 or 2 cans of sliced mushrooms and 3 tablespoons of melted butter. Stuff the cavity and tie the legs together.

4. Rub the outside skin of the turkey with butter, and salt and pepper it well.

5. Line a roasting pan with aluminum foil, put the turkey in, and into the oven.

6. To keep the turkey moist, paint it with melted butter, or pour a bit of white wine over it at intervals of 20 to 30 minutes. When there are enough drippings in the bottom of the pan, spoon this liquid over the turkey in place of the butter or wine.

7. The turkey is done when the thigh joint moves easily as you wiggle a leg back and forth, or when you pierce the thigh with a knife and the juice that runs out is clear, not pink-tinged.

Gravy

1. Remove the turkey, and put it on a warm platter. Surround it with parsley for decoration.

2. Take the rack and aluminum foil out of the roasting pan, and put the pan on top of the stove over a medium flame.

3. Mix 1 tablespoon of flour and 6 tablespoons of water in a jar, and shake well. Pour this into the pan, stirring constantly, and stop when the gravy is the consistency of cream soup. Add salt and pepper to taste, and, if the gravy is colorless, put in 1 capful of (Gravy Master) gravy coloring.

4. Cook, stirring frequently, for at least 5 minutes. If you have not stuffed the turkey, you may want to add a can of sliced mushrooms to the gravy.

Cranberry sauce is, of course, traditional with turkey. To get the sauce out of the can, remove both the top and bottom of the can and the cylinder of sauce will slide out whole.

Leftover Turkey

- Cold sliced turkey is one of the joys of having a turkey. Serve it on a platter decorated with tomato wedges, sliced hard-boiled eggs, and parsley for another meal. Use it in sandwiches, hot or cold.
- To warm up the stuffing, spoon it out of the bird and cook it gently, just long enough to get it hot, in leftover gravy or a can of chicken gravy.
- See the suggestions for Leftover Chicken and all the recipes utilizing cooked chicken. Turkey may be substituted for the chicken in every case, including Chicken Salad (see pages 58 and 162).
- See recipe for Turkey in Black Cherry Sauce.

(LEFTOVER) TURKEY IN BLACK CHERRY SAUCE

Timing of menu: Rice, 30 minutes. Turkey, 20 minutes. Frozen mixed vegetables, 10 minutes.

RECIPE: TURKEY IN BLACK CHERRY SAUCE

white meat slices of turkey
1 large can black pitted cherries
3 tablespoons sherry
nutmeg
cinnamon
powdered clove
ginger

1. Drain the can of cherries, but save the juice. Put the cherries in a saucepan, and add 2 tablespoons of the juice, 2 tablespoons of white sugar, and a teaspoon-tip each of cinnamon, powdered clove, ginger, and nutmeg. Cook this very slowly for 20 minutes.

2. In the meantime, after the cherries have cooked for 10 minutes, put 2 tablespoons of butter and 3 tablespoons of dry sherry in a frying pan. Add the turkey slices to this, and simmer over a very low flame for 10 minutes.

3. Serve the turkey slices, and put the sauce in a separate dish or gravy boat so that it may be spooned over the turkey at the table.

DUCK

For me, all the recipes for duck begin and end with Glazed Duck, for that one recipe is so superb that it seems almost a pity to cook duck any other way. But in the event that not everyone shares my taste, how to roast a duck is also described. Duck has a layer of fat under the skin which melts in the cooking; the duck should not sit in this fat so be sure always to cook it in a pan with a rack. The frozen Long Island ducklings are very good and widely available now. Let thaw in the ice box for 12 hours before cooking. One-quarter of a duck equals one serving.

ROAST DUCK

Timing of menu: Duck, 1½ hours. Wild rice, 30 minutes. Fresh asparagus, 10 minutes.

RECIPE: ROAST DUCK

1. Turn the oven on to 325°.

2. Rub the outside of the duck with salt and pepper. Place in a roasting pan with a rack. Roast the duck for 1½

hours, and then check to make certain it is done by prodding the thickest area of the meat with a fork. If it is tender, not resistant, it has cooked enough.

Gravy

There is too much fat in duck to make good gravy; so it is best not to attempt it.

To Carve

Duck is virtually impossible to slice. Thus, it is served in quarters, being cut in half lengthwise just alongside the backbone and then these halves cut in half. But this, too, is very difficult to do, and you may wish to get the necessary wrestling over with ahead of time by cutting the duck into quarters before it is cooked (easily accomplished with kitchen shears if you have them). If so, just roast in the same fashion as described, laying the quarters on the rack in the roasting pan with the skin side up.

GLAZED DUCK

Remember this version of duck when you are planning a dinner for guests. It is impressive, delicious, and seems to be a new experience for most people.

Timing of menu: Duck, 1 hour and 50 minutes. Sweet potatoes (canned), 20 minutes. Petit pois with a few canned white onions added, 10 minutes.

RECIPE: GLAZED DUCK

1 quartered duck
½ cup orange marmalade
1 can sweet potatoes
2 tablespoons honey
1 teaspoon Gravy Master

1. Turn the oven on to 325°.
2. Cut the duck into quarters. Salt and pepper the pieces, and place them, skin side up, on a rack in a roasting pan.
3. Cook in a 325° oven for 1½ hours.
4. Spread half the orange marmalade over the skin side of the duck.
5. Mix together 2 tablespoons of honey and 1 teaspoon of Gravy Master, and spread half of this on top of the marmalade, painting the pieces of duck in the best fashion possible (some will slide off, but it cannot be helped).
6. Put the sweet potatoes on the rack around the duck, and coat these with the rest of the orange marmalade and the honey mixture in the same fashion.

7. Turn the oven up to 400°, and let the duck and potatoes cook for about 20 minutes more until everything is beautifully glazed.

ROCK CORNISH HENS

Frozen rock cornish hens are a rather new addition to the poultry list and a pleasant one. Since they are small, it is safest to count on one bird per person.

Timing of menu: Baked sweet potatoes, 1 hour. Hens, 50 minutes. Artichokes and tomatoes, 10 minutes.

RECIPE: ROCK CORNISH HENS

1. Allow the hens to thaw in the refrigerator for 12 hours.
2. Turn on the oven to 450°.
3. Inside each hen put 1 peeled clove of garlic, and sprinkle in salt and pepper (about ½ teaspoon of salt and ⅛ teaspoon of pepper). Add ½ teaspoon of thyme.
4. Melt 3 tablespoons of butter in a skillet, and cook the hens in this, turning often, just until they are nicely browned on all sides.
5. Put the hens in a roasting pan without a rack and cook in a 450° oven for 40 minutes, or until they feel tender when prodded with a fork. During this cooking time, have on hand ½ cup of melted butter to which has been added either 4 tablespoons of lemon juice or Cointreau. Spoon some of this over the hens at frequent intervals.
6. When the hens are ready to serve, place them on a platter and pour over them the sauce in the bottom of the pan.

CHAPTER 4 HOW TO COOK FISH

A friend of mine discovered fish at age 25. That is, fish as it should be cooked. His mother, when he was a child, served chunks of fish, head and all, floating in the quantity of water it had been boiled in, which early convinced him that fish, although it might be good for one, was to be avoided at all costs. Fortunately, someone who did not know his aversion to fish invited him to dine on beautifully broiled trout, and now he is an authority on the best seafood restaurants in town, fish having become his most favored food.

If, by any chance, your memories of fish are also of a strong-tasting, unappetizing food, venture the small amount of money necessary to purchase a fish for broiling, cook it, taste it, and decide whether you, too, have not come upon one of the pleasures of this life. It is worth the try because fish is apt to be cheaper than meat, and it is cooked in ways that are simple and quick.

When buying fish the signs of freshness to look for are clear, bright, bulging eyes, shiny scales, and red gills. Press the fish with your thumb; if the flesh feels firm and your thumb leaves no impression, that also indicates that it is fresh. Have the fishmonger cut off the head and tail and split the fish. If possible, buy the fish the same day you plan to have it for dinner; in any event, keep it no longer than 24 hours. To store, wrap it in aluminum foil, and place in the coldest part of the refrigerator outside of the freezing compartment.

Frozen fish, while not completely comparable to fresh, can be very good. Particularly tasty are the frozen rainbow trout that come from Denmark and frozen smelts, which are tiny fish served six to a person and eaten with the fingers. You do not need to thaw fish before cooking; just lengthen the cooking time. If you do thaw it, do it in the refrigerator, out of the freezing compartment, not at room temperature.

To tell when fish is done, gently lift a piece of the flesh near the backbone..When the meat no longer has a transparent or translucent look, it is done. Be careful not to overcook fish.

Fish is traditionally served with wedges of lemon and tartar sauce. Make tartar sauce by cutting pickles into tiny pieces and mixing with mayonnaise.

BROILED FISH

Any fish, up to a reasonable size, may be broiled, for example, mackerel, bluefish, butterfish, smelts, trout. If the fish is whole, turn it once midway through the cooking time. If it is halved, cook it skin side down and without turning. Always place aluminum foil on the broiling pan so as to make the cleaning-up easier.

Timing of menu: Fish, cooking time depends on the size of the fish but about 10 minutes is the average. Boiled potatoes, 30 minutes. Stewed tomatoes, 10 minutes.

RECIPE I: BROILED FISH

1. Turn on broiler to 400° (medium-high).
2. Wash the fish under cold running water, and dry it with paper towels.

3. Salt and pepper the fish. Put aluminum foil in the broiling pan, and pour a small amount of salad oil on it, just enough to keep the fish from sticking. Lay the fish on the foil, flesh side up, and pour an additional small amount of salad oil over the fish to coat it very lightly.

4. Broil the fish until the flesh flakes easily when a portion near the backbone is lifted with the tip of a knife. If the fish is small, make this test after 5 minutes; larger, after 8 minutes.

RECIPE II: BROILED FISH WITH FRENCH DRESSING

1. Follow the directions in Recipe I, but coat the fish lightly with French dressing in place of the oil.

RECIPE III: BROILED FISH WITH WINE

1. Wash, dry, and salt and pepper the fish.
2. Dot the flesh side of the fish with bits of butter.
3. Put the fish under the broiler (400°), and when the butter has melted, moisten the fish with a few tablespoons of dry white wine.
4. When the fish is done, remove it to a warm platter. Pour the juice into a skillet, add a can of drained sliced mushrooms, let the juice boil up, and pour over the fish.

RECIPE IV: BROILED FISH WITH A CRISP SKIN

1. Wash, dry, and salt and pepper the fish.
2. Rub the fish with butter, salt and pepper it, and then dip it lightly in flour. Shake the fish so only a light coating of flour adheres to it.
3. Broil it under a medium-high flame until the flesh flakes easily when tested with a fork.

RECIPE V: BROILED FISH WITH ONIONS AND WINE

1. Wash, dry, and salt and pepper the fish. Paint it with melted butter, and put any extra melted butter in the pan before laying the fish in it. Squeeze the juice of a quarter of a lemon over the fish.
2. Peel and slice an onion thinly, and lay the slices over the fish. Dot the onion with small bits of butter.
3. Put in the broiler under a medium-high flame. After 7 minutes, dribble 3 tablespoons of dry white wine or dry vermouth over all. Cook for another 5 minutes, and test for doneness.
4. Remove fish to a warmed platter. Put the broiling pan over a flame on top of the stove, add 2 more tablespoons

of wine or vermouth, and a few sliced stuffed olives. Let this boil up quickly, and pour the sauce over the fish.

BAKED WHOLE FISH

Any fish from about 1 pound up in size may be baked. The test for doneness is the same as when broiling: gently lift, with a fork or toothpick, a thick part of the flesh near the backbone; if the meat still appears shiny and translucent, it is not yet done. The average baking time is 10 to 12 minutes per pound in a hot (400°) oven. Have the fishmonger split the fish and remove the head.

Timing of menu: Fish, 10-12 minutes per pound. Baked macaroni with tomatoes and cheese, 20 minutes. Fresh spinach, 5 minutes.

RECIPE I: BAKED FISH

1. Light the oven and set it at 400°.
2. Place the split fish skin-side down in a buttered baking dish.
3. Brush the fish well with melted butter, and salt and pepper it. It is optional whether or not you dust it with a very light coating of flour. Another option is to lay a strip of raw bacon on each slice.
4. Bake for 10 to 12 minutes a pound in a 400° oven. Test for doneness after the minimal cooking time. If you like, after the first few minutes of cooking, you can dribble 1 tablespoon of dry white wine or dry vermouth over each slice of fish.

RECIPE II: BAKED FISH WITH TOMATOES AND ONIONS

1. Preheat oven to 400°.
2. Grease the baking dish lightly with a little salad oil.
3. Lay the fish in the dish flesh-side up, and sprinkle it with salt and pepper and thyme. Lay thin slices of onion over the fish and slices of tomato on top of the onion. Dot with bits of butter.
4. Bake in a 400° oven. After 30 minutes, test for doneness.

RECIPE III: BAKED STUFFED FISH

1 good-sized fish
1 small can shrimp
½ cup chopped onions
1½ cups bread crumbs
1 egg
1 cup milk
1 teaspoon Worcestershire sauce

1. Set oven at 350°.

2. Melt 2 tablespoons of butter in a skillet, and lightly cook in this ½ cup of finely chopped onions.

3. Drain a small can of shrimp, and cut the shrimp into small pieces. Add the shrimp to the onions.

4. When the onions have cooked enough to be transparent, add 1½ cups of bread crumbs, and mix in well with the shrimp and onions. Turn the fire off under the pan.

5. Beat 1 egg with a fork just enough to combine the white and yolk. Add this to the pan, along with 1 teaspoon of Worcestershire sauce and 1 cup of milk. Stir everything so that it is well mixed. Stuff the fish with this mixture; that is, spread it on the bottom half of a split fish, and then fold the other half of the fish over it.

6. Place two slices of bacon on top of the fish. Tie two pieces of string around the fish to hold the bacon in place and the fish together.

7. Bake in a 350° oven, and begin testing for doneness after 40 minutes. In the course of cooking, occasionally spoon some of the melted bacon fat over the fish.

FISH FILLETS

Fillet of fish, which is simply boned fish, may be broiled, baked, fried, or poached, and either fresh or frozen fish may be used. If frozen fillets are used, let them thaw in the refrigerator only long enough to separate.

Timing of menu: Fish, broiled, poached, or fried, about 10 minutes; baked, about 35 minutes. Baked corn custard, 30 minutes. Frozen asparagus spears, 8 minutes.

RECIPE I: BROILED FISH FILLETS

1. Turn the broiler on to a medium-high flame.

2. Brush the fillets with melted butter, and sprinkle them with salt, pepper, and paprika.

3. Put under the broiler about 3 inches from the flame. If the fish separates easily into flakes when a piece is lifted with a fork, it is done. Begin testing for doneness after 8 minutes.

4. If you like, a bit of dry white wine may be poured over the fish during cooking. Or grated cheese may be sprinkled over the fillets during the last minutes of cooking.

RECIPE II: POACHED FISH FILLETS

1. Put equal amounts of water and white wine in a skil-

let, from ½ to 1 cup of each depending on the number of pieces of fish. Add ½ teaspoon of salt.

2. When the liquid is just short of boiling, add the fillets. Cook them gently, under the boiling point. Test for doneness after 8 minutes.

RECIPE III: PAN-FRIED FISH FILLETS

1. Put the fillets in a bowl, and add enough milk to cover them. Let them soak for 15 minutes.

2. Spread 2 tablespoons of flour mixed with 1 teaspoon of salt and ⅛ teaspoon of pepper on a piece of paper. Pat the pieces of fillet lightly in the flour, and give them a shake to get rid of any excess.

3. Put 3 tablespoons of salad oil in a skillet, and when it is hot, add the fillets. Cook them until they are nicely browned on both sides, about 8 to 10 minutes.

RECIPE IV: BAKED FISH FILLETS

1. Turn the oven on to 375°.

2. Brush the fillets well with melted butter, and salt and pepper them.

3. Bake for 35 minutes in a 375° oven. Test for doneness.

OR: Pour over and around the fillets a can of tomato sauce before baking.

RECIPE V: FISH FILLETS WITH TOMATOES AND CHEESE

1 pound fish fillets	1 tablespoon grated onion
2 tomatoes	½ cup grated Swiss cheese

1. Butter the bottom of a shallow baking dish, and lay the fish fillets in it. Salt and pepper them.

2. Add 1 tablespoon of grated (or finely chopped) onion. Slice 2 tomatoes, lay them over the fish, and over all put small bits of butter.

3. Broil under a medium flame for 20 minutes.

4. Sprinkle ½ cup of grated Swiss cheese over the fish, and continue broiling until the cheese has melted.

Sauces for Fish Fillets

- Gently cook sliced fresh or canned mushrooms in 1 tablespoon of butter for 5 minutes. Add 2 tablespoons of dry white wine, and cook 1 minute more. Pour sauce over fish.
- Heat a can of (Campbell's) frozen shrimp soup, add 1 tablespoon of sherry, and pour over the fillets.

FISH STEAK

A swordfish steak or a salmon steak, which is a thick slice of fish, may be handled in one of the following ways.

Timing of menu: Boiled potatoes, 30 minutes. Fish steak, 10 to 20 minutes. Frozen mixed vegetables, 10 minutes.

RECIPE I: BROILED FISH STEAK

1. Light the broiler, and put the flame on high.
2. Salt and pepper the steaks, and brush them very liberally with melted butter.
3. Put under the broiler about 3 inches from the flame. Turn when brown on one side, about 4 minutes. After 8 minutes of total cooking time, test for doneness by seeing if fish flakes easily when separated with a fork.

RECIPE II: BROILED MARINATED FISH STEAK

1. Several hours in advance of cooking, put in a bowl ½ cup of dry vermouth, ½ cup of salad oil, the juice of ½ lemon, ½ teaspoon of salt, ⅛ teaspoon of pepper, and a pinch each of marjoram, thyme, and sage. Stir to mix well, and add the steaks. Dunk them around until they are well covered with the marinade, then store the bowl in the refrigerator.
2. When ready to cook the steaks, preheat the broiler, and line the broiling pan with aluminum foil. Broil the steaks under a medium flame, brushing frequently during cooking with some of the sauce. Cook for 7 minutes on each side, and then test for doneness.

RECIPE III: BAKED FISH STEAK

1. Preheat oven to 400°.
2. Brush the steaks liberally with melted butter, or dot them with crumbled bits of butter. Salt and pepper them. Add a pinch of thyme or marjoram if you like.
3. Place each steak in the middle of a piece of aluminum foil large enough to fold around the steak. Seal the foil.
4. Bake in a 400° oven, and test for doneness after 20 minutes.

RECIPE IV: BAKED FISH STEAK IN SHERRY

salmon steaks
1 can sliced mushrooms
½ cup sherry
¼ cup chopped onions

1. Turn oven on to 400°.

2. Place the steaks in a casserole, salt and pepper them, and sprinkle a pinch of tarragon over each.

3. Add 1 drained can of sliced mushrooms and ¼ cup of finely chopped onions, and pour ½ cup of dry sherry over and around the steaks.

4. Bake in a 400° oven. After 20 minutes begin testing for doneness.

SHELLFISH

SCALLOPS

There are several interesting ways of cooking scallops, either the fresh or the frozen ones. The (Red-L) frozen French-fried scallops are good, too, and need only be heated according to the package directions. Serve with tartar sauce. One pound of scallops makes three servings. Frozen scallops need not be thawed before cooking and require the same cooking time as fresh scallops.

Timing of menu: Scallops, Recipes I and II, 6 minutes; Recipe III, 40 minutes. Baked onions, 1 hour. Buttered chopped carrots, 20 minutes.

RECIPE I: SAUTÉED SCALLOPS

1. Heat 2 tablespoons of butter in a skillet with a cut-up clove of garlic.

2. Take out the garlic, and add the scallops. Cook for 6 minutes, stirring them occasionally to turn them over.

RECIPE II: MARINATED BROILED SCALLOPS

1. Several hours in advance of cooking time, put the scallops in a bowl with ½ cup of dry vermouth, ½ cup of olive oil, and a generous sprinkling of garlic salt. Store the bowl in the refrigerator.

2. Preheat the broiler. Spread the scallops on aluminum foil, pour the marinade over, and broil the scallops 3 minutes on each side.

RECIPE III: BAKED SCALLOPS

1 pound fresh or frozen scallops
½ cup chopped onions
1 can frozen cream of shrimp soup
½ cup light cream
1 tablespoon lemon juice
2 tablespoons sherry
1 can sliced mushrooms
nutmeg

1. Turn oven on to 350°.

2. Melt 2 tablespoons of butter in a skillet, and gently cook ½ cup of chopped onions and 1 can of sliced mushrooms until the onions are tender.

3. Add the scallops to the skillet, and cook for a few minutes until they are warm.

4. To the skillet, add 1 can of (thawed) cream of shrimp soup, ½ cup of light cream, 1 tablespoon of lemon juice, 2 tablespoons of sherry, ½ teaspoon of salt, and a sprinkling of pepper and nutmeg. Stir all this together well.

5. Transfer to a casserole, sprinkle bread crumbs and grated American or Parmesan cheese over the top, and bake in a 350° oven for 30 minutes, or until the top is nicely browned.

LOBSTER

Lobsters, as you know, must be purchased alive, and the more vigorous they are, the better. If you are not going to cook them immediately, store them in the refrigerator in a securely closed paper bag. If you are going to cook them immediately and you live not too far from the fish market, you can have the fishmonger cut them in half for broiling. Otherwise, you must do this yourself, and since you may not have the heart, have a kettle of boiling water ready to plunge the lobsters into; boil them for 2 minutes, then take them out and cut them in half ready for broiling. Use poultry shears for this if you have them.

Frozen South African lobster tails can be broiled, although they are not as tender as fresh lobster. When boiled and the meat removed and cut into chunks, the tails make a good start on lobster thermidor or lobster salad. Canned lobster can also be used in these dishes.

BROILED LOBSTER

Timing of menu: Lobster, 10 to 15 minutes. French-fried potatoes, 15 minutes. Green salad.

RECIPE: BROILED LOBSTER

1. Turn the broiler on.

2. If the fishmonger has not split and cleaned the lobster, do this yourself (see above), removing the stomach and intestines but leaving the green liver and the red roe, if any.

3. Brush the flesh sides of the split lobster liberally with melted butter, and repeat this at frequent intervals during the cooking.

4. Broil under a medium flame, shell side down, for 10 to 15 minutes.

5. Salt and pepper, and serve the lobster with plenty of melted butter in which to dip the meat.

RECIPE II: BROILED LOBSTER TAILS

The frozen packages of rock lobster tails usually contain 1 large and 2 small tails, which will feed two people, although not lavishly.

1. Allow the tails to thaw for 2 hours before cooking. If you forget to take them out of the freezing compartment in time, put them in boiling water for 5 minutes.

2. Bend the shells back to crack them; otherwise they will curl up in cooking. Cut out the soft undershell with a pair of scissors.

3. Brush the shell side with salad oil, and put the tails under a medium flame in the broiler with the shell sides up. Broil for 5 minutes.

4. Turn the tails over and brush the meat with melted butter. Broil for an additional 10 minutes, brushing them once again with melted butter in the course of cooking.

BOILED LOBSTER

Follow the same menu as for Broiled Lobster.

RECIPE: BOILED LOBSTER

1. Set a large kettle of water to boil, adding 1 teaspoon of salt for each quart of water.

2. Plunge the lobsters into the briskly boiling water. Allow to cook 8 minutes for 1 pound, 10 minutes for 1½ pound, and 12 minutes for 2 pound lobsters.

3. Cut the lobsters in half, and serve with a generous quantity of melted butter in side dishes.

LOBSTER THERMIDOR

It seems a great pity to do anything with a fresh lobster but broil or boil it; so let us assume that for Lobster Thermidor you are using frozen rock lobster tails (or canned lobster, in which event skip the preparatory directions for cooking the tails). The recipe reads as though it is quite complicated, but although a little care is needed as the ingredients are blended in, it is not really a troublesome dish to make, and the results are splendid.

RECIPE: LOBSTER THERMIDOR

1 package lobster tails for each two servings
1½ cups milk
1 cup heavy cream
2 egg yolks
⅓ cup sherry
½ teaspoon grated onion
½ teaspoon prepared mustard
2 teaspoons lemon juice

1. To a kettle of boiling water sufficient to cover the lobster tails, add 1 tablespoon of vinegar. Boil the tails for 9 minutes.

2. Put the tails under cold water until cool enough to handle. Cut the thin undershell with scissors, extract the meat, and cut it into chunks.

3. In a saucepan, and over a very low flame, melt 4 tablespoons of butter. Put 4 tablespoons of flour in a cup and gradually shake the flour into the butter, stirring constantly as you do so to blend it into the butter without lumps. Cook, still stirring, until the mixture bubbles gently. Add a scant ½ teaspoon of (Gulden's) prepared mustard and stir in.

4. Take the saucepan off the stove and, a little bit at a time, pour in 1½ cups of milk, stirring all the while. Again, the idea is to get this mixed in without causing any lumps.

5. Replace the saucepan on the stove over a minimum flame. The mixture now is quite thin, but it will thicken as it cooks. Stir it continually until it does so.

6. Add 1 cup of heavy cream, stirring in carefully. Grate ½ teaspoon of onion and add this; if you do not have a grater, scrape the cut face of an onion with a knife to get a watery pulp rather than a slice. Add 1 teaspoon of salt and ½ teaspoon of paprika.

7. Separate 2 eggs (see page 22 for how to do this). Beat the yolks with a fork. Take a spoonful of the hot sauce, and add it to the yolks, and then a second spoonful. Mix it, and add the yolks to the saucepan.

8. Stir into the sauce 2 teaspoons of lemon juice and ⅓ cup of dry sherry. Taste at this point to check that the seasonings are as you like them. Add the lobster meat.

9. You can serve as is, or over toast, or fill the lobster shells with the mixture. If you are having this dish for company, everything up to this point can be done in advance and the thermidor put in the refrigerator until 25 minutes before serving time. Then, light the oven and set it at 350°, fill the shells or a baking dish or individual ramekins, sprinkle bread crumbs over the top, and bake for 20 minutes. Place under the broiler for an additional 2 minutes to brown the top.

SHRIMP

Shrimp, deemed enough of a luxury by restaurants so that they charge extra for them, are tedious to clean but otherwise their preparation presents no problem at all. They are excellent cold in a shrimp cocktail or shrimp salad, or hot as the principal ingredient in any number of interesting dishes. When using them cold, follow the directions for Boiled Shrimp and, after cooking, chill them in the icebox. To make the sauce for shrimp cocktail, simply mix together chili sauce and horseradish in the proportion from mild to hot that pleases you. Canned shrimp are very inferior to fresh. Frozen shrimp are better, but still not as good as fresh. Frozen shrimp come both shelled and unshelled. To save work buy them shelled unless the recipe you are using specifies otherwise. Frozen shrimp need not be thawed before using and require the same cooking time as fresh shrimp. One pound of shrimp makes three to four servings.

To Clean: Grasp the inner curve of the shell and simply shuck the shell off, including the tail. If you look at the front end of the shrimp, you will see a black vein running just under the meat along the outer curve. Put the tip of a knife under the black vein and pull. A triangular strip of meat will come off the length of the back and, with it, the black vein. Rinse the shrimp under cold water to wash off any traces of the vein that remain. If you have a cat, he will by now be climbing up your leg, so feed him the strips you pull off; if you don't have a cat, throw them away.

There is a gadget on the market which shells and deveins shrimp in one operation and is much faster than doing it by hand. If you have occasion to cope with shrimp often, you may want to invest in one.

BOILED SHRIMP

For shrimp cocktail or as a start on other recipes involving shrimp.

RECIPE: BOILED SHRIMP

1. Set a pot of water to boil on the stove, and add 1 teaspoon of salt to it.
2. When the water is boiling, put in the shrimp (fresh or frozen), and cook until they turn pink, about 6 minutes.
3. Shell, and devein.

Sauce

Frozen shrimp soup to which 2 tablespoons of dry sherry have been added makes a good sauce for boiled shrimp. Serve over rice or toast.

SHRIMP BOILED IN BEER

Timing of menu: Herb rice, 30 minutes. Shrimp, 10 minutes. Frozen peas, 5 minutes.

RECIPE: SHRIMP IN BEER

1 pound unshelled shrimp (fresh or frozen)
2 cans light beer
½ teaspoon lemon juice
1 clove garlic

1. In a large saucepan, put 2 cans of light beer, and set it on the stove to boil. Add ½ teaspoon of lemon juice, 1 peeled clove of garlic, ½ teaspoon of thyme, 2 bay leaves, and 2 teaspoons of salt.

2. Wash the shrimp and add them when the pot is boiling.

3. Lower the flame, and let the shrimp cook for 6 minutes.

4. Serve the shrimp in a bowl with the liquid, and let each person help himself, peeling and deveining the shrimp as he eats them.

BROILED SHRIMP

Before broiling, shrimp should first be boiled and cleaned. Frozen, already cleaned shrimp may be used. As an intermediate step between boiling and broiling, the shrimp may be marinated for several hours in the refrigerator in one of the sauces described below.

Timing of menu: Potato balls, 15 minutes. Frozen asparagus, 8 minutes. Shrimp, 6 minutes (broiling time, after preliminary preparation).

RECIPE: BROILED SHRIMP

1. Put the shrimp in boiling water with 1 teaspoon of salt, and boil for 4 minutes.

2. Light the broiler.

3. Peel and devein the shrimp. Brush them well with melted butter, and set them on aluminum foil in the broiling pan.

4. Broil for 3 minutes on each side, painting with melted butter once or twice more in the course of cooking.

OR: After boiling and cleaning the shrimp, marinate them in the refrigerator for several hours in one of the following:

- 1 cup of olive oil and 1 cup of dry white wine.
- 1 can of light beer, ¼ teaspoon of dry mustard, and ¼ teaspoon of lemon juice.
- ¼ cup of olive oil, ½ teaspoon of curry powder, and 1 tablespoon of lemon juice.

Remove the shrimp from the marinade, and broil for 3 minutes on each side.

GARLIC SHRIMP

This is very simple and is a good company dish. It serves four to six people. Accompany it with herb rice (available in packaged form), a large mixed salad, and French bread.

RECIPE: GARLIC SHRIMP

2 pounds shrimp (fresh or frozen)
¼ pound butter
2 cloves garlic

1. Cook 2 pounds of shrimp in boiling salted (1½ teaspoons) water for 4 minutes. Peel, and devein them (see page 82).
2. Melt ¼ pound of butter in a skillet, along with 2 cloves of garlic cut in halves or quarters. Cook the shrimp in the butter for 4 minutes.
3. Fish out the garlic, and serve in a large bowl with the butter poured over.

SHRIMP NEWBURG

Either fresh or frozen shrimp may be used for this, but avoid the canned. This amount makes two to three servings.

RECIPE: SHRIMP NEWBURG

1 pound unshelled shrimp
1½ cups light cream
2 egg yolks
2 tablespoons dry sherry

1. Boil 1 pound of shrimp for 4 minutes in enough water to cover, and to which 1 teaspoon of salt has been added. Peel and devein them (see page 82).
2. In a saucepan melt 4 tablespoons of butter. Very slowly shake in 2 tablespoons of flour, stirring all the while to blend the butter and flour smoothly.
3. Take the saucepan off the fire and, while stirring, pour in slowly 1½ cups of light cream. Blend it well so there are no lumps.
4. Put back on a very low flame, and stir until the sauce thickens, which it will do with the heat and the stirring.
5. Separate 2 eggs (see page 22), and beat the yolks with a fork. Add a little of the sauce to the eggs, stir, add more of the sauce, and then put all this back in the saucepan, stirring into the remaining sauce.
6. Add the shrimp to the sauce.
7. Stir in 2 tablespoons of sherry. Taste for seasonings. Serve with rice or over toast.

SHRIMP CURRY

If you like authentic East Indian curry, which involves apples and tomatoes plus a long list of other ingredients, this is not it. But it is good, and it is much easier.

RECIPE: SHRIMP CURRY

Follow the recipe for Shrimp Newburg, steps 1 through 6. Omit step 7 and in place of the sherry, add 1 tablespoon of curry powder. Taste, and if you prefer your curry hotter, add a teaspoonful at a time, until the curry is hot enough for your taste. Serve with rice and chutney.

SHRIMP ESPAÑOL

Timing of menu: Shrimp, 30 minutes. Rice, 30 minutes. Tossed salad.

RECIPE: SHRIMP ESPAÑOL

1 pound shrimp (fresh or frozen)
1 can sliced mushrooms
1 medium onion
1 cup sour cream
2 tablespoons dry red wine
1 chicken bouillon cube
1 cup tomato sauce

1. Add 1 teaspoon of salt to a pot of boiling water, put in 1 pound of shrimp, boil 4 minutes. Peel and devein the shrimp (see page 82).

2. Melt 3 tablespoons of butter in a large skillet. Peel and slice 1 medium-sized onion (or use ½ cup of frozen chopped onions), and cook gently in the butter until the onion is transparent. Add 1 can of sliced mushrooms and 2 tablespoons of dry red wine. Allow to cook a few minutes until about half of the wine has evaporated.

3. Put in 2 more tablespoons of butter, 1 chicken bouillon cube, and 1 cup of (Hunt's) tomato sauce. Stir and let this mixture boil. When it starts to boil, turn the fire down and let it cook gently for 3 minutes.

4. Add the shrimp.

5. When the shrimp are hot (about 3 minutes), add 1 cup of sour cream. Be careful not to let the mixture boil. Serve it as soon as the sour cream has warmed. This amount serves four.

CRAB

Like lobsters, crabs should be energetically alive when you

buy them and should be cooked as soon as possible after purchase. Hard-shelled and soft-shelled crabs are the same creatures, but the soft-shelled crab has recently shed his shell and the new shell has not yet hardened, permitting him to be eaten shell and all. Which is a great convenience, for it is a laborious business to pick the meat out of a crab. It must also be said, however, that it is worth the labor, for the meat is sweet, tender, and delicious. But fortunately, too, crabmeat seems to weather canning and freezing processes the best of all the shellfish (Wakefield's frozen Alaskan King Crab is superb). Use either canned or frozen in the recipes requiring cooked crab if you have not happened to have caught or been given a supply of fresh crabs.

HARD-SHELLED CRAB

Boiled crabs can constitute the main dish of a meal or the meat can be picked from the shells and used in Crabmeat Salad, Crab Stew, or any recipe calling for cooked crabmeat.

Timing of menu: Crabs, 20 minutes to cook, 10 minutes to clean after cooking. A big platter of crabs (at least 2 crabs per person), a large salad, and a loaf of French bread are all that are needed for a meal.

RECIPE: HARD-SHELLED CRAB

1. Put a big kettle of water on to boil, add 2 teaspoons of salt, and a teaspoon of vinegar.
2. Wash the crabs well under cold running water, staying out of the way of their claws.
3. Plunge the crabs head-first into the boiling water. Cook them until the shells turn red, which takes 15 to 20 minutes.
4. Take the crabs out of the water, and when they are cool enough to handle, snap off all the claws and put them on a platter. Pull the upper and under shells of the body apart and hold the body under hot running water to rinse thoroughly. Add the bodies to the platter, and serve with lots of melted butter in which to dip the meat. Nutcrackers and small forks or picks are necessary to extract the meat from within the claws and around the cartilage.

If you are not going to serve the crabs this way but wish to extract the meat to use in other recipes, be forewarned that it takes about 6 crabs to make 1 cup of meat and that getting the meat out is a very long and tedious process. Pick the meat over carefully to be certain that there are no lurking bits of cartilage in it.

SOFT-SHELLED CRAB

The crabs must be purchased alive, and, in general, the smaller they are, the tastier. Soft-shelled crabs are traditionally served on toast. Plan for 1 or 2 per serving, depending on their size.

Timing of menu: Crabs, 10 minutes. Baked corn custard, 30 minutes. Tossed salad.

RECIPE: SOFT-SHELLED CRAB

1. Unfortunately, the crabs must be killed before cooking. This is done by inserting the point of a knife between the eyes, not a job for the faint of heart. Next, clean them by lifting the pointed end of the shell and scraping out the spongy material found underneath. Rinse well in running water, and cut off the tails. Dry the crabs with paper towels.
2. Melt several tablespoons of butter in a skillet; the amount will depend on how many crabs you have to cook.
3. Spread 3 tablespoons of flour on a piece of paper, sprinkle well with salt and pepper, and then dip the crabs in this to coat them lightly.
4. Add them to the hot butter in the skillet and cook briskly until the crabs turn a beige color, which should take about 5 minutes each side. Serve on toast.

SAUTÉED CRABMEAT

Sauté simply means to cook gently, usually in a skillet with butter, and that is all that is involved here. If you are starting with hard-shelled crabs, follow the directions for their preparation. Otherwise, use frozen crabmeat (canned is possible but will not be as good). One package of (Wakefield's) frozen crabmeat will make two servings.

Timing of menu: Crabmeat, 10 minutes. Fresh asparagus, 10 minutes. Corn on the cob, 10 minutes.

RECIPE: SAUTÉED CRABMEAT

1. Melt 2 tablespoons of butter in a skillet, and add the crabmeat. Salt it lightly and cook gently until it is heated through.

OR: Add 1 can of sliced mushrooms, and sauté these along with the crabmeat. Before serving, if you like, add ½ cup of heavy cream to the pan, and cook just enough longer to get it hot; do not let it boil.

OR: After the crabmeat is cooked, take it out of the skillet, and add 2 tablespoons of dry sherry to the pan. Stir, let it bubble up, and pour over the crabmeat.

CRABMEAT STEW

Timing of menu: Rice, 30 minutes. Crab, 20 minutes. Frozen peas, 5 minutes.

RECIPE: CRABMEAT STEW

1 cup fresh, frozen, or canned crabmeat
1 cup cream
¼ cup chopped onions
¼ cup chopped green pepper
½ cup dry sherry

1. Put the crabmeat in a bowl, and pour over it ½ cup of dry sherry. Let this stand in the refrigerator for at least an hour.
2. Melt 2 tablespoons of butter in a skillet, add ⅛ teaspoon of garlic powder, and cook ¼ cup of chopped onions and ¼ cup of chopped green pepper for 5 minutes.
3. Take the onions and pepper out of the skillet. Turn the flame very low. Add 1 more tablespoon of butter, and when it has melted, slowly sprinkle in 2 tablespoons of flour, stirring constantly to blend it smoothly with the butter.
4. Remove the skillet from the stove and slowly pour in, while stirring, 1 cup of cream. When this has been well blended in, without lumps, return the pan to the stove.
5. Add the onions, pepper, crabmeat, and the ½ cup of sherry in which the crabmeat was marinated. Add a pinch of rosemary if you have it, and enough salt to suit your taste. Stir well, and cook for 5 to 10 minutes over a low flame, being careful not to let boil.

CRABMEAT NEWBURG

Timing of menu: Fresh artichokes, 30 minutes. Crab, 20 minutes.

RECIPE: CRABMEAT NEWBURG

1 cup fresh, frozen, or canned crabmeat
1 cup light cream
2 eggs
½ cup dry sherry
1 tablespoon brandy
1 teaspoon lemon juice

1. Melt 4 tablespoons of butter in a heavy skillet. Add 1 cup of crabmeat, and cook it over a low flame for 1 minute.
2. Add 1 teaspoon of lemon juice.

3. Slowly sprinkle 2 tablespoons of flour into the pan, stirring as you do so to blend it in smoothly.

4. Remove the pan from the fire and, still stirring, slowly pour in 1 cup of cream.

5. When this mixture is smooth, add ⅓ teaspoon of salt, a sprinkling of pepper, a dash of powdered clove, and a sprinkling of paprika. Let all of this cook for 5 minutes.

6. Stir in ½ cup of dry sherry.

7. With an egg beater, beat 2 eggs until they just begin to get foamy. Stir them into the skillet quickly.

8. Add 1 tablespoon of brandy and serve immediately.

CREAMED CRABMEAT

A crabmeat dish which is the height of simplicity but yet very good is the following. It serves two.

RECIPE: CREAMED CRABMEAT

1 package frozen crabmeat
2 tablespoons sherry
1 can condensed cream of mushroom soup

1. Let the crabmeat thaw for several hours in the refrigerator out of the freezing compartment, or hasten the process by putting it under cold running water. Pour off all the liquid in the package.

2. Add the crabmeat to 1 can of condensed cream of mushroom soup and 2 tablespoons of sherry. Heat gently, and serve over toast. If you like, frozen asparagus spears that have been cooked for 7 minutes may be laid on the toast first and then the crabmeat poured over.

CLAMS

Clams, too, should be alive when cooked. They are alive if the shells are tightly closed. Throw away any opened shells before cooking; after cooking throw away any that have *not* opened. The smaller clams are apt to be the tastier ones.

STEAMED CLAMS

Timing of menu: Clams, 10 to 15 minutes. If you allow 1 quart of steamed clams per person, this and a salad and a loaf of French bread are all that are needed.

RECIPE: STEAMED CLAMS

1. Scrub the clam shells with a stiff brush under running water, and then put them through several changes of water in a kettle to wash away the sand in them.

2. Cover the bottom of a large kettle with a small amount of water, no more than ½ inch in depth. Add the clams, put a tightly fitting lid on the kettle, and cook until the clams have opened, which takes 10 to 15 minutes. Keep an eye on them, for clams are tough when cooked too long.

3. Serve with dishes of melted butter in which to dip the clams. Everything but the narrow neck is edible.

FRIED CLAMS

Buy soft-shelled clams and have the fishmonger open them for you. Allow six to eight clams per serving.

Timing of menu: Broiled eggplant, 7 minutes. Frozen string beans, 7 minutes. Clams, 5 minutes.

RECIPE: FRIED CLAMS

1. Wash the shucked clams well under running water and put them on a paper towel to drain.
2. Beat an egg with a fork until it is well mixed.
3. Spread bread crumbs on a piece of waxed paper.
4. Melt 4 tablespoons of butter in skillet; allow to get hot.
5. Dip the clams in the beaten egg, and roll them in the bread crumbs.
6. Cook them in the hot butter for 5 minutes, turning once in the course of cooking.

CLAMS IN CREAM

The amount here serves two.

Timing of menu: Clams, 15 minutes. Frozen succotash, 10 minutes.

RECIPE: CLAMS IN CREAM

1 can minced clams
1 cup milk
1 cup heavy cream
1 teaspoon dried onion flakes

1. In a skillet over a low fire, melt 2 tablespoons of butter. Slowly stir in 2 tablespoons of flour, blending well.
2. Pour in 1 cup of milk, a little at a time, stirring to blend smoothly into the paste. Cook gently, stirring, until the mixture thickens.
3. Add 1 drained can of (Doxsee) clams, 1 cup of heavy cream, a good sprinkling of paprika, and salt to taste. Add 1 teaspoon of dried onion flakes.
4. Allow to cook gently for 5 minutes. Serve on toast.

CLAM AND EGGPLANT CASSEROLE

Clams and eggplant make a surprisingly happy couple, as you will find when you try this recipe. This amount serves three.

Total cooking time: about 1 hour.

RECIPE: CLAM AND EGGPLANT CASSEROLE

1 can minced clams
1 large or 2 small eggplants
1 tablespoon chopped onion
1 tablespoon chopped green pepper
½ pint container heavy cream

1. Put a large saucepan of water, with ½ teaspoon of salt, on to boil. Slice the skin off the eggplant, and cut the eggplant into large squares. Cook it in gently boiling water for 10 minutes. When it is tender, take it out of the water, and chop it into small pieces.

2. Open the can of (Doxsee) minced clams and pour the liquid into a pint measuring cup. Add enough heavy cream so that altogether there will be 1½ cups of liquid.

3. In a skillet, heat 2 tablespoons of butter, and add to it 1 tablespoon each of finely chopped onion and green pepper. Cook gently until the onion is transparent.

4. Sprinkle into the skillet 1½ tablespoons of flour, stirring constantly. When the flour is thoroughly mixed in, slowly pour the 1½ cups of liquid in, stirring to prevent any lumps from forming. Continue stirring until the sauce thickens. Taste to see if any seasoning is needed.

5. Add the clams and the eggplant, stirring just enough to blend everything together, and then transfer to a buttered casserole. Put a coating of bread crumbs over the top, and sprinkle with paprika. If you wish, everything up to this point can be done in advance and the casserole put in the refrigerator until about 45 minutes before serving time.

6. Bake in a preheated oven for 30 minutes at 350°, longer if the casserole has been in the refrigerator. The top should be bubbling and lightly browned when you take it out.

MUSSELS

Mussels are not as well-known nor as frequently served as clams, but when steamed in wine, they are a truly fine dish. Curiously enough, it was Rob, whose inability to cook was the genesis of this book, who taught me this. He arrived one evening with a bag of mussels gathered at Jones Beach and the following instructions for cooking them.

Timing of menu: Mussels, 20 minutes. Have a good quantity of these and make a meal of them plus French bread and a tossed salad.

RECIPE: STEAMED MUSSELS

½ to 1 quart mussels per person	2 cups white wine
1 large onion, chopped	1 teaspoon oregano

1. The mussels must be very well scrubbed. Do this with a stiff brush under running water, and then rinse in a kettle in several changes of water. Discard any with opened shells.

2. Place the mussels in a large kettle, pour over them 2 cups of white wine, add the chopped onion (use frozen chopped onions if you have them on hand), and sprinkle in 1 teaspoon of oregano.

3. Put a lid on the kettle, and steam the mussels for 20 minutes. Transfer the entire contents of the kettle to a large bowl, to be placed in the center of the table where each person can help himself. Serve French bread for dunking in the wine sauce.

OYSTERS

If you can inveigle the fishmonger into opening the oysters when you buy them, it makes life easier. If not, use the tip of a sharp knife to cut into the hinged end of the oyster, and when the muscle there has been cut, run the knife all the way around between the halves of the shell. In some parts of the country, only oysters packed in brine are available; these are passable for cooked dishes but will not do for oyster cocktail. If you do have a choice, always buy fresh oysters in preference to any other kind.

BROILED OYSTERS

Timing of menu: Baked sweet potatoes, 1 hour. Frozen peas, 5 minutes. Oysters, 3 minutes.

RECIPE I: BROILED OYSTERS

6 oysters per serving	bread crumbs

1. Turn on the broiler to high.

2. Dip the oysters (shucked) in melted butter, and then roll them in bread crumbs to which salt and pepper have been added.

3. Spread the oysters on aluminum foil, and broil them until lightly browned, which should take about 3 minutes.

RECIPE II: BROILED OYSTERS WITH BACON

6 oysters per serving
½ cup white wine
bacon

1. Put the oysters in a bowl with ½ cup of white wine and ¼ teaspoon of garlic powder. Store the bowl in the refrigerator for ½ to 1 hour.
2. Turn the broiler flame to high.
3. Circle each oyster in ½ of a strip of bacon.
4. Cook under the broiler until the bacon is done.

FRIED OYSTERS

Timing of menu: Zucchini and tomato casserole, 50 minutes. Oysters, 4 minutes.

RECIPE: FRIED OYSTERS

1. Dry the oysters on a paper towel. Salt and pepper them.
2. Beat 1 egg with a fork.
3. Dip the oysters in the beaten egg and then in bread crumbs.
4. For deep-frying, heat 2 cups of salad oil in a heavy skillet, and get it good and hot. For pan-frying, melt 4 tablespoons of butter, and let it heat just short of browning.
5. Put the oysters in the oil or butter and cook for 4 minutes.

CHAPTER 5 CASSEROLES FOR COMPANY

All of the recipes in this chapter have two things in common: they can be cooked in advance and they are fine enough in flavor to please most guests. Too, to the best of my knowledge, they are failure-proof, which is of extreme importance when guests are expected. Make these casseroles an hour ahead, or even two days ahead if you are having weekend guests and want to avoid spending much time in the kitchen. Despite an occasional long list of ingredients, none is difficult to prepare. Each, with the addition of a salad and rolls, is a complete meal in itself or needs only a dish of rice or noodles to go with it. Prepare them in handsome casseroles that can go directly to the table from the stove.

CHICKEN CASSEROLES

Chicken lends itself marvelously well to casserole dishes, and thus the recipes utilizing it are numerous. The best of many follow here. Plan on one-quarter to one-half of a broiler or fryer per person.

CHICKEN AND TOMATOES IN WINE

Total cooking time: 45 minutes. Serve with buttered noodles.

RECIPE: CHICKEN AND TOMATOES IN WINE

1 quartered chicken
2 tomatoes
⅔ cup dry vermouth

1. On top of the stove, melt 2 tablespoons of butter and 2 tablespoons of olive oil (salad oil can be used but olive oil is better).
2. When the oil is hot, add the chicken, as many pieces at a time as will fit in. Brown the pieces of chicken well on both sides, removing the pieces and setting them aside as they become a deep brown color.
3. While the chicken is browning, put a saucepan of water on to boil. Dip 2 tomatoes in the boiling water briefly until the skins split. Take them out and peel them by pulling the skin off. Cut them in half and scrape out the seeds in the middle with a spoon. Then cut the tomatoes into small pieces. (Canned whole tomatoes can also be used, but drain them thoroughly.)
4. When all the pieces of chicken are brown, return any that have been set aside to the casserole, and add the pieces of tomato.
5. Sprinkle in ½ teaspoon of garlic powder, ⅓ teaspoon of salt, and some pepper. Add ⅔ cup of dry vermouth. Put the lid on the casserole, and let cook gently for 20 minutes, or until chicken is tender.
6. Serve with narrow buttered noodles. If some of the chicken and some of the noodles are left over, add the noodles to the casserole and warm up; the dish will be equally delectable the next day.

CHICKEN IN COGNAC AND RED WINE

Total cooking time: about 1 hour and 15 minutes. Serve with rice.

RECIPE: CHICKEN IN COGNAC AND RED WINE

2 quartered chickens
2 tablespoons cognac
¾ cup dry red wine
½ pound mushrooms
1 medium onion
1 chicken bouillon cube
1 teaspoon tomato paste
1 can chicken broth

1. Melt 6 tablespoons of butter in a flameproof casserole, and when it is hot, put in as many pieces of chicken as will come in contact with the butter. Allow the chicken to become nicely browned on both sides. Remove, and put in more pieces until all are browned.

2. Replace all the pieces of chicken in the casserole, warm 2 tablespoons of cognac, pour over the chicken, and set aflame. When the flame has died out, remove the chicken from the casserole.

3. Over a very low flame gently cook in the butter remaining in the casserole ½ pound of peeled, sliced fresh mushrooms and 1 medium onion sliced thin.

4. When the onion is transparent, add 1 chicken bouillon cube. Let this dissolve.

5. Take the casserole off the stove, and sprinkle in 2 tablespoons of flour, stirring well to blend it with the other ingredients.

6. Add 1 teaspoon of tomato paste (canned), 1 can of chicken broth, and ¾ cup of dry red wine. Stir, and return to the stove.

7. Return chicken to casserole, moving it around to saturate it with the sauce.

8. Either now or ½ hour before serving time, put the casserole in a preheated 350° oven for 30 minutes or until the chicken feels tender when pierced with a knife. Taste the sauce for enough seasoning, although it will probably be all right because the bouillon cube is salty.

CHICKEN IN COGNAC AND CREAM

This is another version of chicken with cognac, in a recipe that serves four people.

Total cooking time: about an hour. Serve with herb rice.

RECIPE: CHICKEN IN COGNAC AND CREAM

1 quartered chicken
½ pound fresh mushrooms
2 tablespoons cognac
½ cup heavy cream

1. Melt 4 tablespoons of butter in a flameproof casserole. Salt and pepper the pieces of chicken, and put them in the butter to brown.

2. When all sides of the chicken are a rich brown color, add to the pot ½ pound of sliced fresh mushrooms.

3. Allow to cook over a low flame until the chicken is tender when tested with a knife, about 20 minutes.

Stop here if you are cooking this dish in advance, and after the casserole has cooled, put it in the refrigerator. Return it to the stove 15 minutes before serving time and warm it slowly.

4. About 5 minutes before serving time, warm 2 tablespoons of cognac and sprinkle it over the chicken. Set it on fire.

5. When the cognac has flamed out, add ½ cup of heavy cream and cook very gently, not permitting it to boil, for 5 minutes.

CHICKEN A-RAB

This is a rather exotic recipe that a friend of mine brought from North Africa. The dish is very interesting and very good, but it is an exception to the rule that casseroles improve on being warmed over. It is still perfectly edible but not nearly as good the second day as the first, so try to cook only as many pieces of chicken as will be eaten.

Total cooking time: 2 hours. Serve with rice, an absolute necessity in this instance.

RECIPE: CHICKEN A-RAB

2 quartered chickens (for 6 to 8 servings)
1 onion
½ stalk celery
handful seedless raisins
1 cup dry white wine
2 tablespoons honey
1 teaspoon curry powder
2 apples
handful of almonds
the peel from ½ of a lemon

1. Melt 6 tablespoons of butter in a flameproof casserole, and cook the pieces of chicken, a few at a time, until all are well browned on both sides. Set them aside.

2. In the same butter, adding more if needed, lightly brown 1 medium-sized onion cut into slices and ½ stalk of celery cut in pieces.

3. Put a handful of raisins to soak in a bowl with enough water to cover them, and a handful of almonds in another bowl, also in water.

4. Set the oven at 325°.

5. To the casserole, add 2 tablespoons of honey, 1 heaping teaspoon of curry powder, 1 teaspoon of salt, ⅛ teaspoon

of pepper, and 2 raw apples, peeled, cored, and cut into large pieces.

6. Drain the raisins, and add them to the casserole.

7. Drain the almonds, and squeeze them between the fingers to slip the skins off. Add to casserole.

8. Put the pieces of chicken in the casserole, and pour 1 cup of dry white wine over. Peel ½ of a lemon and add the peel.

9. Put the casserole in a 325° oven, and allow to cook for 1½ hours. Before serving, taste to see if there is enough salt in the sauce.

CHICKEN IN ONION SOUP

From a somewhat complicated recipe, we come to one that could not be simpler. It probably will not sound very good to you on reading it, but it turns out very well, and the onion soup, for some reason, is not identifiable as such. I have been asked for this recipe more times than for any other, I think, and always I give it with some embarrassment and my questioner hears it with some surprise because of its simplicity.

Total cooking time: about 50 minutes. Serve with buttered noodles.

RECIPE: CHICKEN IN ONION SOUP

1 quartered chicken	1 can condensed onion soup

1. Melt 4 tablespoons of butter in a heavy skillet or flameproof casserole. When hot, put the chicken in and turn it so that it becomes nicely browned on all sides.

2. Add 1 can of undiluted (Crosse and Blackwell) onion soup. Allow chicken to cook about 30 minutes, or until tender when tested with a knife.

This can be cooked, taken off the fire, and then returned to the stove just long enough to get piping hot before serving. It seems to be best if the chicken is somewhat overcooked, close to falling off the bones, and it is improved by being made a day in advance.

CHICKEN WITH CHERRIES

Another simple recipe, and a good-looking one when it comes to the table.

Total cooking time: about 45 minutes. Serve with buttered noodles to which a teaspoon of choppea parsley has been added.

RECIPE: CHICKEN WITH CHERRIES

1 quartered chicken	1 can black, pitted cherries
1 tablespoon cornstarch	¼ cup red wine

1. Melt 4 tablespoons of butter in a heavy skillet, salt and pepper the chicken pieces, and cook them in the butter until they are richly brown on all sides.
2. Pour in ¼ cup of dry red wine, put a lid over the skillet, and cook the chicken gently for 20 minutes, or until it is tender when pierced with a knife.
3. Take the chicken out and place it on a hot platter. Stir 1 tablespoon of cornstarch into the skillet, working it into a smooth paste.
4. Open the can of black, pitted cherries, measure out ¼ cup of the juice, and stir it into the pan. Bring this sauce to a boil, and stir until smooth. Discard the rest of the juice in the can, and add the cherries to the skillet. When the cherries are hot, in a minute or two, pour the sauce over the chicken.

BAKED CHICKEN

An easy recipe for six to eight people.

RECIPE: BAKED CHICKEN

2 quartered chickens	1 can sliced mushrooms
1 cup sour cream	½ envelope onion soup mix

1. Preheat oven to 325°.
2. Shake the pieces of chicken in a paper bag with 2 tablespoons of flour, 1 teaspoon of salt, and ⅛ teaspoon of pepper.
3. Melt 4 tablespoons of butter in a flameproof casserole, and in this, brown the chicken on all sides.
4. Mix together 1 cup of sour cream and 1 cup of cold water. Add this to the casserole, along with 1 can of drained sliced mushrooms. Sprinkle a pinch of thyme over all.
5. Cover and bake one hour in a 325° oven. A few minutes before taking the chicken out of the oven, sprinkle ½ of the contents of an envelope of onion soup mix over the top.

PAELLA

Here is a version of Paella which, because it uses mostly canned ingredients, is considerably simpler to put together than the original and highly elaborate Spanish recipe. The amount serves four to six people.

Total cooking time: about 25 minutes.

RECIPE: PAELLA

1 can chicken fricassee
1 can shrimp
1 can crabmeat
1 small can peas
1 can sliced mushrooms
1½ cups uncooked Minute rice
½ teaspoon saffron

1. Put 1¾ cups of water in a large, flameproof casserole, and add to it ¾ teaspoon of salt, ⅛ teaspoon of pepper, ½ teaspoon of saffron (buy it at the herb counter), ½ of a bay leaf crumbled into bits, and ⅓ teaspoon of garlic powder. Add 1½ cups quick-cooking (Minute) rice. Turn heat on under the casserole, and when everything is boiling rapidly, add the lid and cook for 10 minutes.

2. Turn the fire way down, and add 1 can of chicken fricassee, including the gravy in the can. Drain 1 can each of shrimp, mushrooms, and peas, and add them. Drain the can of crabmeat, and pick the meat over to remove any stray pieces of cartilage before adding.

3. Replace lid and cook gently for about 10 minutes.

CHICKEN WITH RICE

Or Arroz con Pollo, another Spanish dish. The amounts given make six to eight servings.

Total cooking time: about 1 hour.

RECIPE: CHICKEN WITH RICE

2 quartered chickens
1 cup frozen chopped onions
1 can whole tomatoes
2 small cans pimento
1 package frozen peas (thawed)
1 small jar stuffed olives
2 chicken bouillon cubes
½ pound link sausage
2 cups uncooked (Uncle Ben's) rice

1. Heat 2 tablespoons of butter and 2 tablespoons of salad oil in a large flameproof casserole and cook the pieces of chicken in this until richly browned on all sides, as many pieces at a time as will fit into the bottom of the casserole. When all the pieces are browned, set them aside.

2. In the remaining oil in the casserole, gently cook 1 cup of frozen chopped onions until they are transparent.

3. Add the liquid from the can of tomatoes to the onions, then cut the tomatoes into small pieces and add them.

4. Add 2 cups of water and the liquid from 2 small cans of pimentoes. Cut up the pimentoes, and add them.

5. Add the liquid from a small jar of stuffed olives, cut the olives in half, and add them.

6. Add 2 cups of (Uncle Ben's) rice, 1 tablespoon of salt, ¼ teaspoon of pepper, and 2 chicken bouillon cubes.

7. Cut ½ pound of link sausages into ½ inch pieces, and add them.

8. Lay the pieces of chicken on top, put a lid on, and cook gently for 30 minutes, running a fork through the mixture occasionally to stir up the rice and make sure it is not sticking.

9. Take off the lid, and add 1 thawed package of frozen green peas (or 1 drained can of peas). Now you have to judge whether or not to replace the lid for the last 10 minutes of cooking. If the mixture has any liquid left, cook it uncovered; if it is just barely moist, leave the lid on. What you want to arrive at is a moist but not soggy concoction.

BEEF CASSEROLES

Beef Stroganoff and Beef Bourguignon are splendid company dishes, hearty but at the same time subtly flavored. Both are easy to make, and neither suffers from being cooked in advance and then reheated a few minutes before serving.

BEEF STROGANOFF

Traditionally this is served with rice, but is also good with noodles or mashed or baked potatoes, anything which will take up some of the delicious gravy. French bread or Brown 'n' Serve Club rolls are almost a necessity too, as is a large green salad. This amount feeds four people.

Total cooking time: about 30 minutes.

RECIPE: BEEF STROGANOFF

- 1 to 1½ pound slice of round steak about ¾ inch thick
- ¼ cup dry vermouth
- 1 can beef gravy
- 1 large onion
- 1 can sliced mushrooms
- ⅔ cup sour cream
- 2 tablespoons chili sauce or catsup
- 1 teaspoon dry mustard

1. Trim all the fat off a 1 to 1½ pound piece of round steak, and then cut the meat into cubes.

2. Heat 3 tablespoons of butter in a heavy skillet over a medium flame. Add the cubed meat and cook, turning the pieces until the meat is brown on all sides (just get the outside brown; do not overcook).

3. While the meat is browning, peel and slice 1 large onion (or use 1 cup of frozen chopped onions). Remove the meat and put the onions in the skillet in its place. Cook them until they are transparent.

4. Add 1 drained can of sliced mushrooms, 1 can of (Franco-American) beef gravy, 2 tablespoons of chili sauce or catsup, a scant teaspoon of dry mustard, ¼ cup of dry vermouth, ½ teaspoon of salt, ⅛ teaspoon of pepper, and put the meat back in. Stir everything up, and taste for a possible need for more salt.

If you are doing this a day ahead or an hour ahead, stop here.

5. Cook very gently, uncovered, for 20 minutes.

6. About 5 minutes before serving time, stir in ⅔ cup of sour cream. Be careful not to let mixture bubble after the sour cream goes in.

BEEF BOURGUIGNON

This, too, may be made as far in advance of the arrival of company as you like, with the cooking being completed while cocktails are served. Traditionally, this is served with boiled potatoes and French bread, but is also good with noodles. This amount makes four servings.

Total cooking time: about 2½ hours.

RECIPE: BEEF BOURGUIGNON

1 pound slice of chuck steak about ¾ inch thick
3 medium-sized onions
½ pound fresh mushrooms
¾ cup dry red wine
½ cup beef bouillon

1. Peel 3 onions and slice them. Cook them gently in 2 tablespoons of butter and 2 tablespoons of olive oil in a heavy skillet or flameproof casserole (4 tablespoons of bacon fat, if you have it on hand, will be even better).

2. While the onions are cooking, trim all the fat off the beef, and cut the meat into cubes.

3. When the onions are transparent, remove them from the skillet and put the meat in. Allow the meat to become brown on all sides.

4. Dust 1½ tablespoons of flour over the meat in the skillet, and a pinch each of thyme and marjoram. Sprinkle in ½ teaspoon of salt and ⅛ teaspoon of pepper. Add ½ cup of beef bouillon and ¾ cup of red wine. Stir everything very well, cover, and allow to cook very slowly for 2½ hours. Add more wine if the liquid seems to be boiling away.

Stop here, after putting the onions back in, if you want to complete the cooking at a later time.

5. About 30 minutes before serving time, add ½ pound of fresh sliced mushrooms. Let everything cook very slowly for 30 minutes, or until you are ready to serve.

CHILI CON CARNE

This recipe is included as a means of coping with those times when you find you have invited twelve people for a Saturday night supper party or when you suspect that any number of the guests invited to a cocktail party will linger on well into the dinner hour.

Total cooking time: about 1 hour and 20 minutes.

RECIPE: CHILI CON CARNE

3 pounds ground beef (chuck)
6 onions
3 large cans tomatoes (20-oz.)
3 large cans kidney beans (20-oz.)
1 small can tomato paste
1 cup beer
2 tablespoons chili powder
½ teaspoon Tabasco

1. While 4 tablespoons of butter are melting in a heavy skillet, peel and slice 6 medium-sized onions. Cook these in the butter until they are transparent.

2. Take the onions out, and put in 3 pounds of ground beef, crumbling it as you add it to the skillet. Stir it with a fork to break up any clumps of meat. Cook until the meat is lightly browned.

3. Transfer the meat (leaving the grease behind) and the onions to a large pot or kettle.

4. Add 3 large cans of tomatoes, 1 can of tomato paste, 1 cup of beer, ½ teaspoon of Tabasco sauce, and 2 tablespoons of chili powder (more if you like it hot). Put a lid on, and let this cook gently for 45 minutes.

Stop here if the dish has been made in advance. About 20 minutes before you plan to serve it, put it back on the fire and let it warm for 5 minutes.

5. Add 3 large cans of kidney beans. Cook gently for 15 minutes.

VEAL CASSEROLE

The following recipe is a fine answer when guests are coming and you wish to serve something different but not exotic. It can be cooked in advance and then warmed just before serving. A platter of noodles is the best accompaniment.

Total cooking time: about 1½ hours.

RECIPE: VEAL WITH BEER

1 pound slice of veal ¾ inch thick (for four people; use 1½ pounds for six)	3 medium tomatoes 1 cup frozen chopped onions 1 can light beer

1. Trim the veal of any fat and cut the meat into cubes.
2. Spread 2 tablespoons of flour on a piece of paper, sprinkle it with salt and pepper, and roll the cubes of meat in this to coat them lightly.
3. Heat 3 tablespoons of butter in a skillet, and put the meat in. Turn the cubes frequently, and cook them just until they are brown on all sides.
4. Take the meat out of the skillet, set aside, and put in 1 cup of frozen chopped onions. Cook them in the butter, adding more butter if necessary, until they are transparent.
5. While the onions are cooking, dip 3 medium-sized tomatoes in boiling water. Take them out the minute the skins split, and peel the skins off. Cut the tomatoes in quarters, and scrape out the seeds with a spoon.
6. Add the tomatoes and meat to the onions. Sprinkle in a pinch each of thyme and marjoram, ½ teaspoon of salt, ⅛ teaspoon of pepper, and add a bay leaf.
7. Pour in 1 can of light beer and let everything cook gently for at least 1 hour, longer if you like. Take out the bay leaf before serving, and taste for the presence of enough salt.

PORK CHOP CASSEROLE

Warming up or warming over improves this casserole, so make it as much in advance as you like. Figure on two chops per person; the center-cut ones are best.

Total cooking time: about 2 hours.

RECIPE: PORK CHOP CASSEROLE

8 pork chops	⅔ cup dry vermouth
4 medium-sized onions	4 tablespoons dry mustard

1. Trim all of the visible fat off the pork chops.
2. Turn the fire on under a large skillet or flameproof casserole, and rub the bottom with 1 or 2 pieces of the fat cut off the chops.

3. Put in as many of the chops at a time as will lie flat, and cook them until they are richly browned on both sides.

4. Mix into a paste 4 tablespoons of dry mustard, 2 teaspoons of salt, and ⅔ cup of dry vermouth.

5. Peel and cut into quarters 4 medium-sized onions. Add the onions and the paste to the casserole.

6. Cover the casserole and cook over a low flame for about 1½ hours.

LAMB CASSEROLES

Here are two lamb casseroles that turn out well and are rather different from the usual.

LAMB CHOP CASSEROLE

Better than broiled lamb chops for company is this dish, for it requires very little attention. Rib or shoulder chops may be used in place of the more expensive loin chops; count on 2 chops per person. The bland flavor of rice provides the best accompaniment.

Total cooking time: about 25 minutes.

RECIPE: LAMB CHOP CASSEROLE

8 lambs chops
1 can small white onions
1 can frozen orange juice (thawed)

1. Trim all the fat and the tails off the lamb chops and put them in a flameproof casserole with 2 tablespoons of butter. Cook them until they are richly browned on both sides. Salt and pepper the chops.

Stop here if you wish to complete the cooking at a later time.

2. Turn on the oven to 350°.

3. Put 1 drained can of small white onions in with the chops.

4. Pour 1 thawed can of frozen orange juice over.

5. Bake in a 350° oven for 15 minutes, occasionally spooning some of the juice over the chops.

GROUND LAMB CASSEROLE

This is best if the ingredients are put together about an hour before cooking time and allowed to stand so that the flavors marry, but it is not essential. Serve with a green vegetable and salad. The amount feeds six people.

Total cooking time: 1 hour.

RECIPE: GROUND LAMB CASSEROLE

2 pounds ground lamb
1 egg
1 cup bread crumbs
1 green pepper
1 cup sour cream
2 tablespoons grated onion
1 medium-sized onion
2 tablespoons chopped parsley

1. Break 2 pounds of ground lamb into small pieces in a large bowl.

2. Beat 1 egg lightly with a fork, and add it to the lamb. Sprinkle in 1½ teaspoons of salt and ¼ teaspoon of pepper.

3. Remove seeds from 1 green pepper and chop it into small pieces. Add this, plus 2 tablespoons grated onion (chop it very fine if you do not have a grater), 1 cup of sour cream, 1 cup of bread crumbs, and 2 tablespoons chopped parsley. Mix all together well and, if convenient, let stand for 1 hour.

4. Rub butter on the sides and bottom of a casserole and press the lamb mixture firmly into the casserole.

5. Turn on the oven to 350°.

6. Peel and slice thinly 1 medium-sized onion. Break the slices into rings by pressing in the center, and then arrange the rings over the top of the casserole. Put some dots of butter on top.

7. Bake for 1 hour in a 350° oven.

SEA FOOD CASSEROLES

Shrimp, lobster, and crabmeat, singly or in combination, are an easy start on casseroles that are simple to put together. Try the recipes given here, and then invent your own, using, as some of these recipes do, frozen cream of shrimp or cream of mushroom soup as the combining ingredient.

LOBSTER CASSEROLE

The recipe as given calls for lobster and asparagus, but shrimp, crabmeat, chicken, or turkey may be substituted for the lobster and peas for the asparagus with just as happy results. The amount serves four.

Total cooking time: 30 minutes.

RECIPE: LOBSTER CASSEROLE

2 cans lobster
4 ounces thin noodles (½ of an 8-oz. box)
1 package frozen asparagus spears
1 can frozen cream of shrimp soup
2 tablespoons dry sherry
¼ cup milk
⅛ teaspoon Tabasco sauce

¼ cup grated Parmesan cheese
1 can sliced mushrooms
2 tablespoons chopped onion

1. Cook 4 ounces (about 4 handfuls; the exact amount does not matter) of thin noodles in boiling salted (1 teaspoon) water for 7 minutes. Cook 1 package of frozen asparagus spears in boiling, lightly salted water for 4 minutes. If the can of frozen shrimp soup has not been thawed, set it in another pot of boiling water.

2. In a skillet, melt 2 tablespoons of butter, and gently cook 2 tablespoons of chopped onions in it.

3. Open and drain 1 can of sliced mushrooms and 2 cans of lobster, breaking the lobster apart. Add these to the onions in the skillet, and cook gently for 2 or 3 minutes.

4. Put in the can of shrimp soup, ¼ cup of milk, 2 tablespoons of dry sherry, and ⅛ teaspoon of Tabasco sauce. Cook slowly, stirring, until everything is well mixed. Taste to see if it needs salt or if you would like more sherry in it.

5. Rub butter over the bottom and sides of a casserole. Put all of the drained noodles in.

6. Arrange all of the cooked asparagus as the next layer.

7. Next, add all of the lobster mixture.

You can stop here, if you wish, and complete the cooking 20 minutes before serving time.

8. Preheat the oven to 400°. Sprinkle ¼ cup of grated Parmesan cheese over the top of the casserole, and bake the casserole, uncovered, for 20 minutes in a 400° oven, or until the top is bubbly and brown.

MIXED SEA FOOD CASSEROLE

This casserole for four can contain just the combination of sea food or can be made into a one-dish meal by first putting a layer of cooked rice or noodles and then a layer of (Le Sueur's) canned peas in the casserole before adding the sea food. If the latter, double the amount of mushroom soup and wine.

Total cooking time: about 30 minutes.

RECIPE: MIXED SEA FOOD CASSEROLE

1 can crabmeat
1 package frozen shrimp (cleaned; not breaded)
1 package frozen scallops
4 tablespoons chopped onion
3 tablespoons dry sherry
1 can condensed cream of mushroom soup
bread crumbs
grated cheese

The shrimp and the scallops should be thawed in the

refrigerator, out of the freezing compartment, for several hours in advance.

1. Melt 2 tablespoons of butter in a skillet and gently cook 4 tablespoons of chopped onions until they are transparent.

2. Drain the can of crabmeat and pick it over to get out any bits of cartilage.

3. Add the crabmeat and the thawed shrimp and scallops to the skillet, plus 3 tablespoons of dry sherry. Cook over a low flame just until the sea food is warm.

4. Add 1 can of condensed cream of mushroom soup. Cook 10 minutes. Taste for sufficient seasoning.

5. Put everything in a casserole or in individual ramekins, sprinkle the top well with bread crumbs and grated Parmesan cheese, and put under the broiler until the top is a golden brown.

SHRIMP AND ARTICHOKE CASSEROLE

This can be made in advance, the day before if you like, but in this event do not combine the sauce with the shrimp and artichokes until you are ready to put the casserole in the oven; warm the sauce before combining. The casserole serves four.

Total cooking time: about 1 hour.

RECIPE: SHRIMP AND ARTICHOKE CASSEROLE

1 pound fresh shrimp
½ pound mushrooms
1 cup milk
½ cup heavy cream
1 can artichoke hearts
4 tablespoons dry sherry
1 tablespoon Worcestershire sauce

1. Cook the shrimp in boiling salted (1 teaspoon) water for 6 minutes. Run under cold water to cool them, and then peel and devein them (see page 82).

2. Turn the oven on to 375° if you are going to complete the cooking at this time.

3. In a skillet over a very low flame, melt 4 tablespoons of butter. Gradually sprinkle in 4 tablespoons of flour, stirring constantly to blend it without lumps into the butter.

4. Take the skillet off the stove and, still stirring constantly, slowly pour in 1 cup of milk and ½ cup of heavy cream.

5. Return to a low flame, keep stirring, and cook until the mixture thickens. Add ¼ teaspoon of salt and a good sprinkling of pepper, and then taste to see if the amount of salt is enough; add more if necessary.

6. In another skillet, while the white sauce is cooking

very slowly, melt 2 tablespoons of butter, slice into it ½ pound of fresh mushrooms, and cook them for 7 minutes.

7. Rub butter around the inside of a casserole. Put the shrimp on the bottom and arrange over them 1 (drained) can of artichoke hearts, and on top of the artichokes put the mushrooms.

Stop here if you are going to complete the cooking later. When you pick up again, warm the white sauce over a very low flame before continuing.

8. Add 4 tablespoons of dry sherry and 1 tablespoon of Worcestershire sauce to the white sauce, stir well, and pour into the casserole.

9. Sprinkle grated Parmesan cheese and a light dusting of paprika over all.

10. Bake 30 minutes in a 375° oven.

BAKED BEAN CASSEROLE

This seems rather an odd choice to end this chapter with, but it is included here because it does so very well, in company with a baked ham, for a buffet supper for a large number of guests.

RECIPE: BAKED BEANS

canned pork and beans
brown sugar
chili sauce or catsup

1. Add 2 tablespoons of chili sauce or catsup and 2 tablespoons of brown sugar for each can of pork and beans. Lay a few strips of bacon over the top of the casserole.

2. Bake, uncovered, in a 325° oven for about an hour.

CHAPTER 6 MISCELLANEOUS MAIN DISHES

If you find yourself wondering about a change from the usual menu, or if your pocketbook happens to be a little thin, browse through this chapter and see what sounds good to you. Almost anything can be done with eggs; mushrooms, heretofore appearing only in a supporting role, are even more delicious when starred; such dishes as spaghetti or spareribs do well even for guests, while tomatoes, peppers, or onions provide tasty packaging for leftovers.

SPAGHETTI

No matter the rumors you have heard, spaghetti sauce need not be an all-day affair. Indeed, clam sauce takes only a few minutes, and meat balls or meat sauce need cook only one-half to one hour. Serve with crusty French or Italian bread, a large green salad, and, of course, grated Parmesan cheese. Spaghetti doubles in amount when cooked; one ordinary-sized package (8 ounces) serves four amply.

RECIPE I: SPAGHETTI WITH MEAT SAUCE

1 box spaghetti
1 pound ground beef
1 onion
1 clove garlic
1 green pepper
1 medium-size can Italian plum tomatoes
1 small can tomato paste

1. Put 3 tablespoons of olive oil or salad oil and 1 whole clove of garlic in a large skillet. Peel and chop 1 onion and 1 seeded green pepper, and cook these gently in the oil until the onions are transparent.

2. Crumble 1 pound of ground beef, and add it to the skillet, separating any chunks of meat with a fork. Cook, stirring occasionally, until the meat is brown.

3. Add to the skillet 1 medium-size can of Italian plum tomatoes, 1 small can of tomato paste, and 1 teaspoon of salt. Let this cook slowly for at least 30 minutes, longer if it is convenient. If the sauce gets too thick, add water. Taste before serving to make sure there is enough salt in it.

4. Cook spaghetti according to the directions on the package, spread it on a platter, and pour the meat sauce over it. But take out the clove of garlic first. To be sure you can find the garlic easily, spear it on a toothpick before putting it in the skillet.

RECIPE II: SPAGHETTI WITH MEAT BALLS

1 box spaghetti
1 pound ground beef
3 slices bread
2 tablespoons milk
1 onion
1 green pepper
1 medium-size can Italian plum tomatoes
1 small can tomato paste
1 clove garlic

1. Put ¼ cup of olive oil or salad oil in a skillet, and while this is heating, cut the crusts off 3 slices of bread, break the bread into small pieces, and soak the pieces in 2 tablespoons of milk.

2. In a bowl, mix the bread, 1 pound of ground beef, and 1 teaspoon of salt. Form into small round balls.

3. Add the meat balls to the skillet and cook them until lightly browned on all sides.

4. Peel and chop 1 onion and 1 seeded green pepper and add, along with 1 whole clove of garlic, to the skillet. Cook gently for 10 minutes.

5. Pour in 1 medium-size can of Italian plum tomatoes and 1 small can of tomato paste, and, if you like, add a pinch of oregano, along with 1 teaspoon of salt and ⅛ teaspoon of pepper. Let everything cook for 30 minutes, take out the clove of garlic, and taste the sauce to see if it has enough salt in it.

6. Cook spaghetti according to the package directions, put the meat balls in the center, and pour the sauce over all.

RECIPE III: SPAGHETTI WITH CLAM SAUCE

1 can minced clams
1 8-oz. package spaghetti
1 clove garlic

1. The thin spaghetti, called spaghettini, does best with clam sauce. Cook it according to the package directions.

2. Five minutes before the spaghetti is due to be done, put 2 tablespoons of butter and 1 sliced clove of garlic in a skillet. Cook the garlic for 1 minute and then take it out.

3. Put in 1 can of (Doxsee) minced clams, including the liquid. Cook for 3 minutes, just long enough to get hot; the clams will be tough if cooked longer.

4. Pour clams and broth over a platter of spaghetti.

OR: If you like red clam sauce, add 1 small can of tomato sauce to the butter in the skillet, and when it is hot, put in the clams and their juice.

Note: None of the prepared spaghetti sauces is really good as is, but all can be doctored to a passable state by adding garlic (clove or powder), a pinch of oregano, some chopped onion, and ground beef that has been browned in olive oil. Some water to thin the sauce will probably be needed, too. Canned spaghetti is fit only for children's lunches.

SWEET-SOUR SPARERIBS

This is tasty enough to consider serving to company, but the occasion must be informal for there is no way to eat spareribs, except with the fingers. Two pounds of spareribs should take care of four people.

Timing of menu: Spareribs, 1¼ hours. Rice, 30 minutes Tossed salad.

RECIPE: SWEET-SOUR SPARERIBS

2 pounds spareribs cut in 2-inch pieces
2 strips bacon
½ cup brown sugar

1 small can pineapple chunks
1 large onion
2 green peppers
½ cup vinegar
2 tablespoons soy sauce
3 tablespoons cornstarch

1. Cut 2 strips of bacon into 2-inch-long pieces and start it cooking in a heavy skillet. Peel and slice 1 large onion.

2. As soon as there is a bit of bacon fat melted in the skillet, add 2 pounds of spareribs cut in pieces and the sliced onion. Cook until the spareribs are brown, turning them as necessary.

3. If the skillet does not have a lid, transfer everything to a flameproof casserole. Add just the juice from 1 can of pineapple chunks. Cover tightly, and cook gently for 40 minutes.

4. Cut 2 green peppers into large slices, and add these plus the pineapple chunks, ½ cup of brown sugar (when measuring, pack it firmly into the cup), ½ cup of vinegar, and 2 tablespoons of soy sauce.

5. Mix together 3 tablespoons of cornstarch and 2 tablespoons of water into a smooth paste, and stir the paste in.

6. Cook, uncovered, until the sauce is thick and brown, which should take about 20 minutes.

CHICKEN LIVERS IN CREAM

If, when buying chicken, you have stored the livers away in the freezing compartment, supplement them with a package of frozen livers and try the following dish.

Timing of menu: Livers, 30 minutes. Stewed tomatoes, 10 minutes. Frozen broccoli, 5 minutes.

RECIPE: CHICKEN LIVERS IN CREAM

or 2 packages frozen chicken livers (½ package per serving)
cup chopped onions
1 cup light cream
3 hard-boiled eggs
½ teaspoon curry powder

1. If 3 hard-boiled eggs are not at hand, start by putting he eggs in a saucepan of cold water, bring the water to a oil, and cook the eggs for 5 minutes after the water begins o boil. Run them under cold water.

2. Melt 2 tablespoons of butter in a skillet and gently ook 1 cup of chopped onions until they are transparent. Jsing a slotted spoon, so as to leave the butter behind, take he onions out of the skillet.

3. Put 1 or 2 packages of frozen chicken livers (thawed nough to separate) in the skillet and cook them over a low

flame for 8 minutes, stirring occasionally so that they brown on all sides. Then set these aside along with the onions.

4. Add 2 more tablespoons of butter to the skillet, and when it has melted, pour in, while stirring, 1 cup of light cream. Let this heat but not boil.

5. Shell the hard-boiled eggs and cut them into quarters. Add them to the skillet, along with the livers and onions. Add ½ teaspoon of curry powder and ½ teaspoon of salt, a sprinkling each of pepper and paprika. Cook gently until the mixture is piping hot but short of boiling.

6. Serve over buttered noodles, spaghetti, toasted English muffins, or waffles.

MUSHROOM DISHES

Fresh mushrooms, firm, large, and white, are a handsome sight in the market, and even if they seem expensive, they should not be passed by, for they can constitute the main dish of a light meal and, thus used, be less costly than meat. Half a pound makes a dinner for two. The recipe for mushrooms and tomatoes, as simple as it sounds, is extraordinarily good. Young mushrooms need not be peeled; if, on the other hand, the mushrooms are old and a little tired, pull the skin off the cap by grasping it on the underside of the edge and stripping it off across the cap.

BROILED MUSHROOMS

Timing of menu: Broiled tomatoes, 20 minutes. Frozen succotash, 10 minutes. Broiled mushrooms on toast, 5 minutes.

RECIPE: BROILED MUSHROOMS

1. Wash the mushrooms (about 6 large per serving) and peel them if necessary. Cut them in half lengthwise.

2. Turn the broiler on to a medium flame.

3. Brush the mushrooms with oil or melted butter. Broil them 2 to 3 minutes on each side.

4. Salt and pepper them and arrange on toast.

BAKED MUSHROOMS

Timing of menu: Chopped carrots, 20 minutes. Mushrooms, 10 minutes. Zucchini, 5 minutes.

RECIPE: BAKED MUSHROOMS

6 large mushrooms per serving   1 cup cream

1. Preheat oven to 425°.
2. Wash the mushrooms, peel if necessary, and remove the stems.
3. Lay the mushrooms, hollow side up, in a baking dish. Sprinkle salt and pepper over, and put a bit of butter in each cap. Pour 1 cup of cream around them.
4. Bake in a 425° oven for 10 minutes.
5. Arrange the mushroom caps on toast and pour the cream over.

CREAMED MUSHROOMS

Timing of menu: Baked potato, 1 hour. Stewed tomatoes, 10 minutes. Mushrooms, 15 minutes.

RECIPE: CREAMED MUSHROOMS

½ to 1 pound mushrooms (6 large mushrooms per serving)
3 hard-boiled eggs
½ can of small white onions
1 dozen stuffed green olives
1 tablespoon dry sherry
1 cup milk

1. First, make a white sauce by melting 2 tablespoons of butter in a saucepan and slowly sprinkling in 2 tablespoons of flour, stirring constantly. When the flour and butter have blended, gradually pour in 1 cup of milk. Keep stirring until the sauce has thickened and is bubbling, and then let it continue to cook over a low flame.
2. In a skillet, melt 2 tablespoons of butter, slice the mushrooms, and put them in. Cook them 5 minutes, and then add them to the white sauce.
3. Also add to the white sauce 1 dozen sliced stuffed green olives, 3 hard-boiled eggs cut in quarters, 8 canned small white onions, 1 tablespoon of dry sherry, 1 teaspoon of salt, and a sprinkling of paprika. Taste to see if more salt and/or sherry are needed. (The olives, eggs, and onions are not essential, and any one or all may be omitted.)
4. Although making for a messy-looking plate, this concoction tastes very good spooned over baked potatoes which have been broken open and mashed down with a fork. Redeem the looks with a jaunty sprig of parsley on top.

MUSHROOMS AND TOMATOES

This dish has my highest recommendation. It is easy and it is excellent.

Timing of menu: Baked corn custard, 30 minutes. Mushrooms, 25 minutes.

RECIPE: MUSHROOMS AND TOMATOES

8 large mushrooms (for two servings)
4 slices of bacon
½ medium-sized can tomatoes
1 tablespoon Worcestershire or A-1 sauce

1. Cook 4 slices of bacon in a skillet until browned and done, about 5 minutes. Take the bacon out.
2. Wash 8 large mushrooms and cut them into quarters.
3. Put them in the skillet in the bacon fat, and add ½ of a medium-sized can of tomatoes, 1 tablespoon of white sugar, 1 tablespoon of Worcestershire or A-1 sauce, ½ teaspoon of salt, and ⅛ teaspoon of pepper. Stir to mix.
4. Cook over a low flame for 20 minutes. Serve on toast, laying the bacon strips on top and sprinkling grated Parmesan cheese over all.

HASH

These two recipes for hash are easily made because they are based on canned hash. The amounts feed one hungry man or two medium-sized appetites.

CORNED BEEF HASH

RECIPE: CORNED BEEF HASH

1 can corned beef hash
⅓ cup sour cream
2 tablespoons dried onion flakes

1. Turn oven on to 350°.
2. Rub butter on the inside of an iron skillet or baking dish.
3. Mix together 1 can of (Broadcast) corned beef hash, 2 tablespoons of dried onion flakes, and ⅓ cup of sour cream. Press the mixture down firmly in the skillet or baking dish.
4. Bake in a 350° oven for 25 minutes.

ROAST BEEF HASH

RECIPE: ROAST BEEF HASH

1 can roast beef hash
3 tablespoons dry red wine
2 tablespoons dried onion flakes
dash A-1 sauce

1. Mix in a bowl 1 can of (Cudahy) roast beef hash,

3 tablespoons dry red wine, 2 tablespoons dried onion flakes, and a dash of A-1 sauce.

2. Put 1 tablespoon butter or bacon drippings in a skillet, and when hot, add the hash. Cook until heated through and a nice brown crust has formed on the bottom. Fold in half and serve.

TUNA FISH

And when all else fails, fall back on a can of tuna fish.

TUNA FISH CASSEROLE

Timing of menu: Tuna fish, 30 minutes. Frozen asparagus spears, 8 minutes.

RECIPE: TUNA FISH CASSEROLE

1 can tuna fish (for two servings)	1 can condensed cream of mushroom soup
4 ounces broad or thin noodles	potato chips
2 tablespoons sherry	

1. Cook 4 ounces of either broad or thin noodles (½ of an 8-ounce box) according to the directions on the package.
2. Turn the oven on to 450°.
3. Rub butter on the inside of a baking dish.
4. Drain 1 can of tuna fish and break the fish into flakes. Use this way or, if you would prefer the fish to taste rather like chicken, put in a sieve and run hot water through it.
5. Put a layer of noodles in the baking dish, a layer of tuna fish, another layer of noodles, and so on, ending with noodles on top.
6. Mix 1 can of cream of mushroom soup with 2 tablespoons of sherry and pour this over the noodles.
7. Crumble potato chips and dust them thickly over the top. Sprinkle paprika over, and bake in a 450° oven about 20 minutes, or until the mixture is bubbly and the top browned.

For other dishes utilizing tuna fish, consult the Index.

CREAMED CHIPPED BEEF

A jar of dried chipped beef is a handy thing to keep in the can cupboard for the times when the refrigerator is suddenly bare.

Timing of menu: Chipped beef, 15 minutes. Frozen mixed vegetables, 10 minutes. Applesauce.

RECIPE: CREAMED CHIPPED BEEF

1 jar chipped beef
1 cup milk

1. Make a white sauce by melting 2 tablespoons of butter in a saucepan and sprinkling in 2 tablespoons of flour. Stir to blend well, and, still stirring, gradually pour in 1 cup of milk. Keep stirring until this mixture thickens.

2. Add 1 jar of crumbled chipped beef, and let cook gently for 10 minutes. Taste and adjust seasoning if necessary.

3. Serve on toast or toasted English muffins.

BAKED STUFFED TOMATOES

Tomatoes are convenient as a case for all kinds of stuffings, including leftovers. Some suggested combinations are given below, but you can also improvise with what is on hand in the refrigerator.

Timing of menu: Baked tomatoes, 20 minutes. Creamed corn, 10 minutes. Frozen peas, 5 minutes.

RECIPE I: TOMATOES STUFFED WITH HAM AND MASHED POTATOES

1 or 2 tomatoes per serving
leftover diced ham
prepared mustard
½ cup leftover or prepared mashed potatoes for each tomato

1. Turn the oven on to 350°.

2. Cut off the tops of the tomatoes and scoop out the pulp that is inside, being careful not to make holes in the walls of the tomatoes. Turn them upside down to drain.

3. Mix together leftover mashed potatoes (or mashed potatoes made according to the directions on a box of dehydrated potatoes) with finely chopped pieces of ham and 1 teaspoon of prepared mustard to each cup of mashed potatoes.

4. Salt the inside of the tomatoes. Stuff them with this mixture, sprinkle a bit of grated cheese and paprika on top, and place them in a well-buttered baking dish. Bake in a 350° oven for 20 minutes.

RECIPE II: TOMATOES STUFFED WITH LEFTOVER RICE

1 or 2 tomatoes per serving
½ cup cooked rice to each tomato
1 can sliced mushrooms

1. Turn on the oven to 350°.

2. Follow the directions in Recipe I for preparing the tomatoes.

3. Melt 2 tablespoons of butter in a skillet, and lightly cook leftover rice and 1 drained can of sliced mushrooms. You can add any leftover, finely chopped meat or any leftover vegetables you like to this mixture.

4. Salt the insides of the tomatoes, stuff them, and bake them in a buttered pan for 20 minutes in a 350° oven.

RECIPE III: TOMATOES STUFFED WITH SEA FOOD

4 tomatoes	1 cup milk
1 can crabmeat, lobster, or shrimp	

1. Turn on the oven to 350°.

2. Prepare the tomatoes according to the directions given in Recipe I.

3. Make a thick cream sauce by melting 4 tablespoons of butter and sprinkling in 4 tablespoons of flour, stirring all the while. When these are blended, gradually pour in 1 cup of milk and stir, cooking over a low flame, until the sauce thickens. Let it cook for 5 minutes. Salt and pepper it to taste.

4. Mix 1 drained can of sea food with the white sauce.

5. Stuff the tomatoes with this mixture, dust the top with bread crumbs or grated cheese and paprika, and place in a buttered baking dish. Bake for 20 minutes in a 350° oven.

OR: Substitute leftover, finely chopped meat for the sea food.

RECIPE IV: TOMATOES STUFFED WITH TUNA FISH

4 tomatoes	1 cup prepared bread stuffing
1 can tuna fish	

1. Preheat the oven to 350°.

2. Prepare the tomatoes according to the directions given in Recipe I.

3. In a bowl, mix together 1 drained and flaked can of tuna fish and 1 cup of (Pepperidge Farm) prepared stuffing. If you like, you can also mix in a few chopped anchovies or olives.

4. Salt the insides of the tomatoes, stuff with mixture, sprinkle grated cheese on top, and place in a buttered baking dish. Bake for 20 minutes in a 350° oven.

OR: Substitute diced chicken or turkey for the tuna fish.

BAKED STUFFED GREEN PEPPERS

Theoretically, green peppers can be stuffed with anything that tomatoes can, but, in practice, to my taste at least, only a meat and rice or a meat and bread stuffing does well with peppers.

Timing of menu: Stuffed peppers, 30 minutes. Broiled tomatoes, 15 minutes. Frozen succotash, 10 minutes.

RECIPE: STUFFED PEPPERS

1 or 2 green peppers per serving
leftover ground or finely chopped beef, lamb, or veal
cooked rice or bread stuffing
1 tablespoon chopped onion per pepper

1. Preheat oven to 350°.
2. Cut off the tops of the green peppers and scoop out the seeds.
3. Melt 2 tablespoons of butter in a skillet, and gently cook the onions until transparent, at which point add the meat and cooked rice or (Pepperidge Farm) bread stuffing and stir so that the butter in the bottom of the skillet is absorbed. If mixture seems too dry, moisten with additional melted butter or a little beef bouillon.
4. Stuff the peppers, place them in a baking dish with a bit of water, and bake for 20 minutes in a 350° oven.

BAKED STUFFED ONIONS

Onions, too, may be stuffed with anything your fancy dictates, but they are best with leftover ground beef or ham. Use medium or large yellow onions.

Timing of menu: Onions, 1 hour and 20 minutes. Baked potato, 1 hour. Green salad.

RECIPE: STUFFED ONIONS

1. Turn on oven to 350°.
2. Use 1 large onion per serving, peel them, and salt them liberally.
3. Wrap each onion individually in aluminum foil and bake for 1 hour in a 350° oven.
4. Pry out the centers of the onions, chop the centers, and mix with leftover meat that has been ground or finely chopped. Add salt and pepper.
5. Stuff the onions with the mixture, put in a buttered baking dish, uncovered, and bake for an additional 20 minutes.

EGGPLANT CASSEROLES

At college we were all too frequently served an eggplant concoction that came to be referred to simply as "train wreck," and it was some time before I learned that eggplant can be a pleasant vegetable and an interesting main dish. If you have any such memories, try either of these casseroles and see if your unhappy memories of eggplant are not dissipated.

EGGPLANT WITH MUSHROOMS AND ONIONS

This casserole serves four.

Timing of menu: Eggplant casserole, 1 hour. French bread. Mixed green salad.

RECIPE: EGGPLANT WITH MUSHROOMS AND ONIONS

1 large eggplant
2 large onions
1 pound mushrooms
1 cup grated American cheese
½ package bread stuffing

1. Turn on oven to 375°.
2. Pare the skin off the eggplant, and cut into slices about ½ inch thick. Dust 2 tablespoons of flour and a good sprinkling of salt and pepper on a piece of wax paper, and dip the slices of eggplant in it.
3. Heat 2 tablespoons of salad or olive oil in a skillet, and cook the eggplant slices 3 minutes on each side. Remove them from the skillet. Set aside.
4. Peel and slice 2 large onions, and cook them in the skillet, adding more oil if necessary. When the onions are transparent, remove them.
5. Wash and slice 1 pound of mushrooms, and cook them for 5 minutes in the skillet, again adding more oil if necessary.
6. Rub a light coating of butter on the inside of a casserole. Put in a bottom layer of eggplant slices, next a layer of onions, next a layer of mushrooms, and then a heavy sprinkling of grated American cheese. Repeat these layers until all the ingredients are used up. For the very top layer, use ½ package of (Pepperidge Farm) bread stuffing, and on the stuffing scatter small lumps of butter.
7. Put a lid on the casserole, and bake it in a 375° oven for 45 minutes.

EGGPLANT PARMIGIANA

As a main dish, this amount serves two.

Timing of menu: Eggplant, 30 minutes. French bread. Tossed salad.

RECIPE: EGGPLANT PARMIGIANA

1 large eggplant
1 small can tomato sauce
sliced Mozzarella cheese

1. Peel 1 large eggplant, and cut it into ½ inch thick slices. Salt and pepper the slices.
2. Melt 2 tablespoons of salad or olive oil in a skillet, and cook the eggplant slices in this for 3 minutes on each side.
3. Put the eggplant into a casserole, pour 1 small can of tomato sauce over, and top with slices of Mozzarella cheese.
4. Put under the broiler until the cheese has melted and is bubbling.

WELSH RABBIT

If you happen to have a half can of beer on hand that has gone flat, here is what to do with it.

RECIPE: WELSH RABBIT

1 pound sharp Cheddar cheese
1 cup beer or ale
1 tablespoon Worcestershire sauce
½ teaspoon dry mustard

1. Melt 1 tablespoon of butter in a skillet over a very low flame. Put in ½ teaspoon of dry mustard, 1 tablespoon of Worcestershire sauce, and a dash each of paprika and cayenne pepper.
2. Add 1 cup of flat ale or beer and allow to cook very slowly until hot.
3. Cut 1 pound of sharp Cheddar cheese into small pieces and add to the skillet. Keep stirring until the cheese has melted.
4. Serve over toast.

EGG DISHES

No matter how bare the cupboard, there are usually eggs on hand. The following recipes are some of the things that can be done to turn them into a meal.

OMELET

Just about anything can be incorporated into or folded into

the center of an omelet, for example, chopped ham, diced chicken, sliced canned mushrooms, cooked vegetables, diced cheese, or chopped parsley, and, for a further touch, condensed cream of chicken or mushroom soup or a can of stewed tomatoes can be poured over. The sauce that is to go on top or anything that is to be folded into the center should be heated separately; if the ingredients are to be mixed into the omelet before it is cooked, then there is no need to warm them in advance. The recipes given serve two people.

Timing of menu: Tomatoes and artichoke hearts, 10 minutes. Omelet, 10 minutes.

RECIPE I: PLAIN OMELET

3 eggs — 3 tablespoons milk

1. Put 1½ tablespoons of butter in a small skillet to get hot.
2. Break 3 eggs into a bowl, and add 3 tablespoons of milk, ¼ teaspoon of salt, and a sprinkling of pepper. Beat lightly with a fork until well mixed. Add any other ingredients you wish at this point.
3. Pour the mixture into the skillet. After a moment or two, lift one edge with a spatula or broad knife and tilt the pan so that some of the runny top slides down underneath. Keep doing this until the bottom of the omelet is lightly tanned and set and the top is set but still creamy, not hard. Fold over and serve immediately.

RECIPE II: FLUFFY OMELET

3 eggs — 3 tablespoons milk

1. Turn the oven on to 375°, and put 1½ tablespoons of butter in a small skillet to get hot.
2. Separate the whites and yolks of 3 eggs (see page 22 for how to do this), and put them in separate bowls.
3. Put ¼ teaspoon of salt in with the whites, and beat them with an egg beater until they are light and fluffy.
4. Beat the yolks until they are frothy.
5. Add 3 tablespoons of milk to the yolks, and then combine the whites and the yolks, overlapping them gently until they are mixed. Add any extra ingredients at this point.
6. Pour into the hot skillet. When the bottom of the omelet begins to set, put skillet and all into a 375° oven, and bake until the top is set. If you wish, slices of American cheese can be laid over the omelet just before it goes into the oven.

BAKED EGGS

Individual custard cups are needed for Recipe I, individual casseroles or a small baking dish for Recipe II. If you do not have them, turn to the Recipes for Poached Eggs instead.

Timing of menu: Eggs, Recipe I, 10 minutes; Recipe II, 25 minutes. Broiled tomatoes, 15 minutes.

RECIPE I: BAKED EGGS WITH HAM, SHRIMP, OR CHEESE

1. Set oven at 350°.
2. Put a pat of butter in each custard cup and line cup with a slice of cooked ham or a slice of cheese or chopped canned shrimp.
3. Break 1 egg into each cup, put a dash of paprika on top, and set the cups in a pan of water. Bake in a 350° oven until the whites of the eggs are firm, about 10 minutes.

RECIPE II: BAKED EGGS WITH SPINACH

4 eggs
1 package of frozen creamed spinach
½ cup grated Swiss cheese

1. Preheat the oven to 350°.
2. Cook the frozen creamed spinach according to the directions on the package.
3. When it is cooked, put the spinach in a small baking dish, and add to it ½ cup of grated Swiss cheese. Mix these.
4. Break eggs, 1 at a time, into a saucer, and slide them from the saucer on to the top of the spinach. Salt and pepper the eggs, and sprinkle them with more grated Swiss cheese. Put a sprinkle of paprika over.
5. Bake in a 350° oven until the eggs are done and the cheese has melted, which should take about 10 minutes.

POACHED EGGS

A few additions make poached eggs as fit for the supper table as the breakfast table.

Timing of menu: Eggs, 10 minutes. Corn on the cob, 10 minutes.

RECIPE I: POACHED EGGS AND ASPARAGUS

1 package frozen asparagus in Hollandaise sauce
1 package frozen waffles
thin slices of cooked ham
4 eggs

1. Cook 1 package of frozen asparagus in Hollandaise sauce according to the directions on the package (or use frozen asparagus spears, cooked, and 1 can of chicken gravy).

2. In a skillet melt 1 tablespoon of butter and put the ham on to heat in it over a low flame.

3. Boil water in a shallow pan. Break eggs into a saucer, and slide them from the saucer into the very gently boiling water.

4. Put waffles in the toaster to warm.

5. When the eggs have set, which will be in about 4 minutes, arrange the waffles on plates, put a slice of ham on each, on top of this the asparagus and its sauce, and top each with a poached egg. Salt and pepper the eggs. A sprinkle of paprika and a sprig of parsley are the finishing touches.

RECIPE II: POACHED EGGS IN TOMATO SAUCE

4 eggs
½ chopped green pepper
½ cup chopped onions
1 small can tomato sauce

1. In a skillet, melt 2 tablespoons of butter, and lightly cook ½ of a chopped green pepper and ½ cup of chopped onions until the onions are transparent.

2. Add 1 small can of tomato sauce to the skillet, plus a dash of garlic powder and a sprinkling of salt and pepper.

3. When the tomato sauce is hot, slide the eggs one at a time into the sauce, first breaking them into a saucer. Salt and pepper them. Cook over low heat, occasionally spooning some of the sauce over the eggs. It will take about 5 minutes for the eggs to set.

4. Serve on toast, with some grated cheese to sprinkle over.

CREAMED EGGS

This sounds, and is, a very simple dish, but there are times when it tastes just right. The recipe is for two servings.

Timing of menu: Eggs, 15 minutes. Stewed tomatoes, 10 minutes. Petit pois, 5 minutes.

RECIPE: CREAMED EGGS

1. Put 4 eggs in a saucepan, add water to cover, and cook them for 5 minutes after the water starts boiling. Run them under cold water until cool enough to shell.

2. In the meantime, melt 2 tablespoons of butter in another saucepan over a very low flame and slowly sprinkle in, while stirring, 2 tablespoons of flour. When the flour and butter

are well blended, gradually add 1 cup of milk, stirring constantly. Continue stirring until the mixture thickens. Add salt and pepper to taste, paprika, and 1 tablespoon of sherry.

3. Cut the eggs in quarters and add them to the sauce. You can also add a can of mushrooms or fresh mushrooms. If the latter, first cook them gently for 5 minutes in butter.

4. Serve on toast or toasted English muffins.

CHAPTER 7 HOW TO COOK VEGETABLES

This chapter should perhaps be entitled how not to *over*cook vegetables, for that is where vegetables most frequently go wrong. Whether fresh, frozen, or canned, vegetables should be cooked for the least possible amount of time and, in the case of green vegetables, in the least possible amount of water. Never should they be permitted to stand in water; if, by mischance, they are done and the main dish is not, pour off the cooking water, put a pat of butter in, and cover the saucepan tightly; just before serving, put them back on the fire for a moment or two, shaking the pot so they will not burn. In storing leftover vegetables, too, just put them in a covered container in the refrigerator, not in water (except for canned vegetables, which may be held over in the juice from the can).

FRESH VEGETABLES

In buying fresh vegetables, it is usually best to choose the smallest ones, for these will be the youngest and therefore the most tender. Look for firm, unblemished vegetables of a bright color. Greens should be crisp and unwilted. Some vegetables, like asparagus, will reveal their age by the presence of seeds; potatoes, onions, and carrots by the presence of sprouts. Try not to keep fresh vegetables too long after purchase, but if they have become wilted in the refrigerator, crisp them by a short soak in cold water before cooking. Do not wash vegetables until you are ready to cook them. Root vegetables, such as potatoes, onions, and beets, can be stored at room temperature, but they will keep longer if there is room for them in the vegetable bin in the refrigerator. Green vegetables last best if placed in a plastic bag and then refrigerated. The plastic bags that come on a roll and in the same type of package as aluminum foil are excellent for storing vegetables and fruit. In cooking fresh vegetables, a pressure cooker is a blessing. If you have one, follow the directions in the recipe book that came with it.

FROZEN VEGETABLES

Frozen vegetables are a great timesaver since they are ready for cooking and need no further preparation. Too, they have the advantage of keeping indefinitely, permitting a supply of a variety of vegetables to be kept on hand, with only the amount needed being cooked at one time, which is a help when the cooking is being done for one or two persons. As every package warns, frozen food that has thawed must not be refrozen; cook it all and then rewarm it if you have too much. The package will give cooking directions. Follow these but use the least amount of time given; for example, if the package says cook 8 to 10 minutes, test the vegetable after 8 minutes, and if it is tender, take it out of the water immediately. Salt the water and have it boiling rapidly before putting the vegetable in. An alternative method of cooking is to thaw the vegetable beforehand just to the point where it separates, i.e., it is no longer one frozen block, and then cook it with a pat of butter in a tightly covered pan. The water that the vegetables themselves give off is sufficient to steam them nicely, and the food value of the vegetable is better conserved in this way. Virtually every type of vegetable is available in frozen form, but some survive the freezing process much better than others. On the whole, green vegetables do well, but I find that the others, such as squash, potatoes, eggplant, and corn on the cob, are far inferior to fresh. As for differences in quality in accordance with brand names, I cannot find any and usually buy a chain-store's brand because it costs less and tastes the same.

CANNED VEGETABLES

Canned vegetables, on the other hand, seem to me to vary greatly in quality, and I have been sorry every time I have bought less than the top grade. Grades are marked on the cans, and I would advise passing up savings of a penny or two in favor of getting the best. Canned vegetables need only be heated, and this is done in the juice from the can. Add salt and pepper and the tip of a teaspoon of sugar to improve the flavor. A slightly more elegant way of warming up canned vegetables is to pour the juice from the can into a saucepan and boil it until it is reduced by two-thirds and then add the vegetable, along with a pat of butter.

Leftover Vegetables

• Most leftover vegetables may be warmed in a little milk; the Italian way of warming them in a skillet in olive or salad oil with a bit of garlic or other herb is very good.

ARTICHOKES

In buying artichokes, choose ones with the leaves still tightly closed; when they begin to open out like flowers, the artichokes are old and tired. Look, too, for an absence of brown, although often the tips of the leaves will be tinged and this, while not preferable, is all right.

FRESH ARTICHOKES

Cooking time: 30 minutes to 1 hour.

To clean: Cut off all but one-half inch of the stem, pull off the outside layer of bottom leaves, and scrape the stem with a knife. Hold rightside up under running cold water, and then turn upside down to drain out the water.

To Cook: Put them in a pot of boiling salted water sufficient to cover them. Cook 30 minutes to 1 hour, depending on size. Test for doneness by piercing the stem with a knife; if the stem is tender, the artichokes are done.

To Serve: Serve hot with individual dishes of melted butter, cold with individual dishes of Hollandaise sauce (see page 206) or Vinaigrette sauce (make this by mixing 3 parts of olive oil to 1 part vinegar and adding salt, pepper, and a touch of dry mustard).

ARTICHOKE HEARTS AND TOMATOES

You do not need me to tell you how wonderful artichokes are, cold or hot, but the combination of marinated artichoke hearts and tomatoes, invented by a friend of mine, may be a new pleasure to you.

1 jar marinated artichoke hearts
2 fresh tomatoes

1. Melt 1 tablespoon of butter in a saucepan, drain 1 jar of (Regina Mia) marinated artichoke hearts and add these. Cut 2 fresh tomatoes into wedges and add these.

2. Cook for about 10 minutes, although it will not matter if they go longer. Taste to see if any salt is needed.

ARTICHOKE HEARTS IN WINE

1 package frozen artichoke hearts
1 cup dry white wine
1 teaspoon grated onion
½ teaspoon lemon juice

Put in a saucepan 1 package of frozen artichoke hearts, 1 cup of dry white wine, 1 teaspoon of grated onion, ½ teaspoon of lemon juice, and 1 teaspoon of salt. Let this come to a boil, then turn the fire down and cook gently for 6 minutes.

Leftover Artichokes

- Serve cold with Vinaigrette sauce, as described above.

ASPARAGUS

Fresh asparagus is incomparable, so use it in the spring when it is available, and settle, not unhappily, for frozen asparagus the rest of the year. Frozen asparagus spears are far better than the cut pieces, but also more expensive. In buying fresh asparagus, avoid limp stalks, too thick stalks, and tops that have begun to go to seed.

FRESH ASPARAGUS

Cooking time: 10 to 15 minutes.

To Clean: Take the stalk in both hands, exert some pressure as though to break it in two, and the stalk will snap at the point at which it begins to be tough and woody. Discard this end. With a knife scrape the stems lightly, pulling off the isolated little triangular leaves, for sand may be lurking behind them. Wash in running cold water.

To Cook: The point with asparagus is not to get the tips soggy, and this can best be avoided by tieing the asparagus into a bunch and standing it on end in 2 inches of boiling salted water. It must be cooked covered so the tips will steam, so either use a deep kettle with a lid or, if you do not have one large enough, put the bunched asparagus in a saucepan and upend another saucepan over it. Cooking time should be about 15 minutes, but test with a knife to see if they are tender before this. Better to have slightly crisp stalks than overdone tips. If the asparagus is cooked without being tied in a bunch, 10 minutes is enough.

To Serve: Serve plain, with a pat of butter on each serving, or with Hollandaise sauce (see page 206).

ASPARAGUS WITH CHEESE

To serve asparagus when there are guests, you may not want to have to worry about last minute timing, in which event you can use this recipe or the one following.

2 packages frozen asparagus spears
bread crumbs
sliced Gruyere or Swiss cheese

1. Cook the asparagus according to the package directions.

2. Rub butter on the inside of a baking dish, and put in alternate layers of asparagus and sliced Gruyere or Swiss cheese. Sprinkle bread crumbs over the top and a dusting of paprika for color.

3. About 10 minutes before dinner is to be served, put in a preheated medium (350° or so) oven and bake until the cheese is melted.

ASPARAGUS WITH SOUR CREAM

2 packages frozen asparagus spears
bread crumbs
1 cup sour cream

1. Cook the asparagus according to the package directions.

2. Place the asparagus in a buttered casserole or baking dish and gently mix in 1 cup of sour cream. Sprinkle the top with bread crumbs and paprika.

3. Bake for 20 minutes in a preheated 350° oven.

Leftover Asparagus

- Warm in a little milk or butter.
- Follow the recipe for Asparagus with Cheese or Asparagus with Sour Cream, reducing the amounts accordingly.

STRING BEANS

Frozen string beans, cut or French-style, are as good as fresh, but canned string beans are to be avoided. String beans are a good choice for company meals, for they lend themselves well to casserole dishes which can be put together in advance and then warmed in the oven at the last minute.

FRESH STRING BEANS

Cooking time: 12 minutes.

To Clean: Break off both tips and discard. Break the beans into pieces about 1 inch long or, to French, cut them lengthwise into strips. Wash in a pot of cold water.

To Cook: Boil them, uncovered, in salted water until tender, perhaps 12 minutes.

To Serve: Serve as is with a dab of butter on top.

STRING BEANS WITH WATER CHESTNUTS

fresh or frozen string beans
1 can water chestnuts

When the beans are almost cooked, melt 2 tablespoons of butter in a skillet, and add 1 drained can of water chestnuts. Cook over a low flame for 3 or 4 minutes. Pour over the cooked string beans.

STRING BEANS WITH MUSHROOM SOUP

2 packages frozen French-style string beans
1 can condensed cream of mushroom soup
1 package dehydrated onion soup or 1 can French-fried onion rings

1. Cook the string beans according to the package directions.
2. Put in a casserole or baking dish, and pour in 1 can of condensed cream of mushroom soup. Stir to mix.
3. Sprinkle over the top 1 package of dehydrated onion soup mix or arrange 1 can of French-fried onion rings over.
4. About 15 minutes before dinner is to be served, heat in the oven.

STRING BEANS IN SOUR CREAM

2 packages frozen French-style string beans
1 cup sour cream
1 can sliced mushrooms
1 tablespoon dried onion flakes

1. Cook string beans according to the package directions.
2. Put in a baking dish or casserole, and mix in 1 cup of sour cream, 1 drained can of sliced mushrooms, 1 tablespoon of dried onion flakes, and ¼ teaspoon of salt, plus a sprinkling of pepper. For an extra touch, cover the top with sliced almonds.
3. Put in the oven to get hot 15 or 20 minutes before dinner is to be served.

STRING BEANS WITH BACON

2 packages frozen French-style string beans
3 slices bacon
4 tablespoons French dressing

1. Cook string beans according to the package directions.
2. At the same time fry, until crisp, 3 slices of bacon. Drain on paper towels.
3. When the beans are done, pour the cooking water

off, and add 4 tablespoons of French dressing. Cook a few additional minutes over a very low flame.

4. When the beans are ready to serve, crumble the bacon and put it over the top.

STRING BEANS WITH VARIATIONS

- Add 1 can of sliced mushrooms the last moments of cooking time.
- Add 2 thinly sliced scallions to the cooking water.
- Drain the beans after cooking, and put in a pat of butter and a good sprinkling of grated Parmesan cheese. Toss the beans with a fork to mix the cheese in.
- Add 1 tablespoon of sour cream to cooked beans just before serving.

Leftover String Beans

- Pour French dressing over the beans and store in the refrigerator. Add to a green salad, or serve as is for salad course.
- Warm in 2 tablespoons of salad oil and 1 halved clove of garlic. Remove garlic before serving.

WAX BEANS

Fresh wax beans, which should be crisp and snap briskly when broken, are prepared and cooked in the same way as string beans. The frozen variety are fine, but, surprisingly, they do not lend themselves to the variations possible with string beans. Cook them according to the package directions and serve them just with a bit of butter melting on top.

LIMA BEANS

Why it should be so, I don't know, but fresh lima beans are tastiest when small and frozen lima beans when large. Thus, I recommend buying frozen Fordhook lima beans and avoiding the packages labeled baby lima beans.

FRESH LIMA BEANS

Cooking time: 20 to 40 minutes.

To Prepare: Lima beans should be shelled at the last moment before cooking, so do not buy already shelled ones. Shell them simply by breaking the pods open and flicking the beans out with your thumbnail.

To Cook: Cook in boiling salted water, uncovered, for 20 to 40 minutes, halting cooking the moment they are tender.

To Serve: Put a pat of butter on top, or melt (Kraft's) Cheez-Whiz as a sauce to go over them.

BEETS

Beets are an excellent and rather neglected vegetable. They are equally good fresh or canned.

FRESH BEETS

Cooking Time: 30 minutes to 1 hour.

To Prepare: Cut off the tops at least 1 inch above the beet proper and leave the bottom root on; otherwise, the color will bleed out of the beets while cooking. Wash them, but do not scrape or peel in any way.

To Cook: Put in boiling salted water to cover and cook with a lid on for 30 minutes to an hour, depending on the size of the beets. To decide when they are done, you will have to pierce one with a sharp knife and feel whether or not the center is still hard.

To Serve: Lift the beets out of the water with a slotted spoon. Stick the prongs of a fork into one end, hold the beet up, slice off the top, and, catching the skin between the knife and your thumb, pull the skin down. This may sound complicated but the skin comes off very readily and the maneuver may be accomplished even though the beets are piping hot. With the beet still impaled on a fork, put it on its side and slice it into a serving dish.

BEETS IN BURGUNDY

1 can sliced beets or 1 cup fresh cooked beets
2 tablespoons Burgundy wine
2 tablespoons French dressing

1. Drain 1 can of sliced beets, and put them in a bowl with a sprinking of salt and pepper and 2 tablespoons each of Burgundy wine and French dressing. Store the bowl in the refrigerator overnight.
2. Heat in a small quantity of the marinade.

BEETS IN ORANGE JUICE

1 can sliced beets or 1 cup fresh cooked beets
½ cup orange juice
grated rind of 1 orange

1. Grate the rind of 1 orange by scraping it against a cheese or onion grater.

2. Put the grated rind, 1 drained can of beets, ½ cup of orange juice, and 1 tablespoon of butter in a saucepan. Cook until very hot, but do not allow to boil.

Leftover beets

- Pickle them for use in salads by adding a few slices of onion and equal parts of vinegar and water, for example, 2 tablespoons of vinegar and 2 tablespoons of water. Store in the refrigerator in a closed jar. Let stand for at least eight hours before serving.

BROCCOLI

Frozen broccoli is easier to cope with than fresh, but if you buy it fresh, look for crisp, firm stems and unwilted heads.

FRESH BROCCOLI

Cooking time: About 15 minutes.

To Prepare: Cut off the bottom of the stalks, pull off large outside leaves, and rinse under cold running water.

To Cook: Like asparagus, it is best if the heads of the broccoli are not in water. Therefore, tie it in a bunch and stand it in a large kettle with a lid or improvise a lid by upending one saucepan over another. Cook in 2 inches of boiling salted (1 teaspoon) water for about 15 minutes, or until the stems are tender when tested with a knife.

To Serve: Serve as is, with melted cheese poured over, with Hollandaise sauce (see page 206), or with mayonnaise to which a little bit of lemon juice has been added.

BROCCOLI WITH BACON

1 package frozen chopped broccoli
2 slices bacon
2 tablespoons vinegar
¼ cup bread crumbs

1. Cook 1 package of frozen chopped broccoli according to the package directions.

2. While the broccoli is cooking, fry 2 slices of bacon and 1 clove of garlic until the bacon is crisp.

3. Take the bacon and garlic out of the skillet; discard the garlic. Add 2 tablespoons of vinegar to the bacon fat. Heat, but do not allow to boil.

4. In another skillet, brown ¼ cup of bread crumbs in 1 tablespoon of butter.

5. Put the cooked broccoli in a serving dish, crumble the bacon on top, pour the vinegar over, and sprinkle with bread crumbs.

Leftover Broccoli

- Warm it up in a little milk.
- If there is just a little bit, marinate it in French dressing and add it to a salad. Or serve it as one of the items on a relish tray.
- Arrange it in a casserole, pour over it condensed cream of celery soup, sprinkle with grated Swiss cheese and bread crumbs, and bake in a 350° oven for 10 to 15 minutes.
- Heat 2 tablespoons of salad oil with 1 sliced clove of garlic. Take the garlic out, add the broccoli and several sliced pitted black olives. Cook until the broccoli is hot. Serve sprinkled with grated Parmesan cheese.

BRUSSELS SPROUTS

Buy the fresh ones and look for firmly closed, unwilted ones.

FRESH BRUSSELS SPROUTS

Cooking time: About 10 minutes.

To Prepare: Cut off the stems and pull off wilted outer leaves. Wash in cold water.

To Cook: Have a pot of water briskly boiling, add 1 teaspoon of salt, drop in the Brussels sprouts, and turn the fire down to the point at which the water is just simmering. Cook the sprouts about 10 minutes, or until tender.

To Serve: Pour a bit of melted butter over.

Leftover Brussels Sprouts

- Place in a baking dish and pour over them ½ can of beef or chicken consommé (or dissolve a bouillon cube in ½ cup of hot water). Sprinkle heavily with grated Parmesan cheese and bake for 10 to 15 minutes in a 400° oven.

CABBAGE

Whether buying white or red cabbage, squeeze the head to

make sure it is firm. The fresher the better, of course, but wilted outer leaves can be stripped away so do not worry too much about them.

FRESH CABBAGE

Cooking time: about 6 to 10 minutes.

To Prepare: Pull off the outer leaves, cut the cabbage in half, and then shred it by making a series of thin, wedge-shaped slices from the center to the outside. Soak the shredded cabbage for 30 minutes in cold water to which 1 teaspoon of salt has been added.

To Cook: Put a fresh pot of water on to boil, add the cabbage, and cook for 6 to 10 minutes, until it is tender.

To Serve: Drain, sprinkle with a bit more salt, and put a pat of butter on each serving.

Leftover Cabbage

- Put in a baking dish with 1 or 2 tablespoons of dried onion flakes and pour condensed cream of chicken soup over (the amounts depend on how much cabbage there is). Sprinkle with grated cheese and paprika and bake in a 350° oven for 15 minutes.
- Substitute sour cream for the soup in the above directions.
- If you have cooked only part of the head and left the rest raw, see the recipe for Cole Slaw (page 157).

RED CABBAGE

Cooking time: about 15 minutes.

To Prepare: Follow the directions for cabbage above.

To Cook: Fry 3 slices of bacon and set them aside. Cook the shredded red cabbage in the bacon fat until tender, about 15 minutes. Serve with the bacon crumbled over the cabbage.

RED CABBAGE WITH APPLES

½ head red cabbage	3 slices bacon
2 apples	

1. Shred or grate the red cabbage so that it is in small pieces.

2. Fry 3 slices of bacon until crisp and then remove them from the skillet.

3. Pare, core, and cut into small pieces 2 apples.

4. Put the cabbage and apples in the bacon fat, add ½ teaspoon of salt, cover the skillet and cook gently until the cabbage is tender, about 15 minutes.

5. Make a sauce by mixing together 1 tablespoon of (Gulden's) prepared mustard, ½ cup of brown sugar, and 1 tablespoon of vinegar. Put this in the skillet with the cooked cabbage and heat briefly. Serve with the bacon crumbled on top.

CARROTS

Carrots are carrots, so there are no particular buying instructions except that the smaller they are, the better. The fresh ones are far better than canned, but canned ones are good to keep on hand to add to stews. Fresh ones keep for weeks in the refrigerator. I can give no rational reason why it should be so but chopped carrots are quite a bit tastier than sliced or whole ones.

FRESH CARROTS

Cooking time: Whole carrots, up to 30 minutes depending on size; quarter-inch slices, 15 minutes; thinly sliced, 10 minutes.

To Prepare: Cut off both ends of the carrot and scrape off the skin with a paring knife. For sliced carrots, cut into quarter-inch slices; for chopped carrots, slice thinly.

To Cook: Bring to a boil a sufficient quantity of water to cover the carrots generously. Add salt. Put the carrots in and boil until tender.

To Serve: For whole or sliced carrots, just put a bit of butter on and a little chopped parsley. For chopped carrots, drain the pan of water, add a pat of butter, and chop the carrots with a knife; tilt the pan toward you so that the carrots pile up against the side and then cut through them repeatedly, with a chopping motion, against the side of the pan.

GLAZED CARROTS

6 to 8 cooked carrots	⅓ cup honey

For every 6 to 8 cooked, small whole or sliced carrots, put 2 tablespoons of butter and ⅓ cup of honey in a skillet.

Flip the carrots in this mixture until they are coated and cook until they are glazed and brown, turning so that they glaze on all sides.

Leftover Carrots

- Warm chopped carrots in a little butter and milk.
- Add sliced carrots to a can of peas.
- Add them to stews or any creamed dish, such as Chicken a la King.

CAULIFLOWER

In buying, choose a small head with a fresh, creamy color that is free of brown spots. Be careful not to overcook either frozen or fresh cauliflower, for it gets soggy easily.

FRESH CAULIFLOWER

Cooking time: Whole cauliflower, about 20 to 25 minutes; flowerets, 10 to 15 minutes.

To Prepare: Remove the leaves, cut off the end of the stem, and soak the head in a kettle of cold water, to which a teaspoon of salt has been added, for 15 to 30 minutes. Leave the head whole or break it into flowerets.

To Cook: Put a kettle of water on to boil, enough water to cover the head or the flowerets, and boil until tender when tested with a knife. If it is a whole cauliflower, test the stem with a knife after 15 minutes; for flowerets, after 10 minutes.

To Serve: Serve it plain with a bit of butter and a sprinkle of paprika or pour melted cheese over.

Leftover Cauliflower

- Arrange the cooked cauliflower in a buttered casserole, lay over it slices of American or Swiss cheese, and sprinkle with bread crumbs. Bake in a 350° oven until the cheese is melted and bubbling. If the top is not yet brown, slide it under the broiler for a minute or two.
- Arrange cauliflower in a casserole, sprinkle over it 2 tablespoons of dried onion flakes and pour in 1 thawed can of frozen potato soup. Dust the top with grated cheese and bake in a 350° oven for 15 minutes. Or substitute frozen shrimp soup for the potato soup.

CORN

The only way to have corn on the cob as it should taste is to grow it yourself and then run with it from the corn patch to the kettle of water boiling on the stove, husking as you go. Failing this, buy it fresh-picked at a nearby farm. Failing this, do your best at the grocery store, your best being never to buy corn already husked, pick out the slenderest ears, and slide a thumbnail under the husk at the top just far enough to get a look at the corn inside; the kernels should be well formed but not hard and fat. Do not buy a large supply of corn, planning to eat it up over several days; buy only enough for one meal and as little in advance of cooking time as is feasible.

As for frozen corn, corn on the cob does not seem to me worth bothering with, but corn niblets are good.

There are two kinds of canned corn, the niblets and cream-style. Del Monte's cream-style is fine, and, in niblets, Le Sueur's shoe-peg corn is head and shoulders above any other brand.

CORN ON THE COB

Have enough water boiling to cover the ears of corn. Husk the ears at the last minute and drop them in the boiling *un*salted water. Cook for 5 minutes, a little longer if the corn is old.

Leftover Corn on the Cob

• Cut the kernels off the cob, and warm the corn in a little milk and butter to which salt, pepper, and a speck of sugar have been added.

CANNED CORN

Canned corn need only be warmed up, which, in the case of niblets, is best done in milk, with a little salt, pepper, and sugar. Or it may be warmed in a little cream of chicken soup. For cream-style, add 1 or 2 tablespoons of milk, ⅛ teaspoon of sugar, salt and pepper, and heat slowly, not allowing to boil.

BAKED CORN CUSTARD

1 large can cream-style corn
2 eggs
2 cups milk

1. Turn on oven to 325°.
2. Put 1 large can of cream-style corn in a buttered bak-

ing dish, and stir in 2 eggs that have been beaten lightly with a fork. Add 1 teaspoon of salt and ⅛ teaspoon each of pepper and sugar.

3. Heat 2 cups of milk just to the boiling point, and add to the baking dish immediately. Stir to mix in.

4. Bake in a 325° oven until the pudding is set, 40 to 60 minutes. It is done when a knife stuck in the middle comes out clean.

If you wish, leftover ground or chopped ham may be added to the pudding before cooking.

EGGPLANT

Eggplant deserves a better reputation than it has, for when well cooked, which is a simple matter, it is delicious. In buying, choose small, firm ones.

FRESH EGGPLANT

Cooking time: 10 minutes.

To Prepare: Slice off the top and bottom and peel the skin off with a knife. Cut the eggplant into slices about as thick as a finger.

To Cook: Eggplant may be either broiled or fried. *To fry:* heat 3 tablespoons of salad oil in a skillet (add a sprinkling of garlic powder if you wish). Spread flour seasoned with salt and pepper on a piece of wax paper, and dip the eggplant slices in this to coat them. Drop the eggplant into the hot oil and cook until both sides are nicely browned, 5 to 10 minutes. *To broil:* spread the eggplant slices on aluminum foil in the broiler. Mix together in a cup ¼ cup of salad oil, ⅛ teaspoon of garlic powder, 1 teaspoon of grated onion, and a little less than ½ teaspoon of salt. Paint the eggplant slices with this mixture. Broil them for 6 minutes. Turn them over, and paint the second sides. Broil for an additional few minutes until tender.

STUFFED EGGPLANT

1 large eggplant
2 cups bread crumbs

1. Cut 1 good-sized eggplant in half lengthwise, and scoop out the pulp to within ½ inch of the shell. Put the shells in a pot or bowl and cover them with cold water.

2. Chop the eggplant pulp, salt and pepper it, and cook for 10 minutes in 1 tablespoon of butter in a skillet.

3. Mix together the pulp and 2 cups of bread crumbs. Drain the water off the shells, sprinkle them with salt and pepper, and stuff them with the mixture. Dust more bread crumbs on top. If the eggplant is for company, this much may be done in advance and the cooking completed later.

4. Bake for 30 minutes in a 350° oven. In serving, scoop out the filling only; the shells are not edible.

Leftover Eggplant

• Arrange cooked eggplant slices in a buttered baking dish, pour some tomato sauce over, and lay slices of Mozzarella or American cheese on top. Broil until the cheese is bubbly.

For other recipes with eggplant, consult the Index.

MACARONI

For plain macaroni, perhaps served with a little butter and grated cheese, follow the directions on the package. For baked macaroni and cheese, the difference in taste between opening a can and making it from scratch is not great enough to warrant the effort. Franco-American seems to me the best brand.

BAKED MACARONI WITH GRATED CHEESE

Put 1 or 2 cans of macaroni into a baking dish. Sprinkle with grated American cheese and bread crumbs, and bake in a 400° oven for 20 minutes. If the top is not brown enough, put under the broiler for a minute or two.

BAKED MACARONI WITH TOMATOES AND CHEESE

This is so good, good-looking, and easy that it does nicely for a company dinner. Empty 1 or 2 cans, or more, of macaroni into a casserole or baking dish. Cover the top with slices of tomato, and lay over these slices of American cheese. Sprinkle with paprika, and bake in a 400° oven for 20 minutes, or until cheese is bubbly.

Leftover Macaroni

• Just warm up, adding a little milk if necessary to prevent sticking.

MUSHROOMS

Mushrooms make a good occasional substitute for potatoes or other vegetables in a dinner menu. In buying mushrooms, size does not matter; just look for unwilted ones with a fresh, creamy color. Canned mushrooms are fine as an ingredient in other dishes, but they cannot stand alone as a vegetable.

FRESH MUSHROOMS

Cooking time: Up to 10 minutes.

To Prepare: Young ones need only be washed; after washing, do not let them sit around with drops of water on them. Older ones can be peeled by grasping the skin on the underside of the cap and pulling it off across the cap.

To Cook: Cut in half and cook gently for 5 to 10 minutes in butter in a skillet. Or brush with melted butter and put under the broiler for 10 minutes.

Leftover Mushrooms

• Heat them gently in a small amount of sour cream and use as a vegetable or sauce.

• Add them to anything: meat, fish, vegetables, soup, what have you.

NOODLES

Keep noodles in mind to use fairly often as a substitute for potatoes, for they are easy and quick to prepare, although not as high in food value, and their unobtrusive flavor often makes them the right companion for an exciting main attraction. Buy wide or narrow noodles, as you prefer, and follow the package directions for cooking.

To dress up noodles, try one of the following:

After cooking, pour melted butter over and a good quantity of chopped parsley. Lift the noodles between two forks several times so that the butter coats all the strands and the parsley is distributed throughout.

Warm 1 drained can of chopped mushrooms in 1 tablespoon of butter and 1 tablespoon of dry white wine. Pour over the noodles and lift the noodles with two forks to coat them well.

Cook 1 drained can of chopped or sliced mushrooms in 2 tablespoons of butter and 1 halved clove of garlic. Take the garlic out before mixing the sauce into the noodles.

Pour melted butter over cooked noodles, lift with two forks to coat them, and then sprinkle grated Parmesan or American cheese liberally over the noodles.

Leftover Noodles

- Add to soups, stews, and creamed dishes.
- Warm up in butter and garlic or in canned beef gravy or in a little milk.

ONIONS

There are white onions, yellow onions, and red onions. Red onions are the mildest and are excellent for salad. White onions are small and make the best vegetable. Yellow onions may be used in any way; when a recipe says onions, yellow onions, unless otherwise specified, are meant. White onions are particularly good boiled; yellow onions are particularly good baked.

BOILED SMALL WHITE ONIONS

Cooking time: Boiled small white onions, 15 to 20 minutes; baked yellow onions, 1 hour.

To Prepare: Cut off both ends and peel off the skin. This can be done somewhat wastefully, but with very little trouble, by cutting through the first layer of onion and then just pulling it off, discarding it along with the skin. Allow about 6 onions per serving. Put enough water to cover the onions in a kettle with 1 teaspoon of salt. When it is boiling add the onions, and cook until just tender, 15 to 20 minutes.

To Serve: Rub a pat of butter over and put on a sprinkle of paprika.

OR: Pour over them melted cheese sauce, white sauce (see page 205), or undiluted condensed cream of mushroom or cream of chicken soup; all of these should be piping hot, of course.

CANNED WHITE ONIONS

Drain the can, salt the onions, and warm them in a little Sauterne wine and a pat of butter for 15 minutes over a low flame.

Leftover Boiled Onions

- Heat them in cheese sauce or one of the soups mentioned above.
- Add them to stews or creamed seafood.

BAKED ONIONS

This is a good thing to do when you are having baked potatoes, for they take the same amount of cooking time. Peel the onions, place each on an individual piece of aluminum foil, put a lot of salt on, and fold the aluminum foil around. Bake them in a 350° oven for an hour, opening the aluminum foil up for the last 15 minutes of cooking.

FRENCH-FRIED ONIONS

Buy frozen or canned French-fried onions, brush them lightly with olive or salad oil, and bake them in a 350° oven for 5 minutes.

PEAS

If you have forgotten what fresh peas taste like, it is worth the effort of shelling them, for they are very good. But so, too, are frozen peas, and the latter are considerably less trouble. Best of all, I think, are Le Sueur's canned peas. These are petit pois, the tiny, early green peas, and they need only warming, although they grow tastier with longer cooking, 15 minutes, say, over a low flame.

FRESH PEAS

Cooking time: 15 to 30 minutes.

To Prepare: Shell the peas, but only the last minute before cooking; do not shell them in advance.

To Cook: Boil in about 1 inch of salted water for 15 to 30 minutes, until tender.

CANNED PEAS

Warm them in the juice from the can, adding salt and pepper and a teaspoon-tip of sugar.

If you like, add small white onions (canned) or a can of sliced mushrooms or some small strips of cooked ham.

PEAS CONTINENTAL

- 1 large can peas, or 1 package frozen peas, cooked
- 1 can sliced mushrooms
- ½ cup chopped onions
- ¼ teaspoon nutmeg
- 2 tablespoons sherry

1. Melt 2 tablespoons of butter in a skillet, and gently cook ½ cup of chopped onions until transparent.

2. Add 1 drained can of peas or 1 package of frozen peas that have been cooked, 1 can (drained) of sliced mushrooms, ¼ teaspoon of salt, ¼ teaspoon of nutmeg, a pinch of marjoram, and 2 tablespoons of sherry. Stir, and cook until the peas and mushrooms are hot.

Leftover Peas

- Slice a clove of garlic, add it to a bit of butter or salad oil in a skillet, and warm the peas in this.
- Add them to any creamed concoction or stew.

WHITE POTATOES

There are no special instructions about buying potatoes, other than to avoid spotted or sprouted ones and not to overlook the little red new potatoes in the spring, for they are delicious when boiled in their jackets. For baking, choose the larger ones and try to have them fairly uniform in size so they take the same amount of cooking time. There is a gadget, consisting of metal prongs, available in ten-cent stores which hastens the baking of potatoes by conducting the heat to the center of the potato. There is also another gadget, called a top-of-the-stove oven, which I find very useful for baked potatoes, onions, squash, and any small dish, such as baked corn custard, because it obviates having to light the oven and getting the kitchen heated up. When baking or boiling or mashing potatoes, I would suggest cooking double the amount needed and then using the extra for fried potatoes or potato cakes the next day. Potatoes do not suffer from being warmed up, and, indeed, are often improved.

Canned potatoes, all the brands of which seem comparable, are useful for some things, for example, for fried potatoes, for roast potatoes, and for adding to stews, and they can be used for potato salad but are not as good as fresh ones. There is no denying that they are a convenience, and it is probably wise to keep a supply on hand on the canned goods shelf.

Frozen potatoes seem to me such a far cut below fresh ones that I would recommend avoiding them. Frozen mashed potatoes are somewhat improved by the addition of evaporated milk and more butter than the directions on the box call for, but they still have a steam-table taste to them. To disguise this, add 4 tablespoons of grated American cheese to 1 package of potatoes. One use frozen mashed potatoes do have, though, is in turning a stew into Shepherd's Pie: warm the stew and the potatoes separately, put the stew in individual casserole dishes, spread the mashed potatoes in a layer over the top, sprinkle them with grated American cheese and paprika, and then put under the broiler to brown. The frozen French-fried potatoes and potato puffs suffer from a sort of heavy greasiness, and I have not a good word to say for them when cooked according to the package directions. However, see the directions for French-fried potatoes for a way of redeeming them.

Packaged dehydrated potatoes, on the other hand, particularly potatoes au gratin and escalloped potatoes, are a great convenience, for it is a lengthy process to make them from scratch, a very simple process to follow the package directions, and the results are quite acceptable. In line with my approach to company meals, i.e., that nothing require last-minute attention, I often have them for guests, mixing the ingredients together in a baking dish beforehand and then just putting the dish in the oven after the guests arrive. Dehydrated mashed potatoes are not up to the taste of freshly made ones, but there is always a package on my kitchen shelf for emergencies, such as laziness. They, too, are improved by using evaporated milk and a larger quantity of both milk and butter than the package directions call for and by a really brisk whipping.

BAKED POTATOES

Scrub the potatoes well with a brush so you can eat them skin and all. Rub them lightly with salad oil, salt the skins if you like, wrap them individually in aluminum foil, and bake in a 350° oven for about an hour. Test for doneness by inserting a knife in the center; if it encounters resistance, let the potatoes bake longer. If you prefer a crisper skin do not use the aluminum foil.

Leftover Baked Potatoes

- See recipe for Fried Potatoes.
- Cut them in small cubes and warm in a little milk and butter.

MASHED POTATOES

1. Put a pot of water on the stove to boil and add a

teaspoon of salt. Pare the potatoes, cut them in quarters (or 1-inch thick slices if they are large), and boil them until tender when pierced with a knife, 10 to 20 minutes. If you cook double the number of potatoes needed, the extra will be ready to be turned into potato cakes for another meal.

2. While the potatoes are boiling, put 2 tablespoons of (plain or evaporated) milk and 1 pat of butter for each potato in a metal measuring cup or small pan and set it over the pilot light on the stove to warm.

3. When the potatoes are done, drain off every drop of water and mash them. This can be done, somewhat laboriously, by squashing them with a fork; more easily, by pressing them through a sieve with the back of a tablespoon; best of all, by putting them through a potato ricer, a gadget available in ten-cent stores or using a regular metal or wooden potato masher. No matter which method you use, the only essential is to get all the lumps out.

4. Add the hot milk and butter, a little at a time, and whip furiously with a fork. Stop with the liquid when the potatoes are at the consistency you like. If you run short of liquid before that point is reached, no damage will be done by adding cold milk. Be sure to taste for enough salt. Add it, if needed, at the whipping stage.

Leftover Mashed Potatoes

- Beat 1 egg lightly and add it to the mashed potatoes. Form the potatoes into cakes and cook them in butter in a skillet until there is a nicely browned crust on both sides.
- Use them to stuff baked tomatoes (see page 116).

BOILED POTATOES

1. Put a pot of water, with 1 teaspoon of salt, on the stove to boil.

2. If you are using new potatoes, i.e., thin-skinned ones, scrub them well, and cook them in their jackets. Small ones may be cooked whole, medium-sized ones cut in half. With old potatoes, peel them before cooking.

3. Begin testing for doneness after 15 minutes by inserting a knife into the center of one potato. Cooking time depends completely on the size of the potatoes.

4. When done, drain all the water from the pot, and put it back over the fire, shaking the pot constantly, to dry the potatoes out a bit.

Leftover Boiled Potatoes

- See the recipes for Fried Potatoes and Potato Salad.
- Cube them and warm them in a bit of milk and butter or in canned beef gravy.
- Add to stews.

FRIED POTATOES

This requires cooked potatoes.

1. Warm 3 tablespoons of salad oil in a skillet.
2. Peel onions and slice, or use frozen chopped onions. The amount to use depends on how well you like onions. They are sweet and delicious this way, so I put in about the same amount of onions as potatoes.
3. Add the onions and sliced cooked potatoes, and cook until both are nicely golden and just beginning to brown.

FRENCH-FRIED POTATOES

Use either frozen French-fries or raw potatoes.

1. If the potatoes are raw, pare them (use old potatoes, not new), and cut them into strips about ¼-inch wide and ¼-inch thick. Soak them in cold water for ½ hour.
2. Put salad oil in a pan to a depth of at least 1 inch. Let it get very hot, but it should not smoke.
3. With frozen French-fried potatoes, ignore the package directions, and cook them, a few at a time, for 1 minute in the hot oil. Transfer them, as cooked, to several thicknesses of paper toweling, and let the oil drain off. Salt well before serving.

With raw potatoes, drop these in, too, a few at a time. Cook until a light brown, and transfer to the paper toweling. When all are a light-brown, turn up the fire under the oil, return all the potatoes to the pan, and cook a minute or two more until they are a golden brown. Drain, salt liberally, and serve.

POTATO BALLS

1. Pare the potatoes and, using a melon-ball cutter, scoop out balls from the potatoes. This leaves behind a latticework of raw potatoes, which should be put in a bowl, covered with cold water, and placed in the refrigerator, to be boiled briefly the next day and made into mashed potatoes.
2. Place the balls in a pot of rapidly boiling, salted water, and cook for 8 to 10 minutes, until tender.

3. Serve as is, with butter and parsley over, or brown the balls lightly in butter in a skillet.

Leftover Potato Balls

- Turn them into French-fried potato balls by following the directions for French-fried potatoes using frozen potatoes.
- Warm them, browning lightly, in butter.

BAKED STUFFED POTATOES

My aunt calls these In-and-Out Potatoes, which is descriptive. Their advantage is that they can be baked in advance, prepared, and then reheated just before serving time.

1. Bake potatoes according to the directions for same.
2. Cut a slit lengthwise in the potatoes and scoop out the centers, leaving the skin intact. Mash the centers thoroughly, getting out all lumps, and then add enough milk and butter to make them smooth. Salt to taste. If you like, sour cream can be used in place of the milk, and/or grated cheese or crumbled Roquefort can be added.
3. Stuff the potato skins with the mashed potatoes, sprinkle paprika over, and bake in a medium oven until the tops are brown, about 10 to 15 minutes.

ROAST POTATOES

Peel and, if large, halve raw potatoes. Boil them for 20 minutes in salted water, and then arrange around a roast for the last 30 minutes of cooking time for the roast.

SWEET POTATOES

Sweet potatoes may be baked, baked stuffed, or mashed. Just follow the directions given for white potatoes, but allow a little more cooking time for baked sweet potatoes, and puncture the skin in several places with a fork before cooking. In canned sweet potatoes, Kelly's seems the best brand, and for an excellent way of using them, see the recipe for Glazed Duck.

GLAZED SWEET POTATOES

1. Drain 1 can of sweet potatoes, and slice the potatoes.
2. Put 4 tablespoons of butter and 4 tablespoons of brown sugar in a skillet and, when melted, add the potatoes.
3. Cook until nicely browned on both sides. If you like, pour a bit of sherry over when ready to serve.

RICE

My best success in avoiding soggy, sticky rice has been with Uncle Ben's brand and by following the package directions exactly. Minute Rice is usually successful, too. The only measure I know of, if you do end up with a somewhat gluey mass, is to put the rice in a warm oven to dry out and allow the grains to separate. Remember that rice swells considerably in the cooking; 1 cup of raw rice may not look like much, but it feeds four people when cooked. 1 cup of Minute Rice will feed two. Frozen fried rice is convenient, but nothing to write home about. The newer combinations of herbs and rice are interesting; follow the package directions in cooking.

Many things may be added to rice after it has been cooked: Onions cooked in butter until transparent, sliced canned mushrooms warmed in butter, cooked crumbled bacon and onions, cooked green pepper, warmed green peas, or chopped tomatoes and onions cooked in butter for 5 minutes. And/or little pieces of leftover meat, such as lamb, ham, or veal, in combination with any of the foregoing.

Leftover Rice

• Fry 1 to 3 strips of bacon, depending on how much rice you have. Remove the bacon, and brown the leftover rice in the fat. Take the pan off the stove and add 1, 2, or 3 raw eggs, again depending on the amount of rice. Return the pan to the fire, and stir constantly until the eggs are cooked. Soy sauce may be added, if you wish, and bits of leftover meat.

SPINACH

Buy only the fresh, as it is perfectly simple to cook and tastes a lot better than the frozen. In buying, look for crisp, green, unwilted leaves. Spinach reduces in bulk enormously when cooked; figure on at least two big handfuls per serving.

FRESH SPINACH

Cooking time: 5 minutes.

To Prepare: Wash well, just before cooking, under cold running water by swishing the leaves around in a kettle of cold water. Nip off the large part of the stems. Shake the leaves a bit to dry.

To Cook: Enough water will cling to the leaves so that no more need be added. Just put the spinach in a saucepan, sprinkle it with salt, and put it over a medium fire. Press it down with a fork a few times to hasten the wilting process which the heat causes. It cooks very quickly and you will know by looking at it when it is done, which is the moment after it is all in the bottom of the pan. Do not overcook even by seconds.

To Serve: The secret of good spinach is to get all the water out of it. Do this by emptying it into a sieve and pressing it down with a fork until you cannot squeeze any more water out. Serve as is or with mayonnaise into which a few drops of lemon juice have been mixed.

SQUASH

Even a confirmed squash-hater can be converted by baked acorn squash, sautéed zucchini, and yellow squash casserole.

BAKED ACORN SQUASH

These keep as well as potatoes and are a fine substitute for same. They do not need refrigeration.

Cooking time: 1 hour.

To Prepare: Cut in half and scrape out the seeds.

To Cook: Put a pat of butter in the center of each half and salt and pepper them liberally. Every cookbook I have ever seen says to add brown sugar, but I take issue, for this just makes them taste like sweet potatoes. Bake for 1 hour, or until tender when tested with a knife, in a 350° oven or in a top-of-the-stove oven over a low flame.

To Serve: Serve just as is.

BAKED YELLOW SQUASH

Cooking time: 30 minutes.

To Prepare: Cut the squash into quarters and remove the seeds. Rub the cut surfaces with butter and sprinkle with salt and pepper. Wrap the quarters in individual pieces of aluminum foil.

To Cook: Bake them in a 400° oven for 25 minutes. Open the foil and cook 5 minutes longer, or until tender when tested with a knife.

YELLOW SQUASH CASSEROLE

2 pounds yellow squash
2 eggs
1 cup American cheese
bread crumbs
3 slices bread
1 can condensed cream of mushroom soup
½ cup chopped onions

1. Pare and cut 2 pounds of yellow squash into pieces and cook in boiling, salted (1 teaspoon) water for 15 minutes.

2. Put the squash in a bowl, and add to it 2 eggs, 1 cup of American cheese (grated or cut in small pieces), 1 can of condensed cream of mushroom soup, and ½ cup of chopped onions. Remove the crusts from 3 slices of bread, and break the bread into bits. Add to the bowl, and mix everything together.

3. Put the mixture in a buttered baking dish, sprinkle bread crumbs on top, and bake in a 325° oven for 1½ hours.

ZUCCHINI SQUASH

Buy firm, rather small ones.

Cooking time: about 5 minutes.

To Prepare: Leave the skin on, wash the squash well, and slice it as you would slice a cucumber. Discard end pieces.

To Cook: Heat salad or olive oil in a skillet. Put in 1 sliced clove of garlic or a sprinkling of garlic powder. Add the slices of zucchini and cook quickly, turning as soon as brown on one side and removing from the skillet as soon as brown on the other.

To Serve: Salt and pepper them, and serve.

ZUCCHINI AND TOMATO CASSEROLE

1 pound zucchini squash
2 tomatoes
½ cup chopped onions
1 cup bread crumbs

1. Melt 2 tablespoons of butter in a skillet with 1 sliced clove of garlic or a good sprinkling of garlic powder. Cook ½ cup of chopped onions in the butter until transparent. Turn off the fire, and turn on the oven to 400°.

2. Add 1 cup of bread crumbs to the skillet and mix well so that the crumbs absorb the butter.

3. Wash the squash and slice into ¼-inch thick pieces.

4. Butter a baking dish, and put in a layer of sliced zucchini, then a layer of sliced tomatoes, then a layer of the bread

crumb mixture, putting salt and pepper on each layer as you go. Repeat the layers until everything is used up, ending with a bread crumb layer.

5. Bake in a 400° oven for 40 minutes.

SUCCOTASH

Use the frozen and, after cooking according to package directions, drain off the water and add 2 tablespoons of cream.

TOMATOES

When buying, choose firm ones, without soft spots and with a good bright color. If they are not quite ripe, leave them out at room temperature for a day or two to ripen. In selecting canned tomatoes, buy the most expensive; there is a great range in quality in canned tomatoes and, hopefully, the most expensive will be the best.

BROILED TOMATOES

When tomatoes are plentiful in the summer, this makes an excellent vegetable course.

Cooking time: about 15 minutes.

To Prepare: Wash, and cut in half. Sprinkle the cut sides with salt, pepper, and white sugar.

To Cook: Put under the broiler as far away from the flame as possible and have the flame fairly low. Cook until tender, which may take about 15 minutes but keep an eye on them to make sure the tops are not burning. If they are underdone, they taste even better that way. If you wish, you can put sliced olives, grated cheese, dried onion flakes, or bread crumbs on the tomatoes before broiling.

STEWED TOMATOES

Use canned tomatoes for this, either those labeled stewed tomatoes and containing green pepper and onion or whole tomatoes which you can cut into smaller size pieces. Just warm up, but what makes a real difference in the taste is the addition of some sugar, ⅛ to ¼ teaspoon depending on the amount of tomatoes. Put salt and pepper in as well, and, if you like, toast a piece of bread, cut it into small squares, and distribute it over the top.

OR: Empty the can of tomatoes into a baking dish, season them, and sprinkle bread crumbs over the top. Bake in a 400° oven for 20 minutes.

CHAPTER 8 HOW TO PUT SALADS TOGETHER

The crucial part of a salad is the dressing, and the crucial part of any French dressing is the oil and vinegar. The thing to remember is the proportion of 3 parts oil to 1 part vinegar, e.g., 3 tablespoons of oil and 1 tablespoon of vinegar. My recommendations are Wesson salad oil or Umberto I olive oil and Chianti red wine vinegar; never use cider or other white vinegars. You can, however, substitute lemon juice in place of the vinegar.

At the risk of being ostracized by those of my friends who take cooking very seriously, let me say that many of the bottled French dressings on the market seem fine to me and I always keep a jar on hand in the refrigerator. As a matter of fact, whenever throughout this book the suggestion is made to marinate one or another thing, such as string beans or tuna fish, in French dressing, it is the bottled dressing I use in such instances. My own preference is not for the creamy, rather orange-looking dressings but for the deep red ones, which are often called "Chef's Style." The variants of French dressing, such as garlic, bleu cheese, and Italian style, are interesting on salads, and the Good Seasons mixes, to which you add the oil and vinegar, allow a last-minute choice of dressings according to what will go well with the particular salad ingredients and the rest of the dinner. In buying mayonnaise, avoid the jar of what looks the same and is called "Salad Dressing"; it is not nearly as good.

In choosing salad greens, look for the freshest, prettiest, most unwilted you can find, and remember that a combination of greens, such as lettuce, chicory, escarole, and endive, is more interesting than just one kind. The ingredients of a tossed salad are whatever you want them to be and may include any combination of the following: slices of green pepper, onions (red, yellow, white, or sliced scallions; red are the mildest), tomatoes (the miniature cherry tomatoes look handsome in the bowl), sliced radishes, watercress, cucumber slices, shredded red or white cabbage, celery (but go easy), thin carrot strips, pickled beets, ripe olives, hard-boiled eggs, or, turning it into a Chef's Salad, strips of cooked ham and/or tongue, or fowl, and cheese.

There are two schools of thought about whether or not to wash salad greens after purchase and before storing them in the refrigerator, but on the whole I tend to think they keep better unwashed. In any event, put them in plastic bags or wrap in Saran wrap before refrigerating. If you prepare carrot sticks or celery strips in advance or have them left over, put them in a glass of cold water in the refrigerator.

The purists say that salads must be made at the last minute, but all that really matters is that the dressing be poured over at the last minute. All the ingredients can be washed and put together in a bowl in advance, the bowl covered with Saran wrap or a damp dish towel, and put in the refrigerator. There is one area in which the purists should be heeded, though, and that is that greens should be torn apart rather than cut with a knife. It does make a difference.

Concerning the care of wooden salad bowls, again there are differences of opinion. There are those who say never to wash them, only wipe them out with a paper towel, but I have been washing mine for years and they are still in perfect condition, kept that way by two things: one, I dry them immediately, never letting them sit around with water on them, and, two, whenever necessary, I rub them with salad oil to restore the sheen.

One further comment: in line with making company dinners as simple, but at the same time as handsome, as possible, I find that a relish tray is a marvelous substitute for a salad. The necessity here is to have a dish or tray that is divided into compartments. Very handsome ceramic ones are to be found in department stores and are, I think, worth the investment. Mine has eight divisions, which I fill with black and green olives, spiced crabapples, carrot sticks, celery, jelly or preserves, radishes, and pickles, a maneuver that takes about all of five minutes. In addition to speed and attractiveness, one further advantage of a relish tray is that most of the things used to fill it keep indefinitely; only the carrots and celery have a short life, while the remainder simply go back into their jars in the refrigerator to await the next occasion. This is in contrast to the makings of a mixed salad, which are perishable and must be bought in much greater quantities than needed for one, even large, salad.

DRESSINGS

FRENCH DRESSING

The following is a basic recipe for French dressing. A bit of garlic powder or a pinch of oregano or tarragon may be added to it, if desired.

RECIPE: FRENCH DRESSING

3 tablespoons olive or salad oil
1 tablespoon vinegar
⅛ teaspoon Gulden's mustard

1. Put salt (a scant ½ teaspoon), pepper, ⅛ teaspoon of Gulden's mustard, and 3 tablespoons of olive or salad oil in a bowl. Beat these ingredients with a fork (with a sort of side-arm motion) for 1 minute.

2. Add 1 tablespoon of vinegar (or lemon juice) and beat until mixed.

If you want to make the dressing at the dinner table, sprinkle salt and pepper on the salad and pour 3 tablespoons of oil over. Toss the greens lightly with a fork and spoon so as to distribute the oil over them. Then add 1 tablespoon of vinegar or lemon juice and toss a bit more.

GARLIC DRESSING

Make this at least several hours in advance and allow to chill in the refrigerator. The dressing will keep indefinitely.

RECIPE: GARLIC DRESSING

1 cup olive or salad oil
⅓ cup vinegar
½ teaspoon dry mustard
4 cloves garlic

Put 1 cup of oil, ⅓ cup of vinegar, 1 teaspoon of sugar, ½ teaspoon of dry mustard, 1½ teaspoons of salt, and 4 sliced cloves of garlic in a jar with a tightly fitting lid. Shake well and chill. Remove the garlic cloves before serving.

EGG AND ANCHOVY DRESSING

This is a rather impressive variation on the usual dressing for a tossed salad. The amount will dress sufficient salad greens for six people.

RECIPE: EGG AND ANCHOVY DRESSING

2 garlic cloves
2 hard-boiled eggs
12 flat anchovies
2 tablespoons wine vinegar
8 tablespoons olive or salad oil
1 tablespoon Worcestershire sauce
2 tablespoons A-1 sauce
¼ cup grated Parmesan cheese

1. Slice the garlic cloves in half and rub the salad bowl well with their cut surfaces.

2. Using a fork, mash together in the salad bowl 2 hard-boiled eggs and 12 flat anchovies.

3. Add 2 tablespoons of wine vinegar, 8 tablespoons of

olive or salad oil, 1 tablespoon of Worcestershire sauce, and 2 tablespoons A-1 sauce. Whip all the ingredients together well with a fork.

4. Add the salad greens, sprinkle them with ¼ cup of grated Parmesan cheese, and toss the salad to coat with the dressing. Serve French bread with this to dunk in the dressing.

ROQUEFORT DRESSING

RECIPE I: FRENCH DRESSING WITH ROQUEFORT

4 tablespoons olive oil
1 tablespoon tarragon vinegar
1-inch square piece of Roquefort cheese
2 tablespoons catsup
½ teaspoon garlic powder

1. Beat together all the ingredients, plus salt and pepper, except the cheese.

2. Crumble a 1-inch piece of Roquefort cheese and add it.

RECIPE II: MAYONNAISE WITH ROQUEFORT

½ cup mayonnaise
¼ cup heavy cream
small piece Roquefort cheese

Stir together ½ cup of mayonnaise and ¼ cup of heavy cream. Crumble the amount of Roquefort cheese that suits your taste and mix it in. Serve over mixed greens.

RUSSIAN DRESSING

This is good over plain lettuce cut in wedges or over sliced hard-boiled eggs and beets arranged on lettuce. Because it does not store well, make only as much as will be used immediately.

RECIPE: RUSSIAN DRESSING

4 tablespoons mayonnaise
1 teaspoon chopped pickles
2 tablespoons chili sauce or catsup

Just mix everything together.

SOUR CREAM DRESSING

Recipe I does well over sliced cucumbers and radishes, Recipes II and III for fruit salad.

RECIPE I: SOUR CREAM AND VINEGAR DRESSING

½ cup sour cream
1 tablespoon tarragon vinegar

Mix together ½ cup of sour cream, 1 tablespoon of tarragon vinegar (other kinds will do), ⅓ teaspoon of sugar, and salt to taste, paprika to color.

RECIPE II: SOUR CREAM AND COTTAGE CHEESE DRESSING

½ cup of sour cream
½ cup creamed cottage cheese

Mix together ½ cup of sour cream and ½ cup of creamed cottage cheese (or in any 1:1 proportions to make the amount needed) and add salt to taste.

RECIPE III: SOUR CREAM AND COCONUT DRESSING

Mix together sour cream and shredded (canned) coconut.

WINE DRESSING

For fruit salads.

RECIPE: WINE DRESSING

2 tablespoons Sauterne or dry sherry
squeeze of lemon juice
¼ cup mayonnaise

Mix together.

GINGERSNAP DRESSING

Use over canned pear or peach halves or any fruit salad.

RECIPE: GINGERSNAP DRESSING

4 gingersnaps
¼ cup sour cream

Crush the gingersnaps as fine as possible, and stir into the sour cream. If done a bit in advance of serving, the gingersnaps will disintegrate completely, making for a very interesting and completely unidentifiable dressing.

VEGETABLE SALADS

To provide a change from the usual tossed salad of mixed greens, the following might be kept in mind.

ARTICHOKE HEARTS

Cook a package of frozen artichoke hearts according to the

package directions. While hot, pour French dressing over, and then chill in the refrigerator.

PICKLED BEET SALAD

Sliced pickled beets (buy them in a jar) combine nicely with sliced hard-boiled eggs, sliced onion rings, or canned asparagus tips. Arrange on lettuce and use French or Russian dressing or mayonnaise.

CARROT AND APPLE SALAD

This looks rather a mish-mash, but it tastes good. Cut an apple into quarters and remove the core. Grate it on a cheese grater right down to the skin and then discard the skin. Pare a carrot and grate it. Mix the grated apple and carrot together with mayonnaise. Add some raisins, if you like.

COLE SLAW

Chop into very small pieces ½ stalk of celery, ½ onion, and ¼ green pepper. Cut a cabbage in half, and shred it by cutting into very thin slices. Mix these ingredients together, along with some sliced stuffed pimento olives. Make a dressing of ½ pint of sour cream, 2 tablespoons vinegar, 1 tablespoon of sugar, ½ teaspoon of salt, and a sprinkle of celery salt and paprika.

CUCUMBER SALAD

Serve sliced cucumbers and onions in Sour Cream and Vinegar dressing (page 155).

OR: Arrange sliced cucumbers and sliced tomatoes on lettuce and pour French dressing over.

OR: Mix chopped fresh mint with yoghurt and serve over sliced cucumbers.

GREEN BEAN SALAD

Marinate leftover cooked green beans or canned green beans in French dressing for at least 1 hour in the refrigerator. Drain and serve with mayonnaise.

SPINACH SALAD

Wash spinach leaves, and set them aside to drain. Fry 2 slices of bacon until crisp. Take the bacon out, and add ¼ cup of vinegar to the bacon fat. Put the spinach leaves in a bowl, pour the sauce over, and crumble the bacon pieces on top.

TOMATO SALAD

Sliced tomatoes are good with French dressing, even better if marinated in the refrigerator for at least an hour in French dressing with a little basil sprinkled over or in a mixture of ½ lemon juice, ½ salad oil.

Possible combinations with sliced tomatoes are sliced cucumbers, sliced onions, or sliced avocado, all with French dressing.

ZUCCHINI AND TOMATO SALAD

Buy small zucchini, wash them well, and then cut them in quarters lengthwise and the quarters in half. Plunge them into boiling salted water and cook for 2 minutes. Take out of the water immediately, put them in a bowl, and add an equal amount of raw tomato cut in wedges. Sprinkle salt and pepper over and a goodly amount of French dressing. An hour's marinating in the refrigerator will make this salad even better, but it is not essential.

VEGETABLES IN LIME JELL-O

This is a salad platter for a luncheon main dish or a cool summer supper.

RECIPE: VEGETABLES IN LIME JELL-O

1 package Lime Jell-o
2 green peppers
1 medium onion
2 teaspoons vinegar
1 teaspoon chopped parsley
1¼ pounds cottage cheese
1 cup mayonnaise

1. Dissolve 1 package of lime Jell-o in 2 cups of boiling water and 2 teaspoons of vinegar in a bowl.
2. Chop in rather fine pieces 2 green peppers, 1 medium-sized onion, and enough parsley to make 1 teaspoon.
3. When Jell-o has cooled, add these to it. Then mix in 1 cup of mayonnaise. Next mix in 1¼ pounds of cottage cheese.
4. Put the bowl in the refrigerator for the Jell-o to set.
5. When ready to serve, arrange lettuce on a platter, dip the bottom of the bowl in hot water, and invert the bowl in the center of a lettuce bed. Decorate with mayonnaise sprinkled with paprika.

FRUIT SALADS

Fruit salads have, unhappily, come to be linked with the ladies' magazines and now seem beyond the pale as a proper accompaniment to a self-respecting dinner. It is surprising, though, how quickly they are eaten and with what relish even by male guests. It is the rare person who does not like fruit, and it is a rare meal that is not brightened by it. Particularly if the main dish is rather heavy, the clear taste of fruit is refreshing. And the salads themselves can be quite simple and elegant. The things to avoid are the chopped marshmallows, nuts, and maraschino cherries that have given them their bad reputation.

AVOCADO SALAD

In buying avocados, avoid soft ones or those with brown spots. Try to find one that gives just a little when pressed with a thumb; if this is not possible, buy a hard one and keep it at room temperature until it is ripe. Peel only as much of the avocado as you are going to use immediately and then wrap the cut edges closely in Saran wrap.

Wedged-shaped slices of avocado, salted and peppered and covered with French dressing are a good salad in themselves. Or add a few onion rings, and/or wedges of tomato.

OR: Alternate slices of avocado and canned grapefruit sections on lettuce. Use Wine dressing, Gingersnap dressing, or French dressing. Canned Mandarin oranges or segments of fresh oranges may be used in addition to or in place of the grapefruit.

OR: Cut large purple grapes in half and take out the seeds. Cut the avocado into small chunks and put in a bowl with the grapes. Sprinkle a bit of sugar and some lemon juice over. Mix in enough mayonnaise to coat lightly, and then serve on lettuce.

OR: Make melon balls of cantaloupe or honeydew with a melon-ball cutter, cut the avocado into small chunks, and pour a little bit of Sauterne over the combination. Add a small amount of mayonnaise, mix, and serve on lettuce.

BANANA SALAD

Having said to avoid chopped nuts, here goes with an exception.

Sprinkle quartered bananas with lemon juice, coat lightly with mayonnaise or sour cream, and roll in crushed peanuts. Serve on lettuce.

OR: Bananas combine well with grapes, oranges, grapefruit, and melon. Just cut in small chunks, combine with other fruit, sprinkle with a bit of sugar and lemon juice, and add mayonnaise or Gingersnap dressing.

FROZEN FRUIT SALAD

Buy a small can of Del Monte Fruit Salad and put it in the freezing compartment for at least a day so that it becomes frozen solid. Cut out both the top and bottom lids of the can, slide out the tube of fruit, slice it thickly, and serve on lettuce with Sour Cream or Gingersnap or Wine dressing.

GRAPE SALAD

All varieties of grapes combine well with other fruits. If they have seeds, cut in half and remove the seeds. Mix with your choice of other fruit, sprinkle on a little lemon juice and sugar, and mix with mayonnaise or use Sour Cream, Wine, or Gingersnap dressing.

GRAPEFRUIT SALAD

Canned grapefruit segments are better for use in salads than fresh grapefruit because they are less sharp in taste.

Add grapefruit segments to a tossed green salad with French dressing.

OR: Arrange on lettuce grapefruit segments and either avocado or banana slices. Dress with Sour Cream, Wine, or Gingersnap dressing.

JELLIED FRUIT SALAD

Lime and lemon Jell-o, because of their tart flavor, are the best choices in a jellied fruit salad. Follow the package directions in their making. Any sort of fresh or canned fruit or fruit combination may be used except fresh pineapple. For a reason someone can probably explain, but not I, fresh pineapple prevents gelatin from setting.

MELON SALAD

Make melon balls, using a melon-ball cutter, from any kind of melon or combination of melons, including watermelon. Soak the melon balls in Sauterne or champagne (flat champagne is fine, if, by some chance, you happen to have any on hand), and let them get very cold in the refrigerator, in the freezing compartment, if you like. Mix with a bit of sour cream and serve on lettuce.

OR: Combine melon balls with avocado or grapes, sprinkle a little lemon juice and sugar over, and mix with mayonnaise. Serve on lettuce.

PEACH SALAD

Canned Elberta freestone peach halves are the best for salad. Serve on lettuce with Sour Cream, Gingersnap, or Wine dressing.

PEAR SALAD

Canned pears are preferable to fresh for salad. Instead of a dressing, roll (Kraft's) Smokelle cheese into balls, dust with paprika, and place in the center of a halved pear arranged on lettuce. Or combine crushed gingersnaps and cream cheese, and roll into balls.

PINEAPPLE SALAD

Use canned pineapple slices, and follow the directions for either Peach Salad or Pear Salad.

OR: Prepare fresh pineapple (see page 183), pour a little green crème de menthe over, and allow to get cold in the refrigerator. Mix a little sour cream or mayonnaise in and serve on lettuce.

MAIN DISH SALADS

On a summer night a salad is a cool and pleasant idea. All of the following are satisfying enough to serve as main dishes, particularly when accompanied by corn on the cob and hot rolls.

CHEF'S SALAD

Anything goes in this salad. Write your own recipe according to what is on hand in the refrigerator.

RECIPE: CHEF'S SALAD

cooked ham or tongue
American cheese
black olives
radishes
mixed greens
hard-boiled eggs
tomatoes
onions

Wash the greens, slice the ham and/or tongue into small strips, crumble or slice the cheese, prepare the other ingredients, mix everything together, and dress liberally with French dressing. Toast cut into small squares or 1 or 2 crumbled bread sticks make an unexpected and interesting addition.

CHICKEN SALAD

Each of the following recipes for chicken salad requires that the chicken spend some time in the refrigerator, so initiate preparations several hours or a day in advance.

RECIPE I: CHICKEN SALAD WITH WHITE GRAPES

4 cups diced cooked chicken (for four servings)
¾ cup mayonnaise
½ cup heavy cream
1 lemon or lime

1. Salt and pepper the chicken, and pour the juice of 1 lemon or lime over it.
2. Whip ½ cup of heavy cream, and mix it with ¾ cup of mayonnaise. Take ½ of this dressing and add it to the chicken. Stir to coat the chicken pieces completely.
3. Press this firmly into a bowl, and put it in the refrigerator for several hours to allow it to get thoroughly chilled.
4. Arrange a bed of lettuce on a serving platter. Turn the bowl upside down in the middle of the lettuce so that the chicken comes out in a neat mound on the platter.
5. With a broad knife, coat the mounded chicken with the remaining half of the dressing. Stud the mound with white seedless grapes, and put a sprinkle of paprika over.

RECIPE II: CHICKEN SALAD MARINATED IN FRENCH DRESSING

1. Salt and pepper a bowl of bite-sized pieces of cooked chicken. Pour over the chicken sufficient (commercial) French dressing to coat all the pieces lightly. Cover the bowl and store in the refrigerator for several hours or overnight.
2. Pour off the French dressing. Add ½ stalk of celery cut into small pieces.
3. Coat the chicken lightly with mayonnaise; the amount to be stirred in depends completely on how much chicken you have. Serve on lettuce with an extra teaspoon of mayonnaise on top and a dash of paprika over, or use to fill tomatoes or avocado halves.

CRABMEAT SALAD

Crabmeat salad may be made in exactly the same way given in Recipe II for Chicken Salad, using either canned or frozen crabmeat, or the following recipe may be followed. One can or package of crabmeat serves two.

RECIPE: CRABMEAT, ARTICHOKE, AND AVOCADO SALAD

1 package frozen crabmeat (thawed)
1 jar artichoke hearts
1 avocado

1. Drain the thawed crabmeat and break it into chunks. Put it in a bowl and add 1 drained jar of artichoke hearts.
2. Peel an avocado, cut it into small pieces, and add it to the bowl. Sprinkle on salt and pepper. Pour some (commercial) French dressing over all, tossing the ingredients lightly to coat them. Put the bowl in the refrigerator for 5 to 10 minutes while you arrange lettuce and wedges of tomatoes on plates.
3. Pour off the French dressing in the bottom of the bowl. Put in just enough mayonnaise to coat the ingredients lightly. Mix and mound on the lettuce.

FRUIT SALAD

This, like Chef's Salad, is any combination of ingredients that strikes your fancy. It will be handsomer in looks, however, if the fruits are not jumbled together but laid out in overlapping islands, with, perhaps, a container of salad dressing in the center, which may be sour cream or mayonnaise thinned with sherry. For the most efficient way of preparing fresh fruit, see Chapter 10.

LOBSTER SALAD

RECIPE: LOBSTER SALAD

1. Cooked or canned lobster may be used. If you start with frozen lobster tails, cook according to the package directions, remove the meat from the shells, and dice it. With canned lobster, drain the meat and break it into chunks.
2. Salt and pepper the lobster meat, and sprinkle it with the juice of ½ lemon. Add some chopped celery, and mix in enough mayonnaise to coat the lobster lightly.
3. Mound on lettuce, or serve in hollowed-out tomatoes or on avocado halves. Or, if frozen lobster tails have been used, fill the shells with the lobster salad.

SHRIMP SALAD

If fresh shrimp are used, plan on ⅓ to ½ pound per serving and prepare them according to the directions on page 82. Frozen shrimp will also need to be precooked; follow the directions on the package. Canned shrimp need only be rinsed well in cold water.

RECIPE: SHRIMP SALAD

1. Put the shrimp in bowl, sprinkle with salt and pepper, and pour enough (commercial) French dressing in to coat all the pieces. Let stand in the refrigerator at least 1 hour, or as much longer as is convenient.

2. When ready to make the salad, pour off the French dressing, add a little chopped celery, and enough mayonnaise to coat the shrimp lightly. Serve on lettuce with tomatoes, or mound on avocado halves.

OR: Skip the French dressing part, thin 1 cup of mayonnaise with 4 tablespoons of dry sherry, and use this as the dressing for the shrimp.

TUNA FISH SALAD

Follow the directions for Shrimp Salad. Hollow out the centers of ripe tomatoes, let them drain, then stuff them with the tuna fish.

PICNIC SALADS

Both of these salads travel excellently, so I have called them picnic salads, which indeed they are, but they also do well at home for buffet suppers.

POTATO SALAD

As you will see, the secret here, as in the sea food salads, is to marinate the potatoes in (store-bought) French dressing. Why this should be a little-known secret, I don't know, but it is a pity that more people are not aware of it, for it is the French dressing in all these salads that keeps them from being bland and flat.

RECIPE: POTATO SALAD

cooked or canned potatoes	1 sliced onion

1. Freshly boiled potatoes, to which the French dressing is added while they are still hot, absorb the dressing best, but canned potatoes will do almost as well. Slice the potatoes into

a bowl. Slice an onion and break the slices into rings by pressing in the center of each slice. Add to the potatoes, and salt and pepper both well. Pour bottled French dressing liberally over. Stir so that the potatoes and onions are well-coated, cover the bowl, and put it in the refrigerator. Actually, the salad will be best if you can do this much the day before and it can stay in the refrigerator overnight.

2. When ready to make the salad, pour off most of the French dressing, add liberal quantities of mayonnaise, mix, and that's all. If you are taking the salad on a picnic, put it in a jar with a screw-top lid. If it is for a buffet supper, line the salad bowl with lettuce leaves, mound the potato salad in the middle, put a tablespoon of mayonnaise on top and sprinkle it with paprika, and tuck around the salad celery and carrot sticks and green and ripe olives.

RICE SALAD

This is the specialty of a friend of mine, whose instructions follow.

RECIPE: RICE SALAD

1 cup cooked rice
1 fresh tomato
3 hard-boiled eggs
1 small can tuna fish
½ cup diced celery

1. One cup of rice boiled "al dente" (still a bit hard) forms the bulk of this dish, in which the following ingredients are also essential: 1 tomato cut in small wedges, ½ cup of diced celery, 3 hard-boiled eggs quartered, and 1 small can of shredded tuna fish.

2. These are the flavoring elements. Any leftovers (cold meats, boiled or raw vegetables) may also be added. The relative proportions are not important, but do not overdo the celery, which tends to overpower everything else.

For the dressing, follow the recipe for French dressing given on page 154.

As a buffet dish, serve as is, without lettuce. For traveling to a picnic, pack in a jar with a screw-top lid, such as a 1-quart mayonnaise jar.

CHAPTER 9 HOW TO PUT DESSERTS TOGETHER

There are some recipes in this chapter, but mostly the directions consist of how to put things together to come up with a good dessert with a minimum of effort. It is usually quite enough to do to put an excellent main course on the table without worrying at the same time about baking a cake. And, as a matter of fact, I have not the faintest idea of how to bake a cake except to follow the directions on a package mix. I do not even do this very often, for the Sara Lee frozen cakes are greatly superior to the best of my efforts. I wholeheartedly recommend Sara Lee Brownies, Spice Cake, Chocolate Cake, and Cream Cheese Cake; they keep well, and they are a great convenience to have on hand for those odd moments when someone drops in. As for other "bought" cakes, sponge and angel food are usually safe, and pleasant things can be done to dress them up, but, short of locating a truly excellent bakery, I would avoid the rest.

Commercially baked pies I feel are hopeless, the only exception being chiffon pies if you can find a good source for them. A delicious substitute, for those times when you grow hungry for a good fruit pie, are Pepperidge Farm frozen turnovers. They puff up into light and juicy concoctions and are wonderful served hot with cold vanilla ice cream beginning to melt over them. Since they take about 30 minutes to bake, you can put them in the oven just before you sit down to dinner, and then, unless you are a very slow or a very fast eater, they will be ready for dessert when you are.

There cannot be any need to comment on the convenience of keeping some ice cream on hand in the freezing compartment, but not everyone may be aware that chocolate, butterscotch, and various fruit sauces are available in cans and jars and will keep indefinitely, after opening, in the refrigerator. Frozen strawberries and raspberries are also delicious over ice cream—thawed first, of course. And for other than children, green crème de menthe and most other cordials are a perfectly simple, yet a bit elegant, topping over ice cream.

Cordials alone may take the place of dessert, as may a Stinger or a Grasshopper. Fruit soaked in wine is also a good choice, as is an assortment of fresh fruit or a mixed fruit bowl (see Chapter 10). Crackers and cheese may be served with the fresh fruit or by themselves. Saltines, slightly warmed, and camembert are a gentle combination after a heavy meal.

In the way of puddings, there are any number of packaged ones available. All suffer from a synthetic flavor, but some disguise can be achieved by using whipped cream or frozen strawberries or raspberries as a sauce.

For a miscellany of dessert suggestions, browse among the following.

PUDDINGS

BROWN BETTY

If you are having a cold supper, say, a salad or cold sliced lamb or beef, it is an interesting reversal to serve a hot dessert.

RECIPE I: APPLE BROWN BETTY

apples
corn flakes
brown sugar
½ cup orange juice (approximate)
raisins
nutmeg and cinnamon

1. Preheat oven to 350°.
2. Rub butter around the inside of a small baking dish. The size of the baking dish will dictate the amount of apples and corn flakes.
3. Put ½-inch layer of corn flakes on the bottom, and dust with brown sugar.
4. Next put a layer of apples that have been pared and sliced thin (cut the apples into quarters, cut out the core, pare away the skin with a knife, then slice the quarters). Dust the apple layer with brown sugar, then with nutmeg and cinnamon. Add a sprinkling of raisins.
5. Repeat these layers until the baking dish is filled. Pour ½ cup of orange juice over.
6. Bake, uncovered, in a 350° oven for 50 minutes. After the cooking is well under way, mix all the ingredients together by stirring with a fork (this need only be done once). Serve hot from the oven with hard sauce (see page 175). If there is any left over, it can be eaten cold or warmed by setting the baking dish inside a larger baking dish with an inch of water in it and heating in the oven.

RECIPE II: PINEAPPLE BROWN BETTY

1 medium-sized can crushed pineapple
8 slices white bread
¼ cup brown sugar
4 tablespoons margarine

1. Turn on the oven to 350°.
2. Toast 8 slices of white bread (stale bread is even

better than fresh if you have it). Cut off the crusts and discard, and then cut the toast into small squares.

3. Butter a baking dish or square, shallow cake tin (a good-sized container is best, so that the layers are spread out rather than piled high).

4. Use half of the toast squares to line the bottom of the baking dish. Spread over these ½ can of crushed pineapple. Sprinkle with half of the ¼ cup of brown sugar. Cut 2 tablespoons of margarine into tiny squares and dot half of these over the sugar. Make a second layer, using the rest of the ingredients in the same order as for the first layer, and then sprinkle nutmeg and cinnamon over the top.

5. Bake in a 350° oven, uncovered, for 50 minutes. Serve hot with vanilla ice cream or hard sauce (see page 175).

CUSTARD PUDDING

Custard is good by itself or topped with fruit: fresh sliced peaches (peel and slice at the last minute; they turn brown quickly), canned black cherries, frozen raspberries or strawberries, or a spoonful of cherry or strawberry preserves. Over the fruit can go whipped cream, or whipped cream can be used alone with the pudding. To vary the flavor of the custard itself, add chocolate bits (these come packaged) or ¼ teaspoon of powdered coffee when putting the ingredients of the pudding together. Custard can be used to "ice" the layers of store-bought sponge cake.

RECIPE: CUSTARD

1 egg
1 cup milk
1½ tablespoons sugar
almond extract

A double boiler is a necessity here, but if you do not have one, improvise by putting an inch or two of boiling water in a saucepan larger than the one the custard will be cooked in.

1. But, first, put 1 cup of milk in the smaller saucepan and heat it directly over the flame. Catch it just as it begins to boil and take it off the fire immediately.

2. In a bowl, beat together 1 egg, 1½ tablespoons of sugar, and a dash of salt. Slowly pour in the milk, stirring the mixture while adding the milk.

3. Put this mixture back in the saucepan and place over boiling water. Let it cook until the mixture has thickened enough so that when you dip a spoon in, it comes out coated. Take the custard off the stove and, after it has cooled a little, add ⅛ teaspoon of almond extract (or vanilla extract). Pour the custard into individual serving dishes.

ICEBOX PUDDING

There are numerous versions of this, and you can invent more of your own.

RECIPE I: ICEBOX PUDDING WITH CHOCOLATE WAFERS

1. Whip ½ cup of heavy cream until stiff, add ¼ teaspoon of sugar and a dash of almond or vanilla extract.
2. On separate dessert plates, place a chocolate wafer, a thin layer of whipped cream, another chocolate wafer, and so on. Use 4 or 5 chocolate wafers for each dessert. Ice the top and sides of each cylinder with the remaining whipped cream.
3. Put in the refrigerator and serve chilled.

RECIPE II: ICEBOX PUDDING WITH CAKE

When a cake begins to get stale, use it up this way.

1. Crumble the cake, and mix it with vanilla ice cream, whipped cream, or vanilla pudding made according to the package directions.

OR: Slice the cake thinly and put ice cream, whipped cream, or pudding between the layers.

2. Chill in the refrigerator (in the freezing compartment if you have used ice cream), and serve with whipped cream on top.

LEMON FLUFF

This, too, requires a double boiler. If you do not have one, see the directions for making Custard Pudding.

RECIPE: LEMON FLUFF

3 eggs
½ cup sugar
3 tablespoons lemon juice
1 tablespoon orange juice
½ pint heavy cream
24 vanilla wafers

1. Separate 3 eggs (for directions on how to do this, see page 22), and beat the yolks briefly with an egg beater. Add a pinch of salt and ½ cup of sugar to the yolks, and beat them well.
2. Transfer to a saucepan, add 3 tablespoons lemon juice and 1 tablespoon of orange juice, and cook in a double boiler until the mixture thickens. Take it off the stove and let it cool.
3. When cool, beat the 3 egg whites until they are stiff and fold them into the egg yolk mixture.
4. Whip ½ pint of heavy cream and gently stir this in also.

5. Crush 24 vanilla wafers and line the bottom of an ice tray with them. Spoon the custard over, and place the ice tray in the freezing compartment.

PLUM PUDDING

Crosse and Blackwell Plum Pudding is superior to any home-made that I have ever eaten; so I recommend a can of this, steamed according to the directions on the can, and served with hard sauce (page 175). Because it is exceedingly rich, the portions served are small, and a can will take care of more people than it would seem from the outside.

VANILLA YOGHURT

This dairy product tastes like vanilla pudding, so it is mentioned here to remind you of its existence. This makes a fine (and healthful) dessert, particularly with frozen strawberries over the top. Try coffee yoghurt, too.

CAKES

As noted, sponge and angel food are the safest buys in cake. If you want to bake your own, there are any number of packaged mixes available, all of which, if you have an accurate oven, turn out well. Packaged icings are, to my mind, far less successful; therefore two easy-to-make icings are included here.

UNCOOKED FROSTING

While this icing does not require cooking, it should be permitted to stand over hot water for 15 minutes after it is made.

RECIPE: UNCOOKED FROSTING

1½ cups confectioners' sugar	flavoring
2 tablespoons butter	

1. Mash the butter in a bowl with a fork until it is well softened, creamy in texture, and without lumps.
2. Add 1½ cups of confectioners' sugar a little at a time, mashing it into the butter. The result must be completely smooth.
3. Add one of the following: 1 teaspoon of orange juice and some grated orange rind; 1 teaspoon of lemon juice and some grated lemon rind; ½ teaspoon of powdered coffee (taste to see if you would prefer a stronger flavor; if so, add more);

or 1 tablespoon of sherry or rum. Mix in very thoroughly, and put the bowl of icing over hot water for 15 minutes. Then beat it until it is cool and the right spreading consistency.

A variation of this icing is to use brown sugar in place of confectioners' sugar (but not with the fruit flavorings).

PENUCHE ICING

RECIPE: PENUCHE ICING

1 cup brown sugar
½ cup butter
¼ cup milk
2 cups confectioners' sugar

1. In a saucepan, melt ½ cup of butter (8 tablespoons) and add 1 cup of brown sugar; the cup of brown sugar should be firmly packed so that you are sure of getting a full measure. Cook this, stirring constantly and over a low flame, for 2 minutes after it begins to boil.

2. Stir in ¼ cup of milk, and keep stirring until the mixture comes to a boil again. Take the saucepan off the stove, and let the mixture cool.

3. Put 2 cups of confectioners' sugar through a sieve to get all the lumps out. When the icing is lukewarm, add the sugar, a little at a time, beating constantly. If the icing does not thicken sufficiently to spread well, put the bottom of the saucepan in a bowl of cold water and beat until thick. If, on the contrary, it becomes too thick, add a trifling amount of hot water to thin it.

CAKE AND ICE CREAM

If the occasion arises when you find yourself called upon to produce a birthday cake, rise to that occasion with one of the following.

RECIPE I: ANGEL FOOD CAKE WITH ICE CREAM AND STRAWBERRIES

1 angel food cake
1 pint vanilla ice cream
1 package frozen strawberries

1. Thaw the strawberries in advance, but do the rest at the last minute. Put the angel food cake on a cake platter, and fill the center hole with vanilla ice cream. Then smooth more ice cream in a layer over the top of the cake.

2. Dot the top with whole frozen strawberries or spoon sliced strawberries over.

OR: If fresh peaches are in season, use peach ice cream and sliced peaches on top.

OR: Vanilla ice cream and chocolate sauce over.

RECIPE II: SPONGE CAKE WITH ICE CREAM

2 layer sponge cake
1 pint ice cream
fruit or chocolate or butterscotch sauce

1. Put a thick layer of ice cream between the two layers of sponge cake, and then coat the top with ice cream.
2. Pour hot chocolate or butterscotch sauce over the top, or use fresh or frozen fruit. Coffee ice cream and chocolate sauce make a good combination.

CAKE WITH WHIPPED CREAM ICING

Make this at least one hour ahead of time.

RECIPE: CAKE WITH WHIPPED CREAM

2 layer sponge cake
2 cups whipping cream
½ cup instant cocoa mix
2 tablespoons crème de cacao

1. Whip 2 cups of heavy cream with an egg beater until it begins to thicken.
2. Add ½ cup of instant cocoa mix (be careful not to use plain cocoa), and then continue to whip the cream until it is quite stiff. Mix in 2 tablespoons crème de cacao.
3. Cut 2 layers of sponge cake in half to make 4 layers. Spread the whipped cream between the layers and over the top and sides. Put the cake in the refrigerator to chill.

FRUIT COBBLER

This can be made with peaches, apples, strawberries, cherries, pineapple, or blueberries, and with either packaged white cake mix or Bisquick. Use either canned or frozen fruit, and drain the juice off before using.

RECIPE: FRUIT COBBLER

1 can or 1 package frozen fruit
½ cup brown sugar
white cake mix or Bisquick

1. In a saucepan, melt 4 tablespoons of butter. Add ½ cup of brown sugar, and cook gently until the sugar has melted.
2. Light the oven, and set it at 350°. Put together the white cake or Bisquick batter by following the directions on the package (follow directions for baking powder biscuits on Bisquick box).
3. Rub butter on the bottom and sides of a cake tin.

Arrange the drained fruit in an even layer on the bottom and pour the butter-sugar sauce over.

4. Gently spoon on top the cake or Bisquick mix.

5. Bake in a 350° oven for the length of time given on the mix package. Let the cake cool slightly and then put a dinner plate on it. Grasping both the plate and the pan, turn over so that the plate is on the bottom. When ready to serve, lift the pan off.

ICE CREAM

See the recipes for Cake and Ice Cream and for Crumb-Crust Pies and the comments at the beginning of this chapter concerning sauces for ice cream. And if you really have a sweet tooth, try the following.

MINT PATTY SAUCE

RECIPE: ICE CREAM WITH MINT PATTY SAUCE

10 chocolate-covered peppermint patties

3 tablespoons cream

1. Let the peppermint patties melt in the top of a double boiler or in a saucepan over boiling water.

2. When melted, stir in 3 tablespoons of cream and blend well. Pour the hot sauce over vanilla ice cream.

SNOWBALLS

RECIPE: SNOWBALLS

1. Crush graham crackers, lemon wafers, or any other kind of cookie that you like and that will break into fine pieces, or crush peanuts, walnuts, or pecans.

2. Roll balls of ice cream in the crumbs until coated and then put in the freezing compartment.

3. Just before serving, pour hot chocolate or butterscotch sauce over.

PIES

Prepared pie crust mixes are on the market, as are pie tins with the bottom crust already made and in place. For filling, you can use canned fruit pie fillings or packaged puddings. Do not have too high hopes for the results, though. My own preference is for crumb-crust pies.

CRUMB-CRUST PIE

The crust may be made with graham crackers, gingersnaps, zwieback, or vanilla wafers; the filling may be custard (see recipe on page 168), prepared pudding mixes, or ice cream; and the topping may be whipped cream or meringue.

RECIPE: CRUMB CRUST

1. Crush finely a sufficient number of graham crackers to make 1⅓ cups of crumbs.
2. Melt ⅓ cup of butter.
3. Add the melted butter and ¼ cup of sugar to the cracker crumbs and mix them together thoroughly.
4. Line a pie tin with this mixture by pressing it firmly against the bottom and sides with the back of a spoon.
5. Bake it for 6 minutes in a 350° oven, then let it cool. Fill with custard, pudding mix, or ice cream. If the latter, do this at the last moment, just before spreading meringue over.

RECIPE: MERINGUE TOPPING FOR PIE

3 egg whites ¼ teaspoon cream of tartar

1. Turn oven on to 450°.
2. Separate 3 eggs (see page 22), making sure no bits of yolk get in with the whites.
3. Beat the whites with an egg beater until they form slight mounds when the beater is raised.
4. Continue to beat, but now begin adding 6 tablespoons of sugar, 1 tablespoon at a time, beating each time until the sugar has dissolved. Continue beating until the egg whites are stiff and will stand up in heavy points.
5. If the pie crust has not already been filled, do this, and then spread the meringue over the top. It will look prettiest if it stands up in points here and there.
6. Pop immediately into a 450° oven and cook for 3 minutes. If the filling is ice cream, take it out after 3 minutes, whether or no; otherwise, if the meringue is not quite golden brown yet, let it go 1 or 2 minutes longer.

FRUIT DESSERTS

For a variety of different ways in which fruit may be served as a dessert, see Chapter 10.

GINGERBREAD

The packaged mixes are excellent. My only recommendation

is to sprinkle in some raisins when making the batter, and top the gingerbread off, when serving, with whipped cream. Keep in mind, too, that gingerbread makes a very pleasant change from rolls if the dinner is a light one.

MERINGUE

Bakeries make quite good meringues, which can be filled with ice cream and then topped with crushed fruit or chocolate or butterscotch sauce for a handsome dessert.

SOUR CREAM DESSERT

A simple but good dessert is a mixture of 1 cup of sour cream and 1 cup of cherry jam or 1 package of frozen strawberries or raspberries. Put this in an ice tray in the freezing compartment for ½ hour, no longer; it should not freeze.

TOPPINGS

Whipped cream or hard sauce does wonders for many different kinds of desserts.

WHIPPED CREAM

There are two things to keep in mind when whipping cream. One is that the cream doubles in amount, i.e., ½ cup of cream makes 1 cup of whipped cream. The second is that the task of whipping cream is made easier if you put the bowl and the beater in the refrigerator ahead of time so that they are cold when you go to use them. Add a trifling amount of sugar during the beating and a few drops of vanilla to the cream after it is whipped.

HARD SAUCE

Hard sauce is simply a combination of sugar and butter with a flavoring agent added. My own preference for the latter is brandy or rum, but vanilla may be used.

RECIPE: HARD SAUCE

½ stick of butter
½ cup granulated sugar
1 teaspoon brandy or rum

1. Let the butter soften at room temperature and then mash it with a fork.
2. Add ½ cup of granulated sugar and 1 teaspoon of

brandy or rum or a dash of vanilla. Continue mashing with a fork until the sugar and butter are blended together. Put in the refrigerator to chill.

CHAPTER 10 HOW TO FIX FRUIT

For reasons both of health and pleasure, it is a good idea always to have some fruit on hand. It makes a fine snack, an excellent dessert, and an interesting accompaniment to main dishes. It may, of course, be eaten raw or cooked, singly or mixed in a fruit bowl. Directions are given in this chapter on how to select fruit in the market and how to cope with it after you have gotten it home.

Canned fruits taste completely different from fresh, but are often very good in their own right and, in the case of pineapple and peaches, are much easier to use for broiling. Of the frozen fruits, strawberries, raspberries, and peaches survive the freezing process well, melon and rhubarb less happily.

FRUIT BOWL

A bowl of mixed fruit makes a handsome dessert and is an easy one to serve guests. Any combination of fruit may be used, as well as a mixture of fresh, canned, and frozen. The one fruit I would definitely include is a box of either frozen strawberries or raspberries, because they are colorful and combine so well with other fruit. If all frozen fruit is being used, an attractive effect can be achieved by putting, for example, peaches, melon balls, pineapple, and raspberries in a bowl while they are still frozen and letting them thaw in the refrigerator; they will not intermix to any extent even after thawing, but will remain in islands of color.

Canned grapefruit, or fresh, is another almost basic component of fruit bowls, particularly if other canned or frozen fruit is used, because the latter tend to be sweet and the grapefruit is a welcome contrast. On the whole, it is probably best to drain the juice of each can of fruit off into a container before emptying the can into the bowl, and then add the mixed juice to the bowl in the right quantity for the amount of fruit; otherwise, there tends to be far too much juice.

If fresh bananas and/or peaches are to be used, add these at the last minute, for they turn brown quickly after peeling. On the other hand, fresh pineapple, berries, melon, grapes, oranges, and grapefruit last well and may be fixed as much in advance as you like.

A bowl of sour cream served separately may be used as a topping for mixed fruit. Yoghurt does better if it is added to the fruit in advance and allowed to chill in the icebox along with the fruit. A friend of mine, Christine by name, holds that raspberries are essential if yoghurt is used, and the quite delicious dessert she makes of raspberries, melon balls, and orange segments, mixed with plain yoghurt and well chilled, was typed up by a guest she had had, labeled "Christine's Summer Delight," and submitted to a newspaper, where it won first prize in a recipe contest.

Shredded coconut looks pretty sprinkled over a bowl of mixed fruit and is a good combination with sour cream. A mound of fruit sherbet in the center of the bowl is another idea, as is kirsch or champagne, flat or bubbly. And don't overlook the decorative effect of mint leaves with any of these additions. A tablespoon or two of undiluted frozen fruit juice is also an interesting topping.

APPLES

There are, as you know, cooking apples and eating apples, and while eating apples may be cooked, it is probably just as well to forego the reverse. Select unbruised apples with a good color. For Apple Brown Betty, see page 167.

BAKED APPLES

RECIPE: BAKED APPLES

1. Put oven on to 350°.
2. Wash the apples thoroughly, and ream out the core with an apple corer or small paring knife. Pare the apples two-thirds of the way down, leaving the last third of the skin in place around the bottom.
3. Place the apples in a baking dish. Sprinkle each apple heavily with sugar, lightly with cinnamon. Add ½ inch of water to the pan.
4. Bake in a 350° oven until tender, every once in a while spooning some of the juice in the bottom of the pan over the apples. Whether they take from 30 minutes to 1 hour to cook depends on the size of the apples.

APPLE RINGS

These are an accompaniment to meat, going particularly well with pork.

RECIPE I: APPLE RINGS

1. Wash apples, core them, and cut into thick slices, leaving the skins on.
2. Cook the slices gently in butter in a skillet until they are tender, about 10 minutes.

RECIPE II: CINNAMON APPLE RINGS

1. Pare and core the apples, and cut them into ½-inch thick slices.
2. Put ½ cup of water and 1 cup of sugar in a skillet, and cook until the sugar has dissolved.
3. Add the apple slices, 2 tablespoons of red cinnamon candies, and some red coloring (both of the latter are available in grocery stores; since the red coloring is just for looks, no harm is done if it is omitted).
4. Cook the apples, turning fairly often, until tender. Serve hot or cold.

APPLESAUCE

For regular applesauce, buy it in a can and serve cold with a bit of cinnamon sprinkled on top.

RECIPE: APPLESAUCE WITH ORANGE

1. Pare, core, and quarter 4 apples. Leaving the skin in place, cut 1 orange in quarters.
2. Cook these in boiling water until the apples are tender.
3. Force the mixture through a strainer, using the back of a spoon; the orange peel will not go through, of course, so discard it as soon as you have gotten it free of the pulp of the orange.
4. Add sugar to taste, and return the mixture to the stove to cook for 3 minutes.

APPLES IN SOUR CREAM

This recipe, which I learned from a European friend, makes a fine light dessert.

RECIPE: APPLES IN SOUR CREAM

1. Fill a medium-sized saucepan three-quarters of the way with water. Add to it 1 tablespoon of sugar, 1 slice of lemon, and 1 clove. Bring the water to a boil.
2. Pare, core, and quarter apples, 1 to a serving, and

put them in the boiling water. Cook them for 2 minutes.

3. Arrange the apples in a shallow dish, and cover them with sour cream. Serve lukewarm.

BANANAS

Choose bananas that are firm and yellow, not green. If not fully ripe, store them at room temperature. When ripe, put them in the refrigerator; the skins may turn brown but the bananas will be all right. Serve them sliced over custard, in mixed fruit bowls, over sponge cake with whipped cream on top, plain in heavy cream, on cereal, and in salads, but always leave the peeling and slicing until the last minute because they turn brown when exposed to the air.

RECIPE: BAKED BANANAS

Bananas may be baked in their skins or peeled.

1. Set the oven at 350°.

2. Bake unpeeled bananas for 30 minutes. Remove one section of the peel, dribble a bit of rum over the exposed part of the banana, and dust with confectioners' sugar.

OR: Peel the bananas, put them in a buttered baking dish, and bake for 25 minutes. Sprinkle the cooked bananas with lemon juice and a light dusting of confectioners' sugar.

RECIPE: BROILED BANANAS

Broiled bananas may be served as a dessert or as an accompaniment to meat.

1. Peel the bananas, slice them in half lengthwise, sprinkle with brown sugar, and put a few dots of butter over.

2. Broil under a medium flame for 10 to 15 minutes.

BERRIES

In buying berries of any kind, look for ripe but unbruised fruit, and buy them not too far in advance, for they do not keep well. When you get the berries home, empty them out of the box and go over them, discarding any green ones and any that are mashed or moldy. Do not wash them until ready to eat. Store them in the refrigerator and use as quickly as possible. If there is space enough in the refrigerator, it is best to spread the berries on a large, flat tin so that they are not touching each other; this is particularly true of strawberries, which will keep much longer this way. To prepare strawberries, cut off the green stem and cut out any brown or very soft spots. Other berries simply need to be washed well; put them in a sieve and let cold water run over them. If strawberries or raspberries are spoiling faster than you can use them, put them in a bowl, mash with a fork, sprinkle some sugar over, add a little bit of water, and refrigerate.

Berries, lightly sugared and with heavy cream to pour over, make a superb dessert. Or they may be added to a fruit bowl or served on sponge cake with whipped cream. Adding them to a muffin mix or Bisquick makes delicious fruit muffins, or see the recipe for Fruit Cobbler on page 172.

GRAPEFRUIT

Perhaps surprisingly, the best-looking grapefruit are not also the best-tasting ones. Those of a perfect yellow color are apt to be thick-skinned and less flavorful than those that have a tracery of tan lines, like a cobweb, over the skin. Indian River grapefruit are to be preferred. Heft the grapefruit in your hand; if it feels heavy in relation to its size, it will be full of juice and good.

If a half grapefruit is to be served, just cut it open. The custom has somehow grown up of slicing each segment free of the dividing membranes and of the skin, as though it were difficult to free just by scooping the segment out with a spoon, which it is not. Cutting the membrane imparts a bitter flavor which is not otherwise present. Grapefruit also, in and of itself, is too good to spoil by the addition of sugar. Hence, the recommendation to cut it in half, put it on a plate, and let it go at that.

If, however, you wish to use fresh grapefruit segments in a fruit bowl, there is a little more to the preparation. Cut off the bottom and the top of the grapefruit to a point where the meat is just exposed. Stand it on one of these flat ends and make a curving slice down the outside just under the skin. Repeat this all the way around, cutting the skin off in strips, and then cut off any little bits of the white of the skin missed by the lengthwise cuts. Take the grapefruit in one hand, with the dividing membranes running parallel to your fingers. Cut right alongside a membrane, and when the knife reaches the center, push it sideways; this will free the segment from the next membrane and allow it to be flipped out. Repeat all around the grapefruit, and then squeeze the pulp left in your hand to get out the remaining juice. This is complicated to describe but very easy to do, and it is the most efficient method of preparation.

BROILED GRAPEFRUIT

This is a different and delicious dessert.

RECIPE: BROILED GRAPEFRUIT

1. Cut grapefruits in half, one half to a serving. With a sharp knife, make a circular cut around the white center core and remove it.

2. Pour off the juice that collects in the hole, and fill it with sherry, port, or green crème de menthe.

3. Put under a very low flame, and broil until the grapefruit is hot and beginning to brown a little. If the flame is low enough, you can put the grapefruit in when dinner is served, and it will be just right at dessert time.

GRAPES

For eating right off the stem, nothing is better than Concord grapes, but because they are rather perishable, they are available only in the early fall. Most other grapes keep very well indeed. Put them away unwashed and in a plastic bag. Before adding seeded grapes to a fruit bowl or salad, cut them in half and flick out the seeds with your thumbnail.

Grapes seem to combine particularly well with bananas, melon balls, and fresh pineapple. If, in serving them alone, you want to dress them up a bit, try the following recipe.

GLAZED GRAPES

RECIPE: GLAZED GRAPES

1. Select a handsome bunch of grapes, wash them well, and let them drain dry.

2. Separate an egg (see page 22) and beat the white with a fork until it is frothy. Paint the egg white over the grapes and then sprinkle with sugar. Chill in the refrigerator.

MELONS

In choosing melons, other than selecting those that are firm and unblemished, there are two things you can do. One is to sniff the stem end of the melon; if it has a good melon smell, it is probably ripe and tasty. The other is to weigh the melon in your hand; the heavier the melon in relation to its size. the juicier it will be.

Melons, for serving, are simply cut in wedges of the size you want and the seeds scraped off with a spoon. They should be chilled before serving, of course, and cut at the last minute. To keep unused melon, cover the cut edges with Saran wrap. Honeydew melon is served with wedges of lemon; cantaloupe tastes best with salt sprinkled over.

For use in salads or fruit bowls, melon balls look prettiest. These are scooped out with a gadget obtainable in ten-cent stores. But the melon may also just be cut into bite-size chunks. Before adding the chunks or balls to a salad or serving them alone as a dessert, put them in a bowl, sprinkle a tiny amount of sugar over, and then some lemon juice; this adds quite a bit to the flavor. Wine, particularly champagne, also does very nice things to melon balls; let soak several hours in the refrigerator and serve well chilled. Light rum is another possibility, and watermelon responds well to bourbon.

Melons can be used as receptacles for mixed fruit. Cut in half, scoop out the seeds, and fill the centers with cut fruit; pour a dash of wine or rum over. In the case of watermelon, and a fair number of guests to eat it, scoop out as much of the melon as will leave the size cavity you want. Combine the cut melon with other fruit and replace in the cavity. Decorate with fresh mint or fruit sherbet.

ORANGES

All the directions for grapefruit, preparing as well as selecting, apply equally to oranges. They too may be broiled, the center filled with port wine, and served hot for dessert. Or segments may be dusted with confectioners' sugar and soaked in light rum for an interesting dessert.

PEACHES

Buying peaches is rather chancy. They may turn out to be marvelously flavorful and juicy or completely dull and tasteless. Your best hope is to sniff them for a good peach smell and to weigh them for heaviness in relation to size. If the peaches are not fully ripe, leave them at room temperature until they are. You can wash them before storing in the refrigerator, but if so, they should be dry before they are put away.

Frozen peaches are quite good, but not the same as fresh. Of the canned peaches, I think the Elberta freestone peaches are by far the best. Canned peach halves are the most suitable for broiling to serve along with meat. They go nicely with lamb chops or with ham. Just put them under the broiler until hot and beginning to brown.

PEARS

Pears are as much of a gamble as peaches. All you can do is pick out unblemished ones, leave them at room temperature to ripen, and then hope that they are juicy, not mealy, when you go to eat them. For broiled pears as a meat accompaniment, use canned halves, and put them under the broiler until hot.

PINEAPPLE

A pineapple that still has green tinges to its skin will ripen at room temperature, but select a fully ripe one if you have a choice. It is quite easy to tell a ripe pineapple by its smell. Sniff the depression in the center of the bottom; if it smells very good, it will taste very good. Too, the juicier the pineapple, the heavier it will feel when hefted.

The pineapple is a rather formidable-looking fruit, but it is easy enough to prepare once you get the hang of it. Cut off the top about 1 inch below the leaves, and cut off about ½ inch of the bottom. Stand it on the bottom and, with a sharp knife, slice just under the skin from top to bottom, following the curve of the pineapple and taking off about a 1-inch strip of the shell with each slice. When all of the shell has been cut off in this fashion, there will still be many "eyes" left. Turn the pineapple on its side and cut it into ¾-inch thick slices. Take each of these slices in turn and cut out the eyes, cutting away as little of the meat as possible. Lay a slice flat and cut it across on both sides of the core. Slice again the other way to cut the core away from the remaining meat, discard the core, and cut the meat into cubes. Do this with all the slices. Put the cubes of pineapple in a bowl, sprinkle a little sugar over and the juice of half a lemon; add 2 tablespoons of cold water, stir, and put in the icebox, covered, to chill.

A hollowed-out pineapple filled with diced fruit that has been soaked in Cointreau, brandy, or rum is an impressive dessert, but it is the devil's own job to get the meat out and leave the shell intact. It is not even much easier if the pineapple, leaves and all, is cut in half, although this, too, looks pretty. Try it if you have a lot of time and patience, but keep your thumbs out of the way.

RHUBARB

I don't hold with rhubarb as a dessert, but I think it makes a wonderful side dish with a meal. Fresh rhubarb is so simple to fix and so much better than the frozen that I recommend you use it whenever it is available. The frozen, which is too sweet for my taste, is somewhat improved by cooking a couple of quarters of lemon along with it. In buying the fresh, choose stalks of a brilliant color and ones that have not gone limp.

RECIPE: RHUBARB

1. Cut off the leaves and about ½ inch of the bottoms of the stalks. Wash well and cut into 1-inch pieces.

2. Put in a saucepan with enough water to cover. Add several slices or quarters of lemon, skin and all, and put in ½ cup of sugar.

3. Bring to a boil, and let cook until it looks like rhubarb should look, that is, a kind of nondescript mess. Taste for sufficient sweetness, and add more sugar as necessary; it can sometimes take a rather surprising amount. It is very, very good served hot, very good served cold.

CHAPTER 11 HOW TO PUT SOUPS TOGETHER

Since this is a cookbook for people who know nothing about cooking but want to do it well and with little effort, one of the things least likely to be missed in it is any dissertation on how to make soups from scratch. Let us leave it to the soup companies to start from scratch, and then let us see what can be done with their products.

BLACK BEAN SOUP

1 can condensed black bean soup
1½ tablespoons sherry
1 can consommé

1. Heat 1 can of black bean soup in a saucepan, and when it is hot, stir in 1 can of consommé and 1 soup can of water. Allow to get piping hot.

2. Just before serving, stir in 1½ tablespoons of sherry.

3. Serve in bowls with a slice of lemon covered with chopped parsley floating on top.

CHICKEN-CELERY SOUP

1 can condensed cream of celery soup
2 soup cans of milk

1 can condensed chicken-noodle soup

Combine the two soups, add 2 soup cans of milk, and heat, but do not allow to boil.

CHICKEN-MUSHROOM SOUP

1 can chicken broth
1 can condensed cream of mushroom soup
whipped cream
prepared horseradish

1. Mix together and heat 1 can of chicken broth and 1 can of cream of mushroom soup.
2. Mix a tiny bit of prepared horseradish into whipped cream, and serve the soup with the whipped cream floating on top.

CREAM OF CHICKEN SOUP

1 can condensed cream of chicken soup
¾ soup can light cream
2 tablespoons sherry
1 teaspoon curry powder

Mix all ingredients and heat, but do not boil.

CONSOMMÉ

RECIPE I: COLD CONSOMMÉ

Ring a change on the usual consommé by serving it in a tall glass over ice, adding 1 tablespoon of dry vermouth to each glass.

RECIPE II: HOT CONSOMMÉ

To each cup of consommé, add 1 tablespoon of sherry.

CORN SOUP

1 can condensed cream of chicken soup
1 small can corn niblets
1 soup can milk
2 slices bacon
½ cup chopped onions

1. Fry 2 slices of bacon in a skillet until they are crisp. Take the bacon out, and in the bacon fat gently cook ½ cup of chopped onions until they are transparent.
2. In a saucepan mix together 1 can of condensed cream of chicken soup, 1 small can of corn niblets, and 1 soup

can of milk. Add the onions. Crumble the bacon and add it. Heat, but do not boil.

CLAM SOUP

RECIPE I: CLAM AND MUSHROOM SOUP

1 can minced clams
1 can condensed cream of mushroom soup
1 soup can milk

Mix together 1 drained can of minced clams, 1 can of condensed cream of mushroom soup, 1 soup can of milk, and a dash of Worcestershire sauce. Heat and serve.

RECIPE II: CLAM AND VEGETABLE SOUP

1 can minced clams
1 can condensed vegetable soup

Mix together 1 can of drained minced clams, 1 can of condensed vegetable soup, and 1 soup can of water. Heat and serve.

RECIPE III: CLAM AND CHICKEN SOUP

1 can minced clams
1 can condensed cream of chicken soup
1 soup can milk

Mix together 1 drained can of minced clams, 1 can of condensed cream of chicken soup, and 1 soup can of milk. Heat and serve.

CRAB SOUP

This, with a salad and rolls, makes a Sunday night supper.

1 can crabmeat
1 can condensed pea soup
1 soup can light cream
1 can condensed cream of tomato soup
6 tablespoons dry sherry

1. Drain the juice from the can of crabmeat, and pick the crabmeat over for any stray pieces of cartilage. Put the crabmeat in a bowl, and pour 6 tablespoons of sherry over it.
2. In a saucepan stir together 1 can of condensed pea soup, 1 can of condensed cream of tomato soup, and 1 soup can of light cream. Heat, but do not permit to boil.
3. Add the crabmeat and wine and heat until all is steaming hot.

LOBSTER SOUP

RECIPE I: LOBSTER AND CHICKEN SOUP

- 1 can lobster
- 1 can condensed cream of chicken soup
- ¾ soup can milk
- 2 tablespoons dry vermouth

1. Drain the can of lobster, and break the meat into small pieces.

2. Mix together 1 can of condensed cream of chicken soup and ¾ soup can of milk. When this has warmed, add the lobster and 2 tablespoons of dry vermouth. Cook until hot but not boiling.

RECIPE II: LOBSTER BISQUE

- 1 can lobster
- 1 can condensed cream of mushroom soup
- 4 tablespoons dry sherry
- 1 can condensed cream of asparagus soup
- 1 soup can light cream

1. Drain the can of lobster, and break the meat into small pieces into a bowl. Pour over it 4 tablespoons of sherry.

2. Mix together 1 can of cream of mushroom and 1 can of asparagus soup, along with 1 soup can of light cream. Heat.

3. Add the lobster and sherry. Heat, but do not allow to boil.

OR: Use 1 can of pea soup and 1 can of cream of tomato soup in place of the mushroom and asparagus soups.

JELLIED MADRILENE

- 1 can madrilene soup
- bleu cheese

Prepare jellied madrilene according to the directions given on the can. Before serving, mix in crumbled bits of bleu cheese. Jellied madrilene must spend eight hours in the refrigerator, so plan accordingly.

ONION SOUP

1. Make the soup according to the directions on the can.

2. Toast 1 slice of French bread for each serving of soup, float it on top of the soup, and sprinkle it with grated Parmesan cheese.

PEA SOUP

1. Make according to the directions on the can.

2. Trim the crusts off 2 slices of bread, and cut the bread into small squares. Fry the bread in butter in a skillet until it is brown. Serve the soup in cups and sprinkle these croutons on top.

SHRIMP SOUP

RECIPE I: CREAM OF SHRIMP SOUP

1 can frozen shrimp soup
¾ soup can light cream
2 tablespoons sherry
1 teaspoon curry powder

Mix all ingredients and heat, being careful not to allow the soup to boil.

RECIPE II: SHRIMP BISQUE

1 can shrimp
1 can condensed cream of tomato soup
1 can condensed pea soup
1 soup can milk
2 tablespoons of light rum

1. Mix together 1 can of condensed cream of tomato soup, 1 can of condensed pea soup, and 1 soup can of milk. Heat gently.

2. Drain 1 can of shrimp and add.

3. At the last moment before serving, stir in 2 tablespoons of light rum.

RECIPE III: SHRIMP AND MUSHROOM SOUP

1 can shrimp
1 can condensed cream of mushroom soup
1 soup can milk
1 tablespoon dried onion flakes
2 tablespoons sherry
dash of Tabasco or Worcestershire sauce

1. Mix together 1 can of condensed cream of mushroom soup, 1 soup can of milk, and 1 tablespoon of dried onion flakes. Heat.

2. Drain 1 can of shrimp and add, along with a dash of Tabasco or Worcestershire sauce. Cook gently until hot.

3. Before serving, stir in 2 tablespoons of sherry.

TOMATO SOUP

Heat according to the directions on the can, and then serve with whipped cream on top, croutons made by lightly frying small squares of bread in butter, or Puffed Rice lightly fried in butter and sprinkled with grated American cheese.

RECIPE: TOMATO AND PEA SOUP

1 can condensed cream of tomato soup	1 can condensed pea soup
	½ cup sauterne

Combine these ingredients and heat.

CHAPTER 12 HOW TO MAKE BREAKFAST

Breakfast is an easy meal to prepare, except that there may be a slight problem in getting everything ready at the same time because it is all last-minute cooking and, too, one may not be at peak alertness at this time of day. Until you get to be an old hand at whipping a breakfast together, it is perhaps best to follow a rather set routine. The following is suggested:

1. *Take the eggs out of the refrigerator.* It is best that eggs be at room temperature before cooking, particularly if they are to be boiled, for the shells crack readily if they are cold. However, all is not lost if you forgot to take them out; hold them for a minute or two under running warm water to warm them up.

2. *Make the coffee.* Do this even if you are having instant coffee, for instant coffee is improved by being cooked. Measure water into a saucepan, and after the water is boiling, add 1 teaspoon of instant coffee for each cup of water. Turn the fire down and allow the coffee to simmer along slowly until breakfast is ready.

3. *Set the table.* Put out cream and sugar, salt and pepper, jam, whatever will be needed.

4. *Prepare the fruit or fruit juice.* Frozen fruit juices, particularly if served with a cube of ice, have a better flavor if 2 and ⅔ cans of water, rather than the full 3 cans, are added. If fruit is being served, such as a half grapefruit, for instance, it is best that it be eaten before the eggs or pancakes or whatever are cooked, so that the latter will not get cold.

5. *Start the cooking.* If you are having hot cereal and toast, start the cereal first. If you are having eggs and toast, the cooking time should be about equal, depending on your toaster; if you are making more than two pieces of toast,

start the eggs only as you put the last two pieces of bread in the toaster. For bacon and eggs, start the bacon ahead of the eggs. Sausages take about 20 minutes; start them before the fruit is eaten. With pancakes and scrambled eggs, cook the eggs only when the last of the pancakes are done on one side. For ham and eggs, start the eggs cooking when the ham is brown on one side. Baked eggs and omelets take quite a bit longer than other types of eggs.

One thing not to forget is to put plates on to warm. Cold plates are ruinous to hot eggs and toast and pancakes.

EGGS

For Baked Eggs, see page 122. For Omelet, see page 120.

With the exception of scrambled eggs, eggs should be cooked gently, not rapidly, and even so they do not take very long. Be careful not to overcook, and remove the egg from the pan the instant the cooking time is up; otherwise, it will go on cooking even though the fire is turned off. Preferably, eggs should be at room temperature before cooking. There is no difference between brown eggs and white eggs; they taste the same.

BOILED EGGS

Cooking time: 4 minutes.

Put enough water in a saucepan to cover the eggs, and when it is boiling briskly, turn the fire down to the point where the water is just bubbling gently. Hold the egg in a spoon above the water for an instant or two so that the steam warms it, then lower it gently to the bottom of the saucepan. Four minutes is the cooking time for soft-boiled eggs; take off or add a ½ minute if you like them softer or harder. Remove the eggs from the water immediately and hold them under cold water just long enough—a few seconds—so that they are not too hot to handle; if the shell remains very hot, the egg will go on cooking.

If, by some mischance, you are one morning confronted with an underdone boiled egg, break a piece of toast into it. The toast will absorb the runny white and make it palatable.

FRIED EGGS

Cooking time: about 4 minutes.

If you are having fried eggs and bacon, cook the bacon first, and when it is done, remove it from the skillet, but leave all of the bacon fat in. Turn off the fire and immediately add the eggs, breaking them into the skillet or one at a time into a saucer and sliding them from the saucer into the skillet. Salt and pepper the eggs and put a lid on them. They will cook very gently in the hot fat and be far more tender and delicious than if cooked with a fire under them. Make toast and whatever else you have to do, then check the eggs. If the whites have not completely set, turn the fire back on and dip up some of the bacon fat with a spoon and dribble it over the eggs.

In the absence of bacon, melt butter in a skillet, about 1 tablespoon per egg, and cook, with a lid on, over the lowest possible flame. Spoon some of the hot butter over the top of the eggs, and as soon as the tops have set, halt the cooking.

POACHED EGGS

Cooking time: 3 minutes.

Put 1 inch of water in the bottom of a skillet; it should be simmering gently, not boiling, when the eggs are added. If you like, ½ teaspoon of vinegar may be added to the water to keep the egg whites together better. Break the eggs, one by one, into a saucer and slide them gently into the water. You can tell by looking at the eggs when they are done, which is as soon as the white has set. Lift them out with a slotted spoon and let the water drain off before depositing them on toast or English muffins.

SCRAMBLED EGGS

This is an unorthodox method of scrambling eggs and is contrary to the rule of cooking eggs slowly, but I think that the results more than justify the method.

Cooking time: no time at all.

1. Put 1 tablespoon of butter in a skillet over a medium flame. Let the pan get quite hot and the butter brown.

2. In the meantime, break eggs into a bowl, 1 to a serving. For each egg, add 4 tablespoons of evaporated milk (regular milk can be used but it will not be as good), ⅛ teaspoon of sugar, and salt and pepper. Beat the mixture with a fork to mix.

3. When the skillet is hot and the butter brown, empty in the eggs. Leave them alone a few seconds and then begin

scraping them off the bottom of the pan with the flat side of a fork. When the eggs have set, which will be almost immediately, they are done.

BACON

Cooking time: about 5 minutes.

Bacon should be allowed to cook slowly over a medium-low flame. Start it in a cold pan, laying it out in strips or, if it won't come apart readily, put a block of slices in and separate them with a fork after they begin to cook. During cooking, occasionally press the slices down with the back of a fork. Turn to cook on both sides. The thing with bacon is that it is done before it looks done; therefore, take it out when your eye tells you it needs to cook one more minute. Put it on paper toweling to drain.

CANADIAN BACON

Fry this gently in butter until it is brown on both sides.

HAM

Used cooked ham, either slices from a baked ham or delicatessen boiled ham, and fry it gently in butter until lightly browned.

SAUSAGE

Cooking time: about 20 minutes.

Puncture the skin of link sausages in several places with a fork. Put the sausages in a skillet, and cover them with water. When the water comes to a boil, turn the fire down and let the sausages cook gently. After 5 minutes, pour off the water in the skillet. Continue to cook the sausages, turning as necessary, until they have browned all around.

TOAST

If you do not have a toaster, you can nevertheless make toast by putting slices of bread under the broiler, and even if you have a toaster, this method may prove to be more convenient when you have a large amount of toast to make, for, done under the broiler, it will all be ready at the same time. Keep the broiler in mind, too, for toasting English muffins or other kinds of muffins that may not fit readily into the toaster.

FRENCH TOAST

Use a baking dish or a bowl with a bottom large enough for a piece of bread to lie flat. Break into the bowl 1 egg and add ½ cup of milk and a sprinkling of salt. Beat with a fork until well mixed. Melt butter in a skillet. Dip a piece of bread into the egg mixture so that it is coated on both sides (but do not soak in the mixture or it will be soggy), and then transfer the bread to the skillet. Cook until it is nicely browned on both sides. The amounts given here are enough for 4 pieces of bread. Serve the French toast with butter melting on top and syrup to pour over.

PANCAKES

Follow the directions on a box of pancake mix. If it strikes your fancy, you can add blueberries to the batter, or, when the pancake is in the skillet, lay a thin slice of boiled ham on the uncooked side, turn, and complete the cooking. You can calculate when to turn pancakes by the presence of bursting bubbles on the uncooked side.

WAFFLES

If you have a waffle iron, follow the package mix directions. If you do not, you will have to settle for the frozen packaged waffles which can be heated in the toaster. Put butter and syrup over them the minute they come from the toaster; otherwise, they tend to be too dry and crisp.

CHAPTER 13 HOW TO FIX LUNCH

A sandwich and soup is a usual menu at lunchtime, and a very good one it is. The choice among soups is wide, every variety being available in cans or dehydrated form. For some suggestions on soup combinations, see Chapter 11. A light soup, such as consommé or chicken-noodle, is pleasant with a grilled sandwich, while the cream soups are in order with, for example, a lettuce and tomato sandwich.

There is not much to be said about the making of simple sandwiches, which, as you know, is a perfectly straightforward process. If the bread is not absolutely fresh, it will taste better toasted, or you can grill the sandwich (see Grilled

Sandwiches) or turn the bread into French toast (see page 193). As a matter of fact, even if the bread is fresh, French toast makes an interesting variation for many plain sandwiches. Another quite good switch from the usual is to soak the lettuce for, say, a sliced egg sandwich or a lobster salad sandwich, in French dressing for a few minutes, using mayonnaise on the bread itself. Sandwiches are usually as palatable as the amount of butter and mayonnaise or mustard or catsup used; it is skimping on these trimmings that makes a sandwich dry and uninteresting. For another change, occasionally try the substitution of watercress or just plain parsley for lettuce. Since fish is an important part of the diet nutritionally, do not overlook sardines, salmon, tuna, and the shellfish as possibilities for sandwiches.

Tuna, salmon, and shellfish also make excellent salad ingredients, and a salad and crackers an excellent lunch. For directions on the preparation of salads, see Chapter 8. Deviled eggs are a pleasant accompaniment to salads, and instructions for these and other luncheon dishes using eggs are given in this chapter.

In my family the favorite for lunch is something we call "Fried Tomatoes," a concoction that, so far as I have been able to discover, is unknown outside the family, although I suspect it to be a Pennsylvania Dutch dish. It is inelegant looking and perhaps will not sound very good in the description, but all of us are devoted to it and so I include it here in the event that anyone else might like to try it.

FRIED TOMATOES

RECIPE: FRIED TOMATOES

2 or 3 ripe tomatoes
milk
fresh bread

1. Melt 2 tablespoons of butter in a large skillet.
2. Slice the tomatoes and lay them in the skillet. Salt and pepper them well, and sprinkle in 1 teaspoon of sugar. Let the tomatoes cook gently over a low fire until they are soft, which should take about 5 minutes.
3. Pour milk over the tomatoes to a depth of about half the skillet, or ¾ of an inch. Heat, but do not allow the milk to boil. Taste for the presence of enough sugar and salt; both are important.
4. Take this mixture to the table in a bowl. Each person helps himself, spooning enough of the mixture over a piece of buttered bread to soak the bread. Seconds, thirds, and fourths are in order in my family.

GRILLED SANDWICHES

If you do not have a grill, grilled sandwiches are readily made in a skillet. Simply butter two slices of bread and then put the filling between them, but with the buttered sides out in the reverse of the usual procedure. Put the sandwich in the skillet over a medium-low heat. Turn when the bread is a golden brown on the underside; the sandwich is done when the second side is ditto.

Anything can be used as a filling. Cheese, which will melt to just the right degree, is the usual, and is even better when a slice or two of tomato is added. For bacon and cheese, cook the bacon first and in a separate pan. For meat sandwiches, such as minced or deviled ham, add catsup when putting the sandwich together; the flavors mix nicely this way. The same is true of sandwiches in which the filling is mixed with mayonnaise, such as lobster or tuna fish; do not, however, add celery or lettuce to the latter.

Grilled sandwiches may also be made under the broiler, in which event they are open-faced sandwiches, that is, they have no top slice of bread. Put the bread under the broiler and toast it on one side only, then lay or spread the filling on the untoasted side and put back under the broiler. Cheese, cheese and tomato, shrimp, lobster, and crabmeat sandwiches are particularly good this way. For the latter, mix mayonnaise with the amount of canned seafood needed for the number of sandwiches you are making before spreading.

Yet another type of hot sandwich may be made by splitting Brown 'n' Serve Rolls (the club rolls are a good shape for this), filling with cheese or chopped meat or seafood mixed with mayonnaise, and baking in the oven until the rolls are brown. Since Brown 'n' Serve rolls keep for a very long time in the freezing compartment of the refrigerator, it is a good idea to have them on hand for, among other emergencies, the times when you run out of bread for sandwiches. Even such plain ingredients as bologna or boiled ham are made interesting when the rolls are buttered and mustard or catsup added before baking.

EGGS

HARD-BOILED EGGS

For a sliced egg or chopped egg sandwich, the eggs must be hard-boiled first. Put the eggs in a saucepan, cover them with water, and put the saucepan over a high flame. When the water begins to boil, turn the fire down to the point where the water is just bubbling gently. Cook for 5 minutes after the water starts boiling, then let the eggs sit in the water for 2 to 3 minutes after the fire has been turned off. Run them under cold water, crack the shells by knocking one end against a hard surface, and peel off the shells.

For a sliced egg sandwich, butter the bread, slice the egg, salt and pepper it, add lettuce and a goodly amount of mayonnaise. For a chopped egg sandwich, cut the egg into tiny pieces, salt and pepper it, add chopped olives if you wish, and mix in mayonnaise.

DEVILED EGGS

Hard-boil the eggs and, after shelling, cut them in half lengthwise. Remove the yolks, put them in a bowl, salt and pepper them, and add some prepared mustard, the amount depending on the number of yolks. Mash the mustard and egg yolks together into a paste. Fill the depressions in the whites of the eggs with this paste, mounding it up a bit, and sprinkle with paprika. If you are planning to take the deviled eggs on a picnic, put the halves of the eggs back together and wrap each egg separately in waxed paper. Deviled eggs, as well as tasting good, look very pretty, so keep them in mind as a decorative asset for cold meat platters or for any type of salad.

FRIED EGG SANDWICH

For a plain fried egg sandwich, fry the egg gently in butter, breaking the yolk after you put the egg in the pan. Cook it lightly on both sides, turning with a pancake turner. Cook it neither too fast nor too long or it will be leathery. Transfer it to a buttered piece of bread, salt and pepper it, and top with another piece of bread spread with mayonnaise or chili sauce.

For a slightly different kind of fried egg sandwich, cut a round hole in a slice of bread (you can do this with the rim of a glass). Melt butter in a skillet, put in the bread, and break an egg into the hole in the bread. When the bread is golden brown on the underside, turn the whole thing over with a pancake turner. Or do not turn over but, instead, sprinkle with grated cheese and put under the broiler until the cheese melts.

SCRAMBLED EGGS

Scrambled eggs as cooked for breakfast are described on page 191, but here are two recipes that alter scrambled eggs enough to classify them as a luncheon dish. The recipes serve two.

RECIPE I: SCRAMBLED EGGS WITH CRABMEAT

4 eggs
½ cup evaporated or regular milk
½ can crabmeat
dash Worcestershire sauce

1. Break 4 eggs into a bowl. Add ½ cup of evaporated or regular milk, salt and pepper, and a dash of Worcestershire sauce, and beat with a fork just until mixed.

2. Melt 1 tablespoon of butter in a skillet.

3. Put ½ can of crabmeat in a separate bowl and pick it over for stray bits of cartilage. Then add it to the eggs, stirring in.

4. Put the egg-crabmeat mixture into the skillet. Keep running the side of a fork across the bottom of the pan so that the uncooked part of the mixture slides down to the bottom. Cooking is complete as soon as the eggs have set, which will be very quickly.

RECIPE II: SCRAMBLED EGGS WITH SWISS CHEESE

4 eggs
½ cup evaporated milk
4 slices Swiss cheese
bread crumbs

1. Break the eggs into a bowl, add ½ cup of evaporated milk, and sprinkle with salt and pepper. Beat with a fork.

2. Butter a shallow baking dish.

3. Melt 2 tablespoons of butter in a skillet, and when hot, add the eggs. Scrape the bottom of the pan with a fork, and the instant the eggs are no longer liquid, take off the fire.

4. Transfer the eggs to the baking dish. Lay 4 slices of Swiss cheese over the eggs, and sprinkle the cheese with bread crumbs and paprika. Put under the broiler until the cheese melts and begins to brown.

POACHED EGGS

Tomato soup and cheese turn these into a luncheon dish.

RECIPE: POACHED EGGS WITH TOMATO SAUCE

1 or 2 eggs per serving
1 can condensed cream of tomato soup
grated cheese
1 piece of bread per egg

1. Put the bread under the broiler and toast on one side only.

2. While the bread is toasting, put 1 inch of water in a skillet, add ½ teaspoon of salt, and when the water is

simmering, add the eggs, either breaking them directly into the water or first into a saucer and sliding them into the water. Cook for 1 minute.

3. Take the eggs out with a slotted spoon, and put them on the untoasted sides of the bread. Pour undiluted cream of tomato soup over each egg and then top with grated cheese.

4. Put under the broiler until the cheese has melted.

CHAPTER 14 HOW TO CONCOCT HORS D'OEUVRES

Because the time spent in fixing hors d'oeuvres is likely to be subtracted from time devoted to the dinner proper, I am of the opinion that hors d'oeuvres should be limited to the quick and the simple. Even if there is a great deal of time that can be spent preparing them in advance, they are apt to be clammy and soggy when removed from under their damp towels in the refrigerator, another argument for bypassing the tiny, open-faced sandwiches that are traditional. Settle, instead, for a bowl of peanuts and/or olives or any of the suggestions which follow.

CRACKERS AND . . .

Smoked Salmon: Buy it, sliced, in the delicatessen. Cut it into cracker-size pieces, arrange on a platter, and decorate with parsley.

Pickled Herring: This is available in jars in the refrigerator case at the grocery story. Vita Herring in Sour Cream seems to me particularly good. Put it in a small bowl in the middle of a platter of crackers.

Liver Paté: A gourmet food shop is usually the best source for a good paté. If you are having a large number of people for cocktails, you can make your own by mashing together 1 pound of liverwurst, ¼ cup of brandy, ½ cup of sour cream, 4 tablespoons of grated onion, and 1 teaspoon of Gulden's mustard.

Sardines: Buy 1 or more tins of the very tiny ones in olive oil. Arrange on a plate, and sprinkle with chopped parsley.

Cheese: Arrange a cheese tray of assorted sharp and smoky cheeses or cheese spreads. There are some interesting spreads on the market involving such things as horseradish and chives and bacon. Shop around among them for the flavors that please you.

Melba toast rounds and the tiny slices of rye bread also go well with any of the above.

POTATO CHIPS AND . . .

Avocado Dip: Peel an avocado and mash it with a fork. Add some onion juice by scraping the cut surface of an onion with a sharp knife. Add the juice of ½ lemon and salt and pepper to taste. Mix well.

Shrimp Dip: Thaw a can of frozen shrimp soup by leaving it in the refrigerator but out of the freezing compartment for 12 hours. Put a small package of softened cream cheese in a bowl, add the juice of ½ lemon, a bit of garlic powder, and mash the cheese until smooth. Add 1 can of shrimp soup and blend together. Store in the refrigerator to chill until ready to use.

Clam Dip: Blend (canned) minced clams with cream cheese, a little garlic powder, and a dash of Worcestershire sauce.

Onion Dip: Mix 1 package of dehydrated onion soup with 1 small container of sour cream.

NOTE: If potato chips or crackers have become a little stale, put them in the oven briefly to restore their crispness.

HOT CANAPÉS

Crabmeat or Shrimp or Lobster: Use the canned varieties. Drain the can and empty into a bowl. Mash the fish into small pieces with a fork. Sprinkle lemon juice over, and add enough mayonnaise to coat lightly. Spread on Melba toast rounds, and put under the broiler for 2 minutes.

Roquefort Cheese: Mash cream cheese and Roquefort cheese together, using three times as much cream cheese as Roquefort. Spread on crackers, and put under the broiler for 3 minutes.

Sharp or Smoky Cheese: Spread on crackers or Melba toast rounds, sprinkle with paprika, and put under the broiler until the cheese melts and begins to brown.

VEGETABLES

Celery: Wash celery stalks, and cut them into 3-inch lengths. Fill the center groove with any of the Kraft's Party-Snack mixes, and sprinkle lightly with paprika.

Cucumber: Pare a cucumber, and cut in slices. Top each slice with a piece of boiled or prosciutto ham or smoked salmon.

Avocado: Peel an avocado and cut it into bite-size pieces. Put a toothpick in each piece, place in a bowl, and pour French dressing over.

Cherry Tomatoes: Cut out the centers of cherry tomatoes and fill with crabmeat, shrimp, or lobster mixed with mayonnaise, or with any of the prepared dips.

Vegetable Plate: Arrange strips of raw carrots, celery, and green pepper, plus raw cauliflower on a platter with a bowl of Russian dressing (page 155) in the center.

FRUIT

Melon Balls: Wrap small strips of prosciutto ham around melon balls and fasten with a toothpick.

Pineapple: Fresh or canned pineapple squares may also be wrapped in prosciutto ham.

EGGS

Deviled Eggs: Make deviled eggs as directed on page 196, but cut a small slice of the white off the bottom of each half so that they will lie on the plate without rolling over.

CHAPTER 15 HOW TO PREPARE BEVERAGES

COFFEE

The absolute essential with coffee is that it be hot, very hot. Thus, if it has been made in advance, put it back on the fire until it just reaches the boiling point before serving, and if it is to be transferred to a decorative pot for serving, fill this pot with hot water beforehand to warm it, emptying it out just before putting the coffee in. If you wish to bring the coffee to the table at the beginning of the meal, a candle warmer is surprisingly efficient at keeping the coffee hot.

Whipped cream and vanilla ice cream make festive substitutes for regular cream. For a utilitarian substitute, evaporated milk does very well. And in a real emergency, powdered milk can be used; just sprinkle it in dry.

INSTANT COFFEE

Use 1 teaspoon to each coffee cup (not measuring cup) of boiling water. Use more than 1 teaspoon if you like your coffee stronger. I happen to prefer Nescafé, but coffee preferences being what they are, perhaps it is best if you try all brands before making up your mind on the subject. Whichever the brand, all instant coffee is considerably improved by some gentle cooking. My own method is to measure the water before dinner is served, put it on the fire, and when it is boiling, add the coffee, turning the fire down immediately. I then leave the coffee on the stove through dinner, over a very, very low flame, turn the fire up when I come back to the kitchen to get the dessert, let the coffee almost reach the boiling point, and serve.

REGULAR COFFEE

A glass coffeemaker is to be preferred over a metal one, and, for the inexperienced, a drip method over percolator. An electric coffeemaker makes 8 cups of coffee excellently, 2 rather badly. Be sure to keep the coffeemaker very clean. Ground coffee, once the tin has been opened, keeps best in the refrigerator, better still if it is transferred to a jar with a lid that closes tightly. The usual ratio in making coffee is 1 heaping tablespoon of coffee to each cup of water.

ICED COFFEE

Brew the coffee double-strength, let cool, and pour over ice.

TEA

HOT TEA

Tea, as any real tea drinker will tell you, must be made with loose tea and in an earthenware pot. True. But I am a confirmed tea drinker and I like tea bags just as well; in fact, better, for I hate to scrape damp and elusive tea leaves out of a pot. So, follow your own inclination. Use 1 teaspoon of tea leaves to 1 cup of boiling water, or 1 tea bag to each cup. If you are using tea bags to brew a pot of tea, use 1 or 2 fewer; 2 tea bags will make 3 to 4 cups of tea.

As for brands, this is too much a matter of taste to make a recommendation, but I would like to suggest that you sometime try Lapsang Souchong. This is not a brand but a type of tea which has an unusual and quite delicious smoky flavor. It must be drunk with cream, though, not lemon. It is not easy to find, but gourmet food shops often carry it. Peppermint tea is an even greater change from ordinary tea, a most pleasant and refreshing one, particularly at mid-afternoon or just before bed at night. This is not to be confused with mint tea, which is just tea with mint added.

ICED TEA

Brew the tea double-strength, let cool, and pour over ice cubes. Serve with fresh mint and lemon.

COCOA

There are times when nothing tastes better than a cup of hot cocoa. But by-pass instant cocoa; it is not nearly so good as making your own. Put in a saucepan 1 cup of milk for each cup of cocoa. Heat the milk, but be careful not to let it boil. While it is warming, measure into a cup 1 level teaspoon of (Hershey's) cocoa and 2 teaspoons of sugar for each cup of milk. With a spoon, dip a little of the milk out of the saucepan and stir it into the cup to dissolve the cocoa and sugar and make it into a thin paste. Pour this paste into the saucepan, stirring to mix. When the milk is hot, the cocoa is done. If there are children to be pleased, put a marshmallow in each cup.

MILK

Milk is milk, and there is nothing to be said about it except that, if you are an adult, it is well to keep in mind the fat-free assets of skimmed and powdered milk. One can quickly get used to the less rich taste of skimmed or powdered milk and not miss regular milk. With powdered milk, it is essential to the flavor that it be cold, so make it up a quart at a time and keep it in the refrigerator. Both skimmed and powdered milk can be used in recipes calling for milk. If you just need a tablespoon or two and there is no milk on hand, there are directions on the powdered milk carton telling how to make up a small quantity.

CHAPTER 16 HOW TO "DOCTOR" BREAD AND ROLLS

There will be no dissertation from me on the virtues of homemade bread and rolls because I am perfectly satisfied with what one can buy in the store, but there are a few things that can be done to dress up ordinary rolls, for example, or turn French bread into garlic bread.

BISCUIT AND MUFFIN MIXES

Bisquick, as I remember it, was one of the first mixes to come on the market, and it remains a very useful product. It can be used for pancakes and waffles as well as biscuits and muffins, and it is probably a good idea routinely to keep a box on hand for the times when you have forgotten to buy rolls or need biscuits to go with a creamed dish or feel that hot muffins are the touch needed to dress up an ordinary dinner. The package gives all the directions you will need, but let me add the suggestion that any one of the following can be stirred into the batter: strawberries or blueberries (this is an excellent way of using up berries that are getting old and tired), canned mandarin orange sections, chopped nuts, ground leftover ham, grated cheese, watercress, canned pitted cherries, or jam or jelly.

Muffin mixes are uniformly good, and there is no preference in brands among them. Whatever strikes your fancy can be added to the batter of these too, with raisins a particularly good choice for bran muffins. Gingerbread mix baked in muffin tins makes fine muffins to go with a dinner of cold sliced ham. Already baked blueberry and bran muffins seem to survive packaging extremely well, so there is no reason not to buy these ready-made if it is more convenient. Simply warm them before serving. If some go stale before all are eaten up, cut them in half, put a pat of butter on each half, and put under the broiler long enough for the butter to melt.

BROWN 'N' SERVE ROLLS

These are a great convenience because they can be stored in the freezing compartment and will keep for weeks, needing only to be browned in the oven before serving. Oven time will vary according to how hot the oven is; plan on 10 minutes but keep an eye on them. If you want a sandwich but there is no bread in the house, cut a Brown 'n' Serve roll in half, put the filling in, and bake until the roll is a golden brown.

Club rolls or the French loaves that come two in a package may be painted before browning with melted butter to which powdered garlic has been added. Or, for a different taste, experiment with adding herbs to the butter.

To turn plain rolls into sweet rolls, melt ½ stick of butter, and mix it with ¾ cup of brown sugar, a sprinkling of cinnamon, and chopped nuts. Spread half of this mixture on the bottom of a pie tin or shallow baking dish (line first with aluminum foil to make for easier cleaning later), put in the rolls, and spoon the remainder of the mixture over them. Bake until the rolls are brown.

BOSTON BROWN BREAD

This is traditionally served with baked beans, but it goes nicely with a lot of other things as well, particularly cold meat platters and salads. Buy it in a can and heat according to the directions on the label.

CINNAMON TOAST

While the bread is toasting, mix together 1 or 2 teaspoons of granulated sugar and a good sprinkling of cinnamon, the amount depending on whether you like a heavy or light cinnamon flavor. Butter the toast, and immediately dust the cinnamon-sugar mixture over.

CHEESE BREAD

Melt butter, and add grated cheese to it. Slice a loaf of French bread down to, but not through, the bottom crust. Paint each slice with the butter and cheese mixture. Wrap the loaf in aluminum foil, and heat in the oven for 10 minutes.

GARLIC BREAD

Melt butter and add to it, if you have a garlic press, 2 crushed cloves of garlic, or use thinly sliced garlic cloves or garlic powder. Slice a loaf of French (or Italian) bread down to, but not through, the bottom crust, and paint each slice with the butter. Wrap the loaf in aluminum foil, and heat in the oven for 10 minutes.

FRENCH BREAD WITH HORS D'OEUVRES SPREADS

Make a center slice the length of a loaf of French bread, but not cutting through the bottom crust. Spread the cut surface of the bread with any one of the prepared hors d'oeuvres spreads, such as chive or clam spread. Wrap loaf in aluminum foil, and put in the oven for 10 minutes.

ROLLS

Cylinders of prepared but uncooked rolls and biscuits (Pillsbury's) are sold in the dairy department of grocery stores. They are handy to have on hand, but once the package is opened, all of the contents must be baked. Directions for baking are on the packages.

The cinnamon rolls sold this way are improved by being

rolled out (use a floured bottle if you don't have a rolling pin), sprinkled with brown sugar and cinnamon and raisins or chopped nuts, rerolled into a cylindrical shape, and then sliced.

CHAPTER 17 HOW TO MAKE TWO SAUCES

There are hundreds of sauces, but you need to know how to make only two. Only one, really, and that is a white sauce or, as it is also called, a cream sauce. This is the basis, or binding element, for dish after dish. Directions for it appear throughout this book in connection with individual dishes, but it will be repeated here so that it can be referred to easily in the event that you are coping with leftovers not referred to elsewhere or you want to try a recipe from some other source and it calls for the use of white sauce.

The second sauce, Hollandaise, is not essential—you could get along perfectly well without knowing how to make it— but it does such nice things for vegetables, which frequently need all the help they can get, that it is included here.

WHITE SAUCE

RECIPE: WHITE SAUCE

1 (thin), 2 (medium), or 3 (thick) tablespoons butter
1 (thin), 2 (medium), or 3 (thick) tablespoons flour
1 cup milk
¼ teaspoon salt
⅛ teaspoon pepper
sprinkle of paprika

A thin, medium, or thick white sauce may be made by varying the amount of butter and flour, 1 tablespoon of each for thin, 2 tablespoons of each for medium, 3 tablespoons of each for thick, with the other ingredients remaining the same. A medium white sauce answers almost every need.

1. Put the butter in a saucepan and melt it over a very low flame.
2. Sprinkle in the flour and stir until the butter and flour are blended smoothly, without lumps.
3. Pour in the milk, a small quantity at a time, and stir constantly. Again, the object is to avoid lumping. Keep stirring until the sauce thickens.
4. After it has thickened, add ¼ teaspoon of salt, ⅛ teaspoon of pepper, and a dash of paprika.
5. Allow the sauce to bubble gently for several minutes.

Taste for sufficient seasoning.

For flavoring, you may, if you wish, add 1 or 2 tablespoons of dry sherry or dry vermouth.

For *mushroom sauce,* add fresh mushrooms that have been lightly cooked in butter until wilted. Or add a drained can of mushrooms.

For *shrimp sauce,* add cooked or canned shrimp cut in small pieces.

For *oyster sauce,* add canned oysters that have been cooked 3 minutes in the juice from the can.

For *clam sauce,* add a drained can of minced clams.

For *egg sauce,* add 1 chopped hard-boiled egg.

For *olive sauce,* add sliced stuffed olives.

For *cheese sauce,* add 4 tablespoons grated cheese.

For *lobster sauce,* add cooked or canned lobster.

For *crabmeat sauce,* add cooked or canned crabmeat.

For *pimento sauce,* add chopped canned red pimentos.

HOLLANDAISE SAUCE

This sauce must be made in a double boiler, and it is a bit tricky because it curdles readily.

RECIPE I: HOLLANDAISE SAUCE

1 stick (8 tablespoons) butter	1 teaspoon lemon juice
3 egg yolks	¼ teaspoon salt

1. Put water in the bottom of a double boiler, leaving a space of 1 inch between the water and the bottom of the upper pan. Do not at any time allow the water to boil.

2. Put 1 stick (8 tablespoons) of butter in the top of the double boiler, and let it melt.

3. Separate 3 eggs (see page 22), and put the yolks in a bowl. Add 1 teaspoon of lemon juice and ¼ teaspoon of salt. Beat with a fork until the yolks are fluffy.

4. Slowly, and stirring constantly, add the egg yolks to the melted butter. Keep on stirring without let-up until the sauce thickens and is hot enough to serve, at which point serve immediately.

If, by some mischance, the sauce shows signs of curdling in the cooking, stir in 1 tablespoon of cream, 2 if necessary.

RECIPE II: MOCK HOLLANDAISE SAUCE

2 tablespoons butter	1 teaspoon lemon juice
4 teaspoons mayonnaise	⅛ teaspoon salt

1. Melt 2 tablespoons of butter until it is bubbly hot.
2. Remove the butter from the fire, add 1 teaspoon of lemon juice and ⅛ teaspoon of salt, and stir in 4 heaping teaspoons of mayonnaise. Serve immediately (do not heat the mayonnaise).

CHAPTER 18 HOW TO COPE WITH EMERGENCIES

Accidents, mishaps, miscalculations, delayed mealtime, unexpected guests, these things can happen to even the most experienced of cooks, so it is well to have in mind some standard preventive and remedial measures. First-aid measures you will already be familiar with, but a few for common kitchen accidents are repeated here. First-aid measures when it is the food that has been subjected to trauma rather than your person are given in so far as these are possible; occasionally something will be burned beyond salvaging, in which event you will have to abandon action in favor of philosophy. If your husband telephones at the last moment to say he has been held up at the office, a little philosophy is also in order, along with a few steps outlined below. In the case of guests, the only sensible course is always to count on them being late, for they so frequently are, and even if they are not, cocktails may go on far longer than you planned. Thus, the best approach to save both your nerves and your dinner is always to plan a menu that is ready when the guests are, not vice versa; to this end, see the chapter on Casseroles for Company.

PREVENTIVE MEASURES

Since prevention is better than Unguentine, a few suggestions, even though they may be obvious, are in order.

Always turn the handles of cooking pots away from the outside of the stove, so that neither you nor someone else brushes past and knocks them off. A scalded foot is no fun.

Keep knives sharp. A sharp knife is less likely to slip than a dull one.

Hot fat is given to spattering. Stay out of range or upend a sieve over the skillet. Drops of water will make fat spatter more, so be careful about letting any get in.

A greasy broiler may catch on fire, and a greasy oven will smoke badly. Scrub the broiler after each use with scouring powder (use aluminum foil to line the broiling pan whenever feasible to make the job of keeping it clean easier). The oven may be kept clean with Easy-Off oven cleaner; follow the directions on the label.

Always use pot holders. Never trust a handle not to be hot.

Don't pour hot liquids into cold jars. For instance, if you need to dispose of the grease in a roasting pan before making gravy, have an empty tin can on hand for the purpose.

Never leave the house with things cooking on the stove, and don't store anything inflammable near the stove, such as paper bags or cereal cartons.

If you go into the living room and sit down to read the paper while dinner is cooking, your chances of getting back in time to catch things before they burn are made infinitely better by a timer. An inexpensive timer can be set for any number of minutes up to an hour and rings a bell when the time is up.

When something spills, even if only water, wipe it up immediately so you don't slip on it.

Keep the kitchen as tidy as possible, putting things back in place as you go along. Confusion is conducive to accidents. It is supposedly the mark of a good cook to have few utensils in evidence by the time the meal is finished cooking, but if you can't stop to wash up saucepans as you finish with them, just stack them out of the way, being sure to put water in them so that they are easier to clean later.

Wear an apron—to avoid stains on your clothing.

Each time you light the oven, make certain that it really *is* lit, not just that the gas is turned on.

REMEDIAL MEASURES

If you cut yourself, hold the cut under running cold water, put an antiseptic on, and bandage it. If it is a small puncture wound, let it bleed a bit before doing these things.

For burns, use Unguentine or a paste of baking soda and cool water. The important thing is to get it on fast. If the burn is other than minor, medical treatment is in order, of course.

In the event of grease catching fire, do *not* throw water on it. Turn off the flame. Leave whatever is burning where it is, that is, don't take it out of the oven or off the stove. If the flame does not go out quickly, which it usually does, throw bicarbonate of soda (baking soda) or salt on it. Pour off the excess grease before resuming the cooking.

Gather up broken glass with wet paper towels or absorbent cotton so that the tiny splinters will stick to the towel or cotton instead of your fingers.

In the case of burned food, meat that is charred on the outside may be perfectly all right on the inside; just cut off the burned portions. With burned potatoes, cut off the burned areas, rinse them off, and put into hot water briefly to warm. With burned vegetables, leave all the burned ones sticking to the pot, rinse the salvagable ones under cold water, and then heat them in a fresh pot of hot water.

Oversalted food may be helped by the addition of sugar.

Sprinkle a few drops of water on stale rolls, wrap them in aluminum foil, and heat in the oven. Or split them, butter them well, and put under the broiler.

For stains, use boiling water on fruit and coffee stains. Use detergent and hot water on grease stains. For candlewax stains on a tablecloth, remove the wax, put a blotter under the stain, and press with a hot iron.

To get rid of the smell of onion on your fingers, rub with a piece of lemon.

To clean burned pans, sprinkle scouring powder in, add water, and allow to soak overnight.

To clean a coffeepot, fill it with water, add a tablespoon of baking soda, and allow it to soak for half an hour.

MISCALCULATIONS

If you run out of sugar, use honey.

If you need just a small amount of flour and there is none on hand, Bisquick can be used.

If a chicken dish must be stretched, run hot water over tuna fish and add it.

Keep powdered milk on hand for the times you run out of milk or cream.

If there aren't enough rolls to go around, see if there is a package of gingerbread mix in the cupboard, or white cake mix. You can add fruit to the latter and bake it in a muffin tin. If you run out of bread, frozen waffles may be able to substitute.

If you have four pieces of chicken and five people, remove the meat from the bones.

Lemon juice can substitute for vinegar in most things, but not vice versa.

Almost anything can be stretched to serve more people by being added to a white sauce or canned gravy or undiluted or very slightly diluted canned soup and served over noodles or rice. With chops or chocolate eclairs, however, the only solution is to claim you don't like them.

DELAYED MEALTIME

If you receive sudden word that dinner must be held up for minutes or hours, how disconcerting the news is depends on what is on the stove. Just as a general rule, nothing that is quick cooking, such as steak, chops, or fish, should be started ahead of time; wait until the prospective diners are assembled before putting these on. If it is a roast that is in the oven when the call comes, let it continue cooking until it is one-half hour away from being done, then take it out of the oven. Roast fowl the same. They can be returned to the oven to finish cooking. Never let anything stay on in the oven even though the fire is off, for the food will dry out. A casserole can be turned off or taken out of the oven and allowed to cool, and then reheated before serving. If it is a soufflé or similar baked dish or omelet, then all is lost, and you had best begin deciding on what cans can be opened.

Many vegetables are a matter of last-minute cooking, and there will be no problem in holding these at the uncooked stage. Baked vegetables should be allowed to go within 15 minutes of being done and then the cooking completed later. If it is anything being cooked wrapped in foil, such as baked potato, it should be unwrapped while it is being held up so that it does not get soggy. The same is true of anything being cooked with a lid; take the lid off while it is cooling; otherwise, steam condenses and drips into it. Vegetables being cooked in water should be completely drained and allowed to cool, later being returned to boiling water to heat and complete the cooking.

Don't interrupt the cooking of any baked goods. Let them go until they are done, then reheat for a moment or two before serving.

If the meal cannot be held up for the absent person, the best that can be done is to wrap his plate in aluminum foil and put it in a very low oven, or, better still, rewarm each thing individually when he arrives, the vegetables in a bit of milk, the meat in gravy or a little butter.

One must, of course, accept with good grace the occasions when lateness for a meal cannot be helped, but the person who decides to make a phone call or start some new task just as dinner is about to be served deserves one's full wrath. Put your foot down early and firmly that if you are going to the trouble of cooking, the others must go to the trouble of being on time at the table. If you can manage somehow to convey it, I think, too, that the cook deserves a kind word about the meal. It may not be a great success every time, but usually at least one thing is particularly good and it is nice to be told so.

Index